Global Sustainability Initiatives

New Models and New Approaches

Global Sustainability Initiatives

New Models and New Approaches

edited by

James A. F. Stoner
Fordham University

and

Charles Wankel
St. John's University

In collaboration with
Shaun K. Malleck, Matthew M. Marovich,
Jurate Stanaityte, and Carolyn F. Stoner

Information Age Publishing, Inc.
Charlotte, North Carolina • www.infoagepub.com

Library of Congress Cataloging-in-Publication Data

Global sustainability initiatives : new models and new approaches / edited by James A.F. Stoner and Charles Wankel ; in collaboration with Shaun K. Malleck ... [et al.].
    p. cm.
  Includes bibliographical references.
  ISBN 978-1-59311-813-6 (pbk.) — ISBN 978-1-59311-814-3 (hbk.) 1. Sustainable development. 2. Management—Environmental aspects. I. Stoner, James Arthur Finch, 1935- II. Wankel, Charles. III. Malleck, Shaun K.
  HC79.E5G59725 2008
  338.9'27—dc22

                                                                2008032790

ISBN: 978-1-59311-813-6 (paperback)
ISBN: 978-1-59311-814-3 (hardcover)

Printed in the United States of America

CONTENTS

PART I

EMERGING MODELS FOR
MOVING TOWARD GLOBAL SUSTAINABILITY

CHAPTER 1

INTRODUCTION

Exploring Issues, Ideas, and Approaches for Moving Toward a Sustainable World

James A. F. Stoner and Charles Wankel

Some observers are convinced that the journey toward a sustainable world will be the greatest challenge ever faced by our species. The editors of this book agree with them. Maybe crawling out of the water onto land and surviving that transition, thus setting the stage for taking the next "step" in our evolution, was more momentous and a tougher task for our slowly evolving species, but our "ancestors" had eons in which to make a success of that challenge. We do not have eons in which to meet our challenge.

Not a few observers think we have a decade at best to make major changes in how we produce, consume, and breed if there is to be a future for our grandchildren that has any meaningful resemblance to the more desirable aspects of our own present and the lives we are currently able to live. The editors of this book are not agreed on the exact number of years that is appropriate for defining how long we have to deal with the current situation, but they do not disagree substantially with the sense of urgency for taking action on the many tasks—some known and many unknown—that must be undertaken.

Global Sustainability Initiatives: New Models and New Approaches
pp. 3–14
Copyright © 2008 by Information Age Publishing

Achieving a sustainable world will require rewriting the current equation that is yielding the unsustainable status of our current world: ever-growing population × unsustainable consumption practices × unsustainable production practices = a world incapable of meeting the needs of our species—and fatal to too many other species.

This volume is one of a great many that are now emerging to suggest possible pieces of the puzzle called "Achieving a Sustainable World." That puzzle and the challenge of finding pieces that fit together is large enough to justify the writing of at least as many books as will be written. There is room in this quest for an awful lot of ideas, experiments, trials, and errors. And there is a desperate need for dialogue in the rich, open, and collaborative sense Isaacs (1999), his colleagues, and so many others use the term.

The authors of the essays in the following chapters have investigated, reported on, and sometimes been actively involved in the innovative ideas and approaches they describe. Like the rest of us, they are aware that we are all engaged, whether or not we like it and no matter how little some of us want to be so engaged, in the adventure of finding out how to make the transformations we need to make. They do not offer a grand scheme for making the "mother of all transformations" that will solve the "unsustainability problem." Instead, they explore a wide variety of approaches to little pieces of the sustainability challenge. Of course some of the pieces may turn out to be a bit larger than others. For example, our air travel habits may constitute a considerably larger piece in that puzzle then many of us realized and much larger than we would like to admit as we reflect guiltily on all the frequent flyer miles we have accumulated and expended over the years. And extreme poverty and the misery (and the terrorism it can breed) is a 2 billion person piece of the problem.

The remaining pages in this chapter offer a brief introduction and some level of highlighting for the contributions of the book's authors in their various chapters. Different readers will find different themes in some of the essays, but hopefully all readers will recognize the challenges we all face and appreciate, as we the editors do, the time and efforts the authors invested to make these fresh, interesting, and provocative ideas, approaches, and projects available to all.

In chapter 2, "Evergreen Brick Works: Planning for Success in a Triple Bottom-Line Enterprise," Ushnish Sengupta, Geoff Cape, Seana Irvine, Pierre Bertrand, and Ann Armstrong present and discuss the early experiences of Evergreen, a Toronto-based environmental charity, as it undertakes a bold and innovative project in downtown Toronto. Evergreen is dedicated to leading Canada's urban greening movement, and the Brick Works project is taking Evergreen well beyond its own accustomed practices and levels of risk. Evergreen was established in 1989 and is constituted by a variety of organizations and projects under a two-part umbrella mission: on one hand, to promote the values that gave rise to the Brick Works—appreciation of and caring for nature, culture, and community; and, on the other hand, to provoke new ideas about relationships among nature, people, and cities. At the Brick Works, these two objectives are pursued through very clear and explicit goals and objectives, and by rigorous programming. The project seeks to become a national and international model of a "zero footprint" production facility that educates the community through a rich variety of visitors' program.

The authors guide us through the project by first describing how the project emerged over time, a discussion that might bring to readers' minds Robert Quinn's delightful strategy-making/emergence phrase "building the bridge as we walk on it" (1996, p. 83). They then present the project's goals, objectives, and anchor programs, followed by a description of environmental and social opportunities the project seeks to realize. Early developments in the project's brief lifetime and plans for the year 2008 are presented. The chapter includes a rich description of how "Triple Bottom-Line Measures of Success" can be defined and used to monitor the progress of the project toward its goals and an early report on how it is doing so far against those measures.

Emerging from Evergreen, a parent organization that has been a highly entrepreneurial not-for-profit leader in environmental initiatives, the Evergreen Bick Works is currently developing into a triple bottom-line oriented organization. In doing so, it is connecting the efforts of not-for-profits, government agencies, and for-profit corporations to achieve social, environmental, and economic goals that engage the public and demonstrate new ways of doing business. Embracing the triple bottom line as a core organizational strategy involves the challenge of finding and maintaining a balance between risk taking and management control. The authors conclude that the challenges being addressed in the project and the project's experiences grappling with those challenges will serve other socially conscious organizations that might undertake similar projects in the future.

In chapter 3, "Hitting Four Birds With One Stone: The Rural Electrification Project for Peace in the Island of the al-Qaeda Front in East Asia," Mari Kondo describes a project that addresses one of the more challenging issues in the world's quest for global sustainability. That issue is the need to alleviate extreme poverty in a sustainable way and, in doing so, to reduce the breeding ground for terrorism created by such poverty and the world's indifference to it. The project she describes is AMORE, a multi-party, partnership-based rural electrification project conducted in the conflict-ridden area of Mindanao, Philippines. In the spirit of the triple bottom-line theme from chapter 2, she frames AMORE as a project seeking four goals: environmental, economic, societal, and political. One of the major partners in the project is Mirant Philippines which joined AMORE as part of its corporate social-responsibility commitment. The project partners include US-AID as part of its Global Development Alliance (GDA) initiative, a public-private partnership for development and alleviation of poverty. The project has many alliance partners of different mandates and characteristics, which makes coordination not an easy task, but the author reports that the parties have used their diversity of interests and perspectives to move the project forward with considerable success.

AMORE is targeted in an area where people are extremely poor and where terrorist activities occur. The electrification project's primary goal is not simply to supply electric power in the areas. Rather, it seeks to be a community development project meant to empower the communities so they can start their own projects for economic growth. The heart of the project is the organization of key people in the communities for peace and development.

Kondo reports the innovations the single AMORE project is using as it seeks to hit the "four birds" of environmental, economic, societal, and political improvement and the results being achieved so far in this quest. Innovation for "sustainable sustainability" is especially important because the target areas are so poor and so unsafe. Although AMORE has been an innovative project from the start, its continued success calls for further innovation and refinement of its existing program.

Bonnie Richley's chapter, "Learning to Cooperate: A Model at the Nexus of Business and Society and its Impact Around the World," speaks to a task critically important in moving toward a sustainable world: learning how to create the social innovations that will be needed to bring about and sustain that movement. Her chapter analyzes how visitors to one of the world's most successful cooperatives, Mondragon Corporacion Cooperativa (MCC) came to Spain's Basque Region to learn from the cooperative and how they then employed those lessons in social innovation. Richley's focus is unique in that it does not focus on the unique structure of the MCC, geared toward participative and democratic business management, but rather on how the MCC's social innovation is diffused throughout other businesses and organizations that have sought to learn from the for-profit business.

Richley chose to use positive organizational scholarship (POS) and appreciative inquiry (AI), which examine "theories of excellence, positive deviance," and other exemplary organizations, as the research and teaching tools with the best framework for assessing how social innovations diffuse. She finds these approaches for enabling social innovations to occur particularly appropriate for her exploration because they reflect the desire of MCC visitors to learn from the company's positive example. Richley builds much of her discussion on interviews with nine individuals who had visited MCC, could articulate how and what they had learned, and could represent how they applied it. Her interviews focused on positive learning experiences and high-point stories, drawing out common themes in why these individuals sought to learn from the cooperative and how they applied the lessons they learned.

Richley found that, for many visitors, a combination of internal and external factors led them to seek out MCC and its lessons in social innovation. She identifies the phases through which the visitors progressed—searching for, discovering, and experiencing the innovation—and recognizes that this process was driven by the values and objectives of the individuals. For the nine interviewees, visiting the MCC was valuable because it is a "grounded" yet "feasible and successful" innovation and "seeing is being." According to Richley, these findings show that social entrepreneurs may, in adopting innovations, be likely to engage in an ongoing process of changing innovations to conform to their own specific values and goals.

In chapter 5, "Convergence of For-Profit and Not-for-Profit Organizational Practices," Martin Stack, Laura Fitzpatrick, and Tim Keane discuss the traditional, oversimplified portrayal of for-profit businesses (FPOs) and not-for-profit organizations (NPOs) and note how this portrayal is becoming progressively less accurate in some and perhaps many cases. They note that these two types of institutions are often seen as being completely different in terms of focus (making profits versus furthering broader social purposes) and organizational efficiency (efficient versus unsophisticated). The authors argue that this traditional view, which places FPOs and NPOs on "opposite sides of a continuum stretching from … organizations motivated purely by narrow, profit maximization concerns to … 'less sophisticated' nonprofits … motivated by a more noble … concerns," is inconsistent with the focus of many NPOs on efficiency and constituent concerns and with the rewards that welcome FPOs that address social concerns. They illustrate the emerging convergence of these two types of institutions by describing a FPO and a NPO that are each making greater contributions to global sustainability in their local domains by leaning to become a bit more like the other in terms of focus and efficiency.

In grounding their observations in the literature, Stack and colleagues first review contemporary responses by Michael Porter and Charles Handy to Milton Friedman's well-known argument that the only social responsibility of business is legal profit maximization. According to Porter, businesses can justify contributions in community engagements when it is in the company's long-term business interests, as shown by the educational initiatives of the Cisco Network Academy. This position moves a bit away from Friedman's admonition to focus solely on making profits, but not very far. Handy moves much further, shifting the focus from firms onto the community and suggesting profits should be evaluated in light of corporate environmental and social interests.

Having reviewed this literature, the authors discuss how two entities—Water Partners, a not-for-profit committed to bringing potable water to impoverished communities suffering from its absence, and Fertigator Technologies, a for-profit lawn care firm with environmentally friendly products and services—demonstrate the interplay of ideas and organizational strategies between NPOs and FPOs. Water Partners, in seeking to address the poor's widespread lack of safe and affordable water, has drawn on a variety of for-profit practices to increase its own scope of operations and impact. It has begun to identify those able to pay for water projects, shifting gifted projects to communities unable to pay for them; to utilize efficient micro-lending techniques to enable communities to pay for projects, and to create a more business like structure by employing individuals to communicate with corporate contributors. Fertigator Technologies, on the other hand, became a successful for-profit venture after it shifted its business model toward one more focused on the contributions its products, technologies, and services could make to a more sustainable physical environment, and the financial benefits to its customers of doing so. In this shift toward a more environmentally sensitive way of being, it focused on marketing environmentally positive "green" technologies, started directing its marketing communications to end users who were more concerned about the need to alleviate environmental issues and benefited more directly from the company's products than the company's distributors did, and shifted its activities to a specific region (southeastern Florida) where the needs for its technologies are particularly clear and pressing. The two examples demonstrate how NPOs and FPOs can learn from one another and how their structures and interests can be more closely aligned than oversimplified distinctions between the two might suggest.

Jenni Goricanec's and Roger Hadgraft's chapter 6, "What Is Sustaining Practice? How Is it Learned?" delves into theoretical and practical dilemmas of bringing the *problematique* of global sustainability into higher education in a systemic way. In doing so, they address the obvious and very pressing need to transform the world's educational institutions from ones that "work harder and harder to do better and better that which should not be done at all," to paraphrase Peter Drucker's wise caution about managing (Stoner, 1976). Instead of training young people to make successful personal careers in institutions that are part of a production and consumption paradigm that is rapidly destroying the planet's capacity to support the survival of our species and many others, universities, and all other learning environments, need themselves to learn how to enable their participants to contribute to the great transformations in population size and consumption and production processes that will need to occur if a sustainable sustainability is to be achieved.

As a starting point for their discussion, the authors introduce the philosophical background of "nature of our predicament": the environment and its systemic characteristics, such as turbulence, unpredictability, interconnectedness, and ubiquity. These systemic properties will shape how educational goals will have to be achieved in tomorrow's universities. Where will the systems considerations approach meet the need to evaluate objective reality? The dangers of real life *maladaptive* responses of *system-in-its-environment* follow from, as the authors demonstrate, the necessity for organizations (corporations, governments, nations) to take proactive stances to adapt to turbulence and uncertainty of change. So-called second order maladaptive responses—monothematic *dogmatism, stalemate,* and *polarization*—deserve special attention when applied to interpreting efforts to change any university system, not just the Australian ones they discuss.

In the section that serves as a bridge between theoretical and practical concepts ("Within the context of our predicament—universities") they discuss the experiences they and others had as they undertook two distinct organizational change and transformation initiatives. One involved developing a new educational program oriented toward the Asian market which would create learning situations and curricula consistent with the pressing current need to develop skills, tools, and commitments for creating a more sustainable future. The second was directed toward conceptualizing and developing *Akademos*—an alternative model of education in 2000 which would also address those same basic educational needs for building a sustainable world. The analysis of these two initiatives allowed the authors to generate a series of indicators specific to university environments. In chapter sections that follow, reader are offered four rich stories that describe the process of idea-development and implementation-design for four unique programs (two undergraduate and two postgraduate) that focus on sustainable practice and moving it beyond knowledge and *learning* to transformation and *doing*. Practical insights that the authors draw from evidence in the cases show how, through the use of these practical models and approaches, a sensible balance can be achieved to guide students through processes of inquiry, reflexivity, and exploration toward proactive stances in generating transformative practices and, finally, leadership of the future.

In chapter 7, "Transport Sustainability and the Airport City," Michael B. Charles and Paul H. Barnes discuss how air travel, air cargo, and just-in-time logistic systems have led to the creation of unsustainable aerotropolises, or airport cities, that operate "more or less independently of the[ir] conventional (or 'host') city." The authors call attention to the damage done by airplane construction, fossil fuels from airplanes and related ground vehicles, and aerotropolis construction. This damage includes destruction of valuable habitats, noise pollution, release of GHG emissions, and other serious consequences that necessitate envisioning a more sustainable model. Such a plan, however, cannot be "one-size-fits-all," according to the authors, who divide aerotropolises into space-rich and space-poor and examine the numerous issues airport cities must address to achieve sustainability.

Some aerotropolises are planned more independently of cities, such as Australia's Brisbane Airport and Thailand's Suvarnabhumi Airport (production of which was on hold at the time of writing because of political instability) and other "build it and they will come" airports. However, most develop out of existing structures and are surrounded more closely by existing neighborhoods and developments, such as the Netherlands' Shiphol. Because of this basic difference, some airports will struggle to contain impacts on natural communities and others will work harder to contain their impacts on residential and commercial ones.

Guidelines that have been developed by some industry groups, Charles and Barnes note, appear not to have been constructed for community-specific needs, but rather to reduce complaints and to create a one-size-fits-all approach. Instead, the authors suggest that a truly sustainable model be suggested, which would address governance, transport and connectivity, services, environment, equity, economy, housing and the built environment, and social aspects and culture in community specific terms.

They propose that emerging space-rich aerotropolises be evaluated in their own right, as potentially sustainable communities—with consideration of their quality of governance arrangements, transport and connectivity, services, environment, equity, economy, housing and the built environment, and social aspects and culture. Merging community (airport) specific needs with broader sustainability goals, they argue will appropriately move us away from industry guidelines, which serve only to "limit negative responses to airport activities."

In chapter 8, "Sustainable Aviation: Challenges and Solutions in a Carbon Constrained World," Dawna L. Rhoades "takes off" from the airport discussion in the preceding chapter by continuing and expanding the exploration of the role of aviation in global warming into other domains. Her discussion and analyses demonstrate how differences in aviation markets and governmental actions around the world influence the impacts of the aviation industry on the global environment. She observes how the position of aviation in the United States and the resulting governmental actions (and nonactions) relative to the industry have yielded different types and extents of its impacts on the world compared to the impacts of aviation in other global regions. The contrast is especially clear when the actions of the European Union are considered, where the industry is seemingly committed to follow through with the EU Emissions Trading Scheme set by the European Commission. The chapter also explores and sheds light on where inefficiencies stem from in specific segments of the aviation industry in the United States—airlines, manufacturers, airports, general aviation, airspace, and air cargo.

Rhoades then discusses how the aviation industry segments tackle the demands to participate in sustainability negotiations and what voluntary and mandated actions are relevant to the goal of reduction of GHG emissions. Beyond the obvious answer of need to create and put into place new technologies that would reduce fuel and energy consumption, and new types of alternative fuels, these include process redesign in how airports are operated, and holistic approaches toward GHG issues. However, while recent research has reported on best practices, produced advice, and offered specific guidelines, there are a number of reasons why implementing systemic environmental initiatives has not yet achieved popularity.

By failing to take a proactive stance, airlines in the United States may be risking much of the competitive advantage they have. At least two risk factors that threaten the airlines' futures are the high probability that environmental regulations will be tightened and the possibility that U.S.-EU multilateral service agreements will not be conducive to the U.S airlines' competitive success. Although some sectors of the aviation industry in the United States are addressing climate change proactively, the industry as a whole, and the airlines in particular, have much do to catch up with European aviation's posture on the environment and its implications for global sustainability.

The possibilities of holistic solutions are further explored in chapter 9, "Closed-Loop Supply Chain Management For Global Sustainability," where Matthew J. Drake and Mark E. Ferguson look into extending traditional understanding of supply chain management (that includes "forward flows" from suppliers to end users) to the broader view of it: closed-loop supply chain management (that also incorporates "reverse flows" of products returned by end users). The authors demonstrate how viewing management of reverse flows solely as a cost center can be shifted to an empowering perspective of value-creating opportunity. The dilemma that remains here is that from a societal point of view, various supply chain management practices may still remain suboptimal: traditional business models are based on increasing consumption, while sustainable society is only possible via decreased per-capita consumption.

While reverse flows may originate from a variety of sources, the value that U.S. companies realize from engaging reverse flows of their product is mainly based on self-organizing principles (as opposed to the European Union where comprehensive producer responsibility legislation is in force). That is, companies implementing closed-loop supply chain management strategies can gain tangible benefit, such as reduced costs of reverse flows management, but also intangible benefit, such as enhancing their brand by promoting their environmental and social consciousness. In practice, commitment to include reverse flows into supply chain management means adopting specific strategies related to product acquisition, operational planning, and pricing and demand management: subsequent sections of the chapter discuss a number of such strategies, illustrated by examples of companies that successfully turned reverse flows into competitive advantage. Strategic choices are discussed in the logical order of reverse flows stages, and include: waste-stream system versus market-driven system, use of automation and financial incentives in the product acquisition stage; organizing reverse logistics networks and manufacturing planning operational planning and costing stage; and development of decision-support models in the pricing and demand management stage.

In concluding sections, the authors point toward truly vanguard practices where companies have been able to reduce consumption of their products with no negative impact, or even higher profitability by bundling services into the products. These examples establish closed-loop supply chain management as a vital element in a true definition of business sustainability.

In chapter 10, "Construction and Demolition Debris Recycling for Sustainable Local Economic Development," Lynn M. Patterson explores the changing attitudes of local economic agencies toward construction and demolition (C&D) recycling and demonstrates how promising this largely overlooked opportunity for environmental improvement actually is. While most local communities have historically placed their primary emphasis on economic growth, and traditional paths to such growth, with little interest in the complex implications of such growth, Patterson indicates that many are becoming more socially and environmentally aware. For many of those communities, C&D recycling presents a good economic opportunity for a new form of effective and environmentally friendly development. However, Patterson notes that little research has been done to explore the relationship between local economic development agencies and C&D recycling.

In particular, the chapter explores the extent to which local economic development agencies are aware of the economic benefits of C&D recycling. These include profitability and the increase in related economic activities, job growth, and employment for less skilled workers and for those "at risk." In addition to the more traditionally recognized benefits of C&D recycling there are other and broader social/sustainability benefits that can arise. These include reduced landfill dependency, lowered emissions from landfills, reduced pollution from landfill leaching, and reduced need for the use of virgin materials. Some of the common barriers to entry facing C&D recycling industries are also discussed: low landfill fees, subsidized virgin materials, apathy toward wastefulness and waste, and weak markets for recycled materials.

Patterson conducted a national survey of local economic development agencies to determine how they view the introduction of C&D recycling. The survey covered communities serving 100,000 or more persons. The information provided by the 207 survey respondents suggests that attitudes are changing toward recycling and there is increasing awareness that recycling can be economically, as well as socially, beneficial to communities. However, her survey also shows that few agencies have more than one or two employees devoted to recycling. While agencies feel recycling can provide economic benefits to some areas, the same agencies are less likely to support recycling industries in their own town.

Despite this gap between attitudes and action, some agencies (though only 8% of Patterson's sample) do support recycling industries. This support traditionally takes the form of (1) recruitment efforts, (2) site/location assistance, (3) marketing aid, and (4) financial assistance. Other agencies provide less traditional assistance in the form of creating building guides for C&D materials or other means. Yet, even supporters of C&D recycling were also frequently found to be uncertain of local recycling regulation and landfill capacity issues, suggesting that other values drive recycling support. Patterson ends the chapter by summarizing her interpretations of her findings—that there is a growing interest in sustainability and recycling-based development and there is an increased willingness to be flexible in pursuing opportunities that arise, despite the currently low support rates.

The final chapter in the book, Sam Wong's Chapter 11: "Wrestling With the Hard Realities—Unintended Consequences and Disappointing Outcomes in a U.K. Water Project," calls attention to two aspects of the global sustainability challenge: environmental sustainability and social justice. In the course of doing so, he provides a sobering reminder of just how subtle and fine-grained the task of moving toward an environmentally sustainable world in socially just ways can be. Wong investigates the difficulties present in the adoption of sustainable technologies in poor communities through the rubric of a case study of the adoption of sustainable rainwater and greywater technologies in northwest England. His case example demonstrates that the success of sustainable technologies has more to do with the subjective attitudes of the communities adopting them than many assume, pointing to the importance of bottom-up transformation to developing and implementing sustainable technologies and practices.

Wong's case study documents attempts made to induce a poor, mainly elderly community to adopt a greywater and rainwater recycling system. The ways key decisions about the system were made, the ways it was "marketed" to the residents, and the failure to understand how community members felt about the proper use of different types of water all contributed to the ultimate failure of the initiative. Wong concludes that such a failure reveals that sustainable innovation must be analyzed against the background of broader psychological, institutional, and societal dynamics.

REFERENCES

Isaacs, W. (1999). *Dialogue and the art of thinking together.* New York: Random House/Currency.

Quinn, R. E. (1996). *Deep change: Discovering the leader within.* San Francisco: Jossey-Bass.

Stoner, J. A. F. (1978). *Management.* Englewood Cliffs, NJ: Prentice Hall.

CHAPTER 2

EVERGREEN BRICK WORKS

Planning for Success in a
Triple Bottom-Line Enterprise

**Ushnish Sengupta, Geoff Cape, Seana Irvine,
Pierre Bertrand, and Ann Armstrong**

This chapter describes the benefits and challenges of developing a triple bottom-line approach as a core business strategy for a sustainable social enterprise. Evergreen Brick Works is a CDN$55 million multiyear project to redevelop a heritage site into a revenue-generating center for environmental excellence. The Evergreen Brick Works is an ambitious project undertaken by Evergreen, an environmental organization that engages in the urban greening of schools and other civic spaces. The environmental and social goals for the Brick Works build and extend beyond the parent organization's social mandate and core competencies.

Evergreen's ambitious plan for the Brick Works carries significant risk, and at the same time, provides a unique opportunity for demonstrating the successful transformation of a nonprofit organization into a revenue-generating social enterprise. The Brick Works project provides Evergreen with a unique opportunity to measure its progress toward sustainability

Global Sustainability Initiatives: New Models and New Approaches
pp. 15–32

and to serve as a model for the sustainable practices that it seeks to propagate. Evergreen's mission statement explains the profound sustainable changes the organization aims to achieve over the long term:

> Evergreen's mission is to bring communities and nature together for the benefit of both. (Evergreen, 2008)

EVERGREEN BRICK WORKS

Evergreen Brick Works is a $55 million project to redevelop a 100 year-old abandoned downtown Toronto brick factory into an innovative triple bottom-line enterprise. The project integrates efforts of nonprofit organizations, government agencies, and corporations to achieve social, environmental, and economic goals that engage the public and demonstrate new ways of doing business. Located on a 12-acre site, within the ravine system of downtown Toronto, Evergreen Brick Works will comprise almost 200,000 square feet of building space in 15 heritage buildings and one new building available for use by a variety of community partners and private tenants. An architect's rendering of Evergreen Brick Works is provided in Figure 2.1.

Source: Image courtesy of DTAH.

Figure 2.1.   Evergreen Brick Works birdseye view.

HISTORY OF THE PROJECT

Evergreen is a charity with a strong entrepreneurial streak. Since its inception in 1989, Evergreen has embraced the bold vision of becoming a leader in Canada's urban-greening movement. Evergreen has evolved into an organization that leverages corporate sponsorships with multinationals like Toyota, Home Depot, Wal-Mart, and Unilever for most of its funding. In 2002, exploring opportunities for reaching new audiences for its programs and tiring of the ongoing project-based funding model, Evergreen began to examine business approaches that aligned with its mission. The concept of starting a native plant nursery to supply the increasing demand for native plant materials quickly emerged as an idea worth pursuing. Employing at-risk youth helped to flesh out the nursery into a triple bottom-line social enterprise—one that would serve environmental and social mandates with a built-in business component. Gradually, additional programs were added, including farmers' markets, office space, event facilities, cultural programs, and a variety of youth initiatives.

In the spirit of "emerging strategy," Evergreen stumbled on the Don Valley Brick Works site as a potential home for the nursery. In comparison with the current plans to transform the site into a large-scale venue for exploring nature, culture, and community, the original plans were relatively modest and were restricted to one building. However, the natural and cultural significance of the Brick Works, coupled with Evergreen's mandate of bringing nature back to our cities, quickly gave rise to opportunities and synergies that would have been impossible to predict at the outset. In many respects, the project has continued to evolve and gain momentum as new partners have joined, and as Evergreen has developed a greater appreciation of both the complexity and potential of the site.

The intent of creating a social enterprise remains a driving principle of this project and one which Evergreen monitors closely as business and master plans continue to evolve. What is better understood now is that a nonprofit organization undertaking a triple bottom-line development of this scale is an exciting undertaking for which Evergreen has found few comparative models worldwide. Ultimately, success will be measured not only by Evergreen's ability to raise capital and create attractive architecture, but also by its ability to offer compelling programs that support Evergreen's mandate and the ongoing operation of the Brick Works. As Drucker has noted, innovation often comes from an unexpected event, which can be a symptom of a unique opportunity (Drucker, 1993).

THE BRICK WORKS' MAIN GOAL

The main goal for Evergreen Brick Works is to inspire visitors to become active participants in shaping a more sustainable future through education that inspires action. The goals of the interpretive program—provide a sense of place, make connections to the city, and demonstrate the benefits of nature firsthand—should contribute to this main goal of inspiring positive actions directed at creating a more sustainable future. Achieving the program goals and objectives will make Brick Works worth a visit. Visitors may come with a specific destination in mind, but feeling the spirit of the place and making a connection to the site will be their unexpected reward.

Provide a Sense of Place: For visitors, a sense of place emerges through an emotional connection to the history of an area, its wildlife, and its legends. To provide a sense of place, the project will pursue three objectives that involve (1) describing what makes Evergreen Brick Works unique, (2) examining the natural history of the area, and (3) drawing attention to Evergreen's work in the community.

The interpretive program must reinforce these objectives through the voice of the text, the imagery selected, and the physical design of the displays.

Make Connections to the City: Over the years, the Brick Works has served many purposes that have shaped the city. The interpretive program should provide notable insights into the regional impact of sustainability, industry, and geology as they relate to the Brick Works.

Demonstrate the Benefits of Nature Firsthand: As a leader in the urban-greening movement, Evergreen is in the midst of transforming an abandoned industrial space into a unique community place that connects visitors with nature. To inspire action, the interpretive program should demonstrate the social and environmental benefits of this transformation.

Purpose Statement

A purpose statement was designed to introduce Evergreen Brick Works' goals and desired outcomes. It informs the entire project and the interpretive program. It reads:

- Evergreen Brick Works will provoke new ideas about the relationship between nature, people, and cities.
- By capitalizing on the Brick Work's unique natural and industrial heritage setting and engaging and educating the community about diverse nature-based experiences, people will be able to witness the

benefits of nature firsthand, giving them a renewed sense of place and inspiring them to become active participants in shaping a more sustainable future

PROJECT GOALS AND OBJECTIVES

Evergreen developed the following sets of goals and objectives to inform the planning and programming of the entire Brick Works site.

Overall Project Goals

- Transform an industrial heritage site into the greenest facility in North America.
- Establish Evergreen Brick Works as a multipurpose, multiprogram site that serves as a model of economic, environmental, and social sustainability.
- Strengthen Evergreen's profile as a national leader in Canada's environmental sector.
- Build Evergreen's capacity to operate efficiently and effectively.

Project Objectives

- Design and operate Evergreen as a "zero footprint" facility.
- Operate Evergreen Brick Works on an economically self-sustaining basis.
- Deliver unique and innovative programs focused on motivating sustainable behavioral change.
- Attract new program participants, volunteers, members, and donors to support Evergreen's mission.
- Create new revenue streams to support Evergreen's programs.

PROGRAM GOALS AND OBJECTIVES

The following set of program goals and objectives are specific to programming and the interpretive experiences at Evergreen Brick Works.

Program Goals

- Create a destination center for Torontonians and visitors alike looking to have fun and learn while saving the world.
- Empower people with the knowledge that their actions do matter and they can be part of creating a more sustainable future.
- Transform an abandoned industrial space into a unique community place that connects visitors with each other, the soil under their feet, and with a unique heritage property that helped build our city.
- Foster new partnerships among traditionally unaligned agencies that together, can create rich educational programs that encourage sustainable living.

Program Objectives

- Raise public awareness about the importance of nature in our cities and the need to create more sustainable cities.
- Provide people with the inspiration, training, and resources to reduce their "ecological footprints" and help shape a more sustainable future.
- Provide employment opportunities for at-risk youth that build confidence, team and life skills, and improve their opportunities for finding employment.
- Provide opportunities for people to work and learn together.
- Appeal to families looking to spend time together in meaningful and affordable ways.
- Deliver programs that speak to the site's unique geology and industrial heritage.
- Deliver programs that demonstrate the relationships between urban sustainability and issues such as health, the arts, food, and urban ecology.
- Strengthen Evergreen's position as a national leader in Canada's urban greening movement.
- Use the operation of the facility as a stage for demonstrating environmental best practices.
- Use the programs as a revenue-generating stream that helps support facility operations.

Evergreen's Supportive Anchor Programs

As part of the overall project, Evergreen will offer a wide menu of environmental, arts and culture, leadership development, and food programs and services to contribute to the success of the site and to create a unique visitor experience. Anchor programs will include

- Evergreen Gardens—a large scale native plant nursery, garden center, and demonstration garden that will also offer skating in the winter;
- Farmer's and artisan's marketplace pavilions—offering local and organic foods and crafts that connect producers and artisans with consumers and two skating facilities in the winter;
- Food marché—offering local and prepared foods;
- Children and adult discovery center—offering educational and experiential exhibits and play areas for people to learn about and connect with nature;
- Jamie Kennedy Foundation—a foundation to be established by Jamie Kennedy, famed Toronto restaurateur and caterer, that will offer similar programs to those of the James Beard Foundation in New York City;
- Conference and event facilities;
- Administration space for Evergreen and other social entrepreneurs;
- Annual program of festivals and events related to the program goals and objectives; and
- Overall, a stronger habitat from which to develop, market, and deliver Evergreen's core programs.

ENVIRONMENTAL AND SOCIAL OPPORTUNITIES

Evergreen Brick Works is designed to provide a number of opportunities for realizing environmental and social benefits. They include Evergreen Gardens, developing partnerships and shared programs, providing administrative space for non-for-profit organizations, implementing a strategy related to food, developing a discovery center, developing Brick Works Park, and incorporating green technologies in its operations.,

Evergreen Gardens

Within Evergreen Gardens, visitors will be provided with opportunities to learn best practices from the latest innovations in home and school ground greening, restoration projects in parks and public lands, and pesticide-free landscaping. Visitors will be able to increase their knowledge of native plants and buy plants to return to their communities to implement

Source: Image courtesy of Ferruccio Sardella.

Figure 2.2.   Evergreen Gardens.

green school grounds, restore local parks and public lands, and practice pesticide-free landscaping for gardens. An artist's rendering of Evergreen Gardens is provided in Figure 2.2.

Partnerships and Programs

Evergreen will partner with community organizations that share environmental and social values to provide programs and learning opportunities.

In collaboration with the YMCA, the native plant nursery and demonstration garden will offer at-risk youth jobs and skills training. The YMCA is the largest provider of youth employment in Toronto. The youth employment program will be targeted to at-risk youth who face systemic barriers to employment. At-risk youth are often early school leavers, who have not completed postsecondary education. A structured employment training program for young people provides hands-on training and support, including job preparation, assistance in securing a job, and assistance in keeping a job including individual and group counseling.

Evergreen Brick Works will provide a variety of employment opportunities, including garden center jobs, restaurant jobs, and commercial sales and service jobs. Job skills are developed with the help of an adult mentor to help ensure that youth are less likely to fall out of the labor market. Outcome research indicates that at-risk youth who enter a structured program develop early engagement in labour market, return to further education and/or formal training, and experience an easier transition to permanent jobs (Outward Bound, 2007).

Outward Bound Canada will set up ropes courses, climbing walls, and minicamps. Outward Bound currently runs courses for students outside the city, but at cost of $150 per day, these are expensive for many school children. Evergreen Brick Works will enable Outward Bound to provide programs at a more reasonable cost for climbing wall activities and it will make Outward Bound available to public schools such as the Toronto School Board. Outward Bound's facilities at the Brick Works will facilitate team building, individual confidence, working in groups, and trusting others. Outcome research indicates that at-risk youth who are involved in Outward Bound activities have a greater high school retention rate (Outward Bound, 2007).

Administrative Space for Nonprofit Organizations

The only new building in the facility will be a four-story addition that will contain almost 40,000 square feet of office space which shall serve as the new home base for Evergreen. It will also provide colocation with other social entrepreneur and not-for-profit organizations. The colocation will provide a structured program enabling tenants to interact formally and informally, reduce costs through shared space and core services, share knowledge, and collaborate on approaches to addressing environmental issues.

Food Strategy

A large-scale farmers' market will provide visitors with the opportunity to purchase local and organic produce and to learn about slow food processes.

Internationally renowned chef Jamie Kennedy, through a foundation and restaurant to be located at the Brick Works, will bring internationally and locally renowned chefs to provide patrons with the best in slow food and cuisine both in the restaurant and through programming events elsewhere in the facility. The Children's Discovery center will also provide children with hands-on exhibits and play areas that allow them to see where food is cultivated, harvested, and prepared.

Source: Image courtesy of Ferruccio Sardella

Figure 2.3.   Children's playground.

Discovery Center

In an age of indoor play, canceled recess, and virtual realities, the family-friendly Discovery Center will provide an experiential learning laboratory that will connect children of all ages with nature. The Discovery Center will immerse children in a multisensory, low-tech experience that starts in the local past and moves toward the global future. This experience will extend beyond the nearly 10,000 square feet internal area to an innovative outdoor play area located in the chimney courtyard on the north side of the facility. An artist's rendering of the children's playground is provided in Figure 2.3.

The second floor mezzanine of the Discovery Center will provide people of all ages with educational and experiential exhibits on a variety of ever-changing topics related to nature and communities.

Brick Works Park

Evergreen Brick Works is located at the center of the Toronto ravine system, a series of ravines that traverse the city and connect with Lake Ontario. The 30 acre Brick Works Park is located immediately to the north of the old factory site and was created by filling in the old quarry that fed the brick factory. The Toronto ravine system and Brick Works Park will be important elements of Evergreen's strategy at the site even though they are not officially a part of the space Evergreen is leasing from the city. Both will allow visitors to travel to Evergreen Brick Works by foot, bicycle, and other nonpolluting forms of transportation and in the process, provide additional green recreational space for city residents.

Green Technology

The Brick Works will incorporate the latest in green design technologies for the efficient use of water and energy. The facility will incorporate green roofs, photovoltaic panels, biomass heating, living walls, and naturalized landscapes. The administration building at the Brick Works will strive for a "platinum" level of LEED certification. The LEED Canada Rating System has been developed by the Canada Green Building Council to recognize "leadership in energy and environmental design."

EVERGREEN AT THE BRICKWORKS EXPERIENCE —AS OF NOVEMBER 2007

Evergreen has taken a bootstrap approach to building experience, expertise, and funding ability to implement the Brick Works project. The risks associated with the project revolve around the three main components: design and construction, programming, and legal/finance. Coordinating and finding the right balance between the three has been the primary challenge in developing the plans for the site, heightened by the fact that Evergreen had to design around an existing set of derelict buildings that were not originally constructed for their new purposes. Evergreen has primarily seconded employees from its core programs to take on the necessary roles for the project either on a full-time or part-time basis. Some additional employees have also been brought in, such as a general manager, to supplement skills sets that were not sufficiently present.

Volunteers have also been added to Evergreen's board and Brick Works Board Committee with expertise in real estate development, architecture and finance to bolster experience and to offer advice. Finally, a multitude of contracted parties in the architecture, interpretive design, and construction industries have been engaged to move the project forward. All of these changes involved much learning and stress on the core Evergreen staff and programming at a time when that programming is accelerating its growth due to the increased focus on the environment and the increasing visibility and reputation of Evergreen.

In order to learn more about the viability of its intended programs, Evergreen structured a series of programs and events at the facility during 2006 and 2007 using the outdoor pavilions and one of the smaller buildings that had been recently renovated by the city.

Summary of 2006 Brick Works Programs

Evergreen's 2006 programs at the Brick Works were considered a solid success, involving more than 5,000 participants through the following activities:

- Two large festivals called Doors Open and Harvest Family Fun Day;
- An ambitious program of planting and stewardship activities involving planting beds and the Brick Works Park;
- The opening of an Interpretive Showroom; and
- A broad menu of smaller events, walks and talks with a variety of partners. These included a First Nations Spring Ceremony, yoga events, photography workshops, native plant gardening workshops, and numerous site tours.

2007 Goals and Objectives

Evergreen had two key goals for the spring-summer-fall programming in 2007:

1. Learn by doing, iron out kinks, and build Evergreen's capacity for its ultimate management of Evergreen Brick Works.
2. Build community support and awareness for Evergreen Brick Works.

Its objectives included (1) generating revenues associated with third party events and various program activities, setting the stage for Evergreen's triple bottom-line enterprise, (2) developing relationships with key event suppliers, farmers, and so on, creating the solid base of networks required for the ultimate operation of the Brick Works, (3) demonstrating Evergreen's commitment to "walking the talk" in terms of green operations, quality public education programs, and creating a collection of fun, colorful, and dynamic multiprogram activities, (4) gearing most of the activities to the "family audience" while hosting specific activities tailored to youth and new Canadian audiences, and (5) generating enthusiasm among existing and potential donors that this is a fabulous project to support.

Programs included introducing Evergreen Gardens; launching the Brick Works Farmers' Market as a weekly, Saturday morning market; layering different activities running simultaneously on an ongoing basis; placing greater emphasis on having three large events (Doors Open, a Summer Food Celebration, and Harvest Family Fun Day), and increasing the number of space rentals of the pavilions to corporations and not-for-profits.

Overall, the season was a great success and provided Evergreen with valuable learning, attracting more people than Evergreen ever expected (over 20,000) and basically serving as a proof of concept for many elements of Evergreen's plans.

PLANS FOR 2008

The plans for the 2008 season will move the bar even further for Evergreen by being more focused on fewer but larger, better managed, and more profitable events and programming. These will include an expanded Farmer's Market, a few festival/picnic like events, one major fundraiser for Evergreen, and the native plant nursery. Evergreen will also increase its presence at the site through signage, banners, and so on. The season is expected to end somewhat earlier than in 2006 and 2007 as construction is expected to start in September 2008.

Organizational Change

Evergreen is continuing its change from a highly entrepreneurial not-for-profit to a triple bottom-line oriented organization. The Brick Works project requires an organizational culture that allows risk taking, balanced with management control. Evergreen is developing this balance between the flexibility required to manage constant change, and the organizational processes required to mitigate the many new risks emanating from the project.

Involvement of the Board

Evergreen's board and its committees have provided strong positive ongoing support for the Brick Works project. Evergreen has highly evolved governance practices with clear separation between the Board and operations. The board has taken steps to increase risk and financial management processes and has agreed to incur up to $12 million in interim financing to bridge the gap between private pledge payments and the expenditure of funds on construction. Evergreen has been able to recruit new board and committee members with required financial, development, and legal backgrounds.

Evergreen Staff Involvement

One of the challenges of taking on a large project like the Brick Works is finding staff with the required skills. Most of the people assigned to the Brick Works project are internal Evergreen staff who have additional Evergreen program responsibilities. Through these secondments and split responsibilities, the focus on the Brick Works has caused some management and staff to be concerned that core programs would be neglected. However, Evergreen management has mitigated this risk by utilizing capital funding for the Brick Works so that current programming is not jeopardized and maintaining strong internal communications so that staff have the confidence that core programs will be supported over the long term. In addition, the plans for the Brick Works include many elements that will allow Evergreen to leverage and market its core services to a greater extent.

TRIPLE BOTTOM-LINE MEASURES OF SUCCESS

The evolution of Evergreen Brickworks' performance measures includes the conversion of the Brick Works Values Charter (see Table 2.1) into specific performance measures for Evergreen and the various subtenants and licensees at the site. The framework will expand beyond the Brick Works to include Evergreen's significant national set of programs in Learning Grounds, Common Grounds, and Home Grounds primarily centered around design, stewardship, and grant administration.

Financial Measures of Success

The primary financial benchmark is to achieve self-sufficiency which, based on financial projections, should occur by the fourth year of operations once the estimated $12 million in interim financing is repaid. Financial self-sufficiency will require increasing revenues and profits, as well as reducing costs for the triple bottom-line enterprise while achieving measurable environmental and social objectives.

The Brick Works faces a number of financial challenges in the early stages. Evergreen has invested a substantial amount of its own resources and finances and has incurred the opportunity cost of not investing these resources into its existing programs. Initial capital for the project has been raised through $30 million in government grants and $7 million in private donations. Another $18 million in private donations remains to be pledged.

Table 2.1.   Brick Works Values Charter

Who we are:
- We are a community of organizations whose mission and values celebrate the three core themes of the Brick Works—nature, culture and community.
- We are organizations that operate in a financially, socially, and environmentally responsible manner.
- We strive for excellence in our respective fields.

Why we are here:
- We honour the history and sense of place that define the Brick Works and recognize the important role it plays promoting the conservation of Toronto's natural and cultural heritage.
- We bring together our shared values that include trust, transparency, and inclusiveness to all of our work.
- We believe that working together creates synergies that can make a more significant contribution than if we were working on our own.

Therefore, we are committed to:
- Inspiring social change by demonstrating leadership and innovation.
- Making our cities more livable by reducing the impacts of our operations on the natural environment and showcasing best practices.
- Working collaboratively in the spirit of the shared values that underlie the Brick Works to ensure its success and inspire its future growth.

Nursery and Garden Center: The nursery and garden center at the Brick Works will be operated as a profit center and provide visitors with the opportunity to purchase a wide variety of native plants, as well as other plants and garden products. Evergreen will also offer its Home Ground private home landscape design services through this center. The garden center will be located along both the interior and exterior spaces of three buildings at Evergreen Brick Works including Evergreen Gardens, which will serve as a demonstration garden.

The number of plants bought from the nursery will be a measure of financial and environmental success. An increase in the number of native plants purchased and planted will result in a more sustainable ecosystem. The environmental benefits of education efforts can and will be measured. Evergreen has long-term experience in sustainable planting events at schools and communities. Therefore, environmental measures of success should include increases in the number of planting events based on learning at the nursery and Evergreen Gardens, as well as the number of trees and plants utilized in planting events.

Environmental benefits are looked at in terms of their benefits to human health. Evergreen's research and programs to date have explored the wide range of benefits that accrue from the presence of nature—improved access to shade, decreased vandalism, increased aptitude for learning, more physical activity, and greater sense of community belonging (Dyment, 2005; Evergreen, 2006; Raffan, 2000). These benefits have the opportunity to proliferate by using Evergreen Brick Works as a test case and demonstration vehicle.

Partners and Programs: Partners using program space will pay a rental fee that will provide revenues for Evergreen. For cost recovery purposes, the partners will charge a fee to visitors taking part in programs. Evergreen Brick Works provides a number of unique services and products for visitors interested in sustainable lifestyles and will therefore be an attractive location for businesses providing sustainable products and services. Customers who visit the Brick Works for a sustainable product or service will be likely to purchase products and services from other colocated organizations providing additional complementary sustainable products and services.

The number of visitors participating in programs, workshops, and outreach events will be a financial as well as an environmental measure of success. Follow-up surveys of visitors and participants will provide feedback on the use of the knowledge gained from Evergreen Brick Works. The ability to mobilize a number of volunteers participating in each event will be an important measure of success that will both support Evergreen's mandate, as well as reduce operating costs.

The influence of Evergreen and its partners on public policy will be an important long-term measure of success. The number of municipalities engaged in workshops will be tracked, as well as the resulting affect on municipal, provincial, and federal government policies.

In conjunction with its partners, Evergreen has established a number of social measures of success for its at-risk youth program. The number of participants engaged in an employment or training program will be one measure of success, since participation in a program increases the potential for long-term employment. An intermediate measure of success will be the number of program participants gaining employment. Long-term measures of success will include length and variety of employment. Stakeholders, including government agencies, will be interested in long-term social cost savings achieved through, for example, the reduction of requirements to provide employment benefits and social services to individuals who are no longer at risk.

Administration Space: Rental revenue from leasing administration space to other social entrepreneurs and nonprofits will provide one of the largest revenue streams for Evergreen. Rental revenue will be used for the ongoing operating costs. Tenants will benefit from long-term savings in energy and water usage through green building design. Tenants will also benefit from colocation and opportunities for interaction with other innovative organizations. Evergreen Brick Works provides a number of specialized products and services for visitors interested in sustainable lifestyles and, therefore, will be an attractive location for businesses providing sustainable products and services.

Opportunities for collaboration and results from collaboration opportunities will be tracked. The number and variety of tenants will be an important financial and social measure of success. The number of events involving multiple Brick Works tenants will be a measure of the opportunities for collaboration, while the number of joint ventures or partnerships formed between tenants will be a long-term measure of success for collaboration.

Food Strategy: A large-scale farmers' market will provide revenues for local and organic producers. Producers will provide revenue through a basic fee for use of space. Visitors attracted to the Brick Works by the farmers' market will be likely to use other products and services at the Brick Works, including the garden center, the Discovery Center, the marché, and the restaurant and café.

The number and variety of producers participating in the farmers' market will be an environmental and financial measure of success. An increase in the volume and variety of organic produce purchased will enable sustainable organic farming at larger scales. The number of patrons for the restaurant and café will also be a measure of environmental and financial success. An increase in the number of people consuming prepared slow food will lead to a corresponding reduction in the consumption of "fast food" and its harmful health and environmental effects.

Gateway to the Ravine System: The Brick Works Park will be connected to other parks in Toronto, providing additional routes of access for visitors, therefore increasing visitor traffic to the site. Outdoor recreation activities, such as biking and skating, provide opportunities for ancillary businesses such as bike and skate rentals. The number of visitors to the Brick Works arriving through sustainable modes of transportation will be tracked through traffic studies.

CONCLUSION

Evergreen Brick Works provides Evergreen, a Canadian environmental charity, with the opportunity to increase the scope and impact of its successful and growing program of design, planting, and grant administration services. In the process, it is pushing itself to move from a nationally recognized and entrepreneurial not-for-profit to a full-fledged triple bottom-line organization, an organization with a new national, green-design-leading base in the heart of Canada's largest city. Evergreen's current and future challenges and insights from implementing the project and changing its core organization and programs will serve as valuable lessons learned for other not-for-profits and socially conscious private sector organizations contemplating similar projects.

REFERENCES

Drucker, P. F. (1993). *Innovation and entrepreneurship*. New York: Collins.

Dyment, J. E. (2005). *Gaining ground: The power and potential of school ground greening in the Toronto District School Board*. Toronto, Ontario, Canada: Evergreen.

Evergreen. (2006). *Small wonders: Designing vibrant, natural landscapes for early childhood*. Toronto, Ontario and Vancouver, British Columbia, Canada: Evergreen and Toyota Canada.

Evergreen. (2008). *Evergreen mission statement*. Retrieved July 17, 2008, from http://www.evergreen.ca/en/about/about.html

Outward Bound. (2007). Retrieved June 14, 2008, from http://www.outwardbound.org/

Raffan, J. (2000). *Nature nurtures: Investigating the potential of school grounds*. Toronto, Ontario and Vancouver, British Columbia, Canada: Evergreen and Toyota Canada.

CHAPTER 3

HITTING FOUR BIRDS
WITH ONE STONE

The Rural Electrification Project for Peace in the Island of the al-Qaeda Front in East Asia

Mari Kondo

Alliance for Mindanao Off-Grid Renewable Energy program (AMORE) is a U.S. Agency for International Development (USAID) project started in 2002, with the collaboration of the Mirant Philippines Foundation. AMORE has introduced renewable energy to poor, remote, conflict-affected communities in Mindanao, in the southern part of the Philippines. Through strong community participation, the project tries to hit four birds with one stone: (1) environmental sustainability through the provision of clean renewable energy systems; (2) social sustainability by mending the war-torn social fabrics of the communities; (3) economic sustainability through the development of indigenous microbusinesses; and (4) political sustainability through the promotion of peace at the grassroots level. While the project addresses environmentally sustainable energy, it also has global relevance in another domain, promoting peace through collaboration of the public and private sector in al-Qaeda's area of acknowledged influence in Asia. Perhaps even more importantly, it shows how multinational corporations, through their

Global Sustainability Initiatives: New Models and New Approaches
pp. 33–60
Copyright © 2008 by Information Age Publishing
All rights of reproduction in any form reserved.

corporate social responsibility undertakings, might possibly contribute to world peace. The chapter describes innovative aspects of the project and lessons that can be learned from its experiences.

INTRODUCTION

This chapter reports on a program called AMORE, or Alliance for Mindanao Off-Grid Renewable Energy, a USAID project started in 2002. This project is one of several programs USAID conducted successfully under its Global Development Alliance (GDA) initiative (U.S. Agency for International Development [USAID], 2008). GDA is a public-private development partnership. The private foundation Mirant Philippines joined the project as one of the leading partners and as one of it corporate social responsibility initiatives.

Mindanao is the second largest island in the southern part of the Philippines, the largest Christian nation in Asia. Mindanao is also home to the country's largest Muslim population, which has had a long history of struggling for independence. While many believe the root cause of the struggle in Mindanao is religion, that view may be inaccurate. Instead, some are convinced that it is poverty—particularly in the area where the Muslim population resides—that is the major source of discontent and conflict (Human Development Network, United Nations Development Program, and New Zealand Agency for International Development, 2005). In recent years a growing number of antigovernment and/or terrorist organizations have emerged in Mindanao, which is now considered by some to be the al-Qaeda front in East Asia (Collier, 2006).

The chapter discusses AMORE, the rural electrification project led by USAID, Winrock International, Mirant Philippines Foundation, and other organizations. The project has introduced renewable energy, mainly solar housing systems, in poor, remote, conflict-affected communities in Mindanao that cannot be connected to the power grid. The report is based on data from fieldwork conducted in the areas by a Filipino researcher, interviews with officers in Manila,[1] and a survey of documents and available published literature.

Although AMORE may look like a simple electrification project, this project tries to hit four birds with one stone. The project seeks to contribute to the following:

1. Environmental sustainability—by providing clean renewable energy systems (mainly solar energy);

2. Social sustainability—by mending the war-torn social fabrics of the communities (including former guerillas and now empowered Moslem women);

3. Economic sustainability—by developing indigenous microbusinesses in the communities and providing hope for development (so the guerillas will stop kidnapping and fighting); and

4. Political sustainability—by promoting peace at the grassroots level and lessening antagonism against Christians and, especially against the United States.

The project has global relevance, because it addresses environmentally sustainable energy use, promotes peace in one of al-Qaeda's acknowledged areas of influence in Asia, and involves collaboration with a foreign governmental agency and local private sector institutions. Even more important, the project shows how multinational corporations, through their corporate social responsibility undertakings, can contribute directly and concretely to world peace by contributing to global sustainability at the local level. The project is innovative in many ways, and provides various lessons.

The chapter is organized in the following manner: After this brief introduction, the Philippines as well as the Mindanao conflicts are introduced in the next section. The third section discusses rural electrification and Mirant Philippines. The fourth and fifth sections describe the project and its organizational arrangements. The sixth and seventh sections discuss project innovations for sustainability and the achievements of the project. The eighth section discusses the challenges experienced and the areas needed for further innovation.

THE PHILIPPINES AND THE MINDANAO CONFLICT

The Republic of the Philippines is one of the largest archipelagos in the world, composed of more than 7,000 islands. The total land area of the Philippines is about 300,000 square kilometers, making it slightly smaller than the British Isles. The two largest islands, Luzon and Mindanao, account for about two thirds of the overall land area. The Mindanao, the southern island group, is about the size of Greece and its nearest neighbors are Malaysia and Indonesia. The Philippines is known as the "Christian country in Asia," with about 81% of its people being classified as Roman Catholic and 11% being considered Protestants or as members of other Christians' faiths. About 5% are Muslims and 2% are classified as being involved in other faith traditions (Central Intelligence Agency, 2008).

Historically, the first settlers in the Philippines were of Malay origins. In the fifteenth century, the first Islamic sultanate was established in Sulu. Islam quickly spread throughout the archipelago reaching all the way to the Luzon. When the Spaniards came in the sixteenth century, they colonized the Philippines and converted the majority of the population to Christianity, except the population of Mindanao and Sulu. The current Mindanao conflict has long historical roots, around 5 centuries since the time the Spaniards came to the Philippines (Schiavo-Campo & Judd, 2005; Stark, 2003).

After Philippine independence in 1946, conflict intensified in the late 1960s when Christian settlers were sent to Mindanao by the central government and disputes over land and other natural resources became serious. From the 1960s to 1990s, the Moro National Liberation Front (MNLF) guerillas represented the Muslim population in its fight against the Philippine government (Schiavo-Campo & Judd, 2005).

In 1989, the Autonomous Region in Muslim Mindanao (ARMM) was formed. ARMM is a region located in the southwestern portion of Mindanao which includes the mainland provinces of Maguindanao and Basilan, and the traditional island centers of Muslim economic, political, and cultural activities, Sulu and Tawi-Tawi. Most of the conflicts were reported around this region (Schiavo-Campo & Judd, 2005).

In spite of various peace negotiations, the armed conflict continued and it is now the Moro Islamic Liberation Front (MILF) guerillas who fight against the central government. It is said that MILF has some relations with the Indonesia-based Jemaah Islamiyah, which is regarded as the al-Qaeda front, though the relations may be sporadic and loose. There are also bandit type of criminals or terrorists, called Abu-Sayyaf in the area. There are various reasons for the conflicts. It is largely believed that the religious differences are only partial reasons; other more serious reasons include the prevalence of clan conflicts called Rido among Muslim population, widespread banditry, conflicts among Christians, inequalities, among others (Kamlian, 2005; Schiavo-Campo & Judd, 2005).

The cost of these conflicts is serious. Since the 1970s, 120,000 deaths and displacement of more than 2 million people have occurred. Poverty has worsened and kidnap-for-ransom has become common. Discouragement of investment in the region and in the Philippines has been serious. (Schiavo-Campo & Judd, 2005).

With a population of more than 2.4 million predominantly Muslim inhabitants in 2000, according to the National Statistic Office (NSO), the ARMM is by far poorest region in the Philippines. The NSO indicates that three fifths of the households used kerosene for lighting, while about 28% used electricity. About 31% of the households drew water for drinking from a spring, lake, river, or from rain. In the case of Tawi-Tawi, only

Table 3.1.   Selected Social Indicators

	Philippines	*NCR (Metro Manila)*	*ARMM*
Functional literacy rate (2003)	83.79	92.41	61.19
Infant mortality rate (2003)	30.00	24.00	41.00
Poverty incidences families (2000)	33.70	8.70	62.90

Source: Philippine Institute for Development Studies (2008a, 2008b, 2008c).

about 2% used community water systems (National Statistic Office, 2003). In an interview, an officer of the Mirant Foundation estimated that the human development/basic service level of Moslem Mindanao is around one tenth that of the National Capital Region (Metro Manila region). Public expenditures per capita for human development were only two thirds of the Philippines national level in 2001 (World Bank, 2003). The selected social indicators below which compare the Philippines as a whole, the National Capital Region, and ARMM, show the deprived status of the region.

RURAL ELECTRIFICATION AND THE MIRANT PHILIPPINES FOUNDATION

Rural electrification is considered globally as a tool to address the problems of social inequity and poverty; electricity can be a catalyst for growth and a better life. In 2002, the World Bank conducted a thorough study of rural electrification in the Philippines, measuring the social and economic benefits. A diagram of how electrification may benefit a community, prepared by the Mirant Philippines Foundation based on the said study of the World Bank (2002), is shown in Figure 3.1. As the diagram indicates the acquisition of electrical appliances can help bring intermediate benefits ranging from improved living comforts to livelihood possibilities. These in turn can translate into basic services enhancements that can include education, communication, health, and even productivity improvements.

In the 1960s, the Philippine government declared the total electrification of the country as a national policy objective. At that time, less than 18% of the country had electricity. The electricity distribution in urban areas, which could be profitable due to population density, is conducted by private firms, but the private firms were not interested in rural electrification. Therefore, in the 1960s rural electric cooperatives were established. The strategy was to establish rural electric cooperatives in

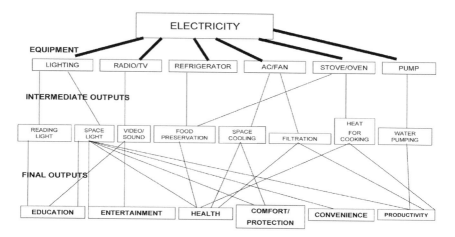

Source: Mirant Philippines Foundation (internal document).

Figure 3.1.   Relationships between electricity use and energy services.

contiguous areas with populations of around 100,000 people. By 1980 there were more than 120 electric cooperatives or distribution utilities scattered around the country. The focus was given to the electrification of barangays ("barangay" is the basic unit of local administration in the Philippines, somewhat equivalent to a "village"). (World Bank, 2002).

The Philippines experienced martial law under President Marcos, a dictator, from the early 1970s to the early 1980s. In 1972, the National Power Corporation (NPC) became the sole generator of power in the country (Sharma, Madamba, & Chan, 2004). During the Marcos period and the political turmoil afterwards, the Philippines could not come up with an effective energy policy. By the late 1980s, the NPC could no longer cope with the increasing demand for power. By the 1990s, the country was suffering from daily 4- to 12-hour blackouts that crippled industries and other businesses (Toba, 2007).

In the early 1990s, the Philippines faced a severe electricity crisis. However, neither the Philippine government nor NPC could build additional power plants on their own because of lack of borrowing capacity and poor credit ratings in global capital markets. To solve this problem, the government launched an aggressive campaign involving the private sector, foreign funding agencies, and other related organizations to invite private power producers to build power plants and to sell power to NPC so that the gap between supply and demand could be filled. At this time Hopewell, a predecessor of Mirant Philippines, came to the Philippines as one of the first independent power producers (IPPs) (Toba, 2007). Mirant Philippines subsequently became the largest independent power producer.

To encourage the quick entry of IPPs, the government provided generous concessions to the prospective IPPs (Toba, 2007). These concessions are deemed to be responsible for the high cost of electricity in the Philippines up to the present. IPPs, especially Mirant which decided to enter the Philippines early, enjoyed hefty concessions and high profits. Because of their high profits, the Philippine government required IPPs to give mandatory contributions to rural electrification efforts.

In the Philippines, rural electrification is important for its country-wide economic development. At the same time, it is important politically. Rural electrification, especially the number of barangays electrified, is one of the measurements of the effectiveness of a president in the Philippines in alleviating poverty and narrowing inequalities. In spite of this emphasis on rural electrification, according to Mirant, in 2001, 8,534 barangays still remained without electricity.

For rural electrification, the Philippine government has severely constrained resources so it needs to rely on private sector investments. In 2001, an act of the Philippine Congress created a unit within its Department of Energy (DOE) that would focus on achieving this goal. The agency is named the Electric Power Industry Management Bureau. The bureau's mission was to achieve 100% electrification. Funds come from a mandatory contribution by the IPPs equivalent to 1% of every peso earned from power purchased by the NPC. Those revenues are put into a holding fund to be used for development projects. The DOE launched the O-*Ilaw* (literally means "light") program for rural electrification which set the stage for a private-public partnership that sought to bring light to the countryside. The O-*Ilaw* program was further extended and renamed the Expanded Rural Electrification Program. To support the DOEs' rural electrification program, Mirant Philippines Corporation committed to electrify 1,500 barangay at a cost of U.S.$27,000,000 or Php1.5B. The program is called Project BEACON, and has been implemented and managed by Mirant's social development arm, Mirant Philippines Foundation. The AMORE program constituted part of the commitment of Mirant Philippines Foundation to rural electrification.

The Mirant Philippines Foundation, which was established 2001, was led by the country's recognized veterans of corporate social responsibility activities in the Philippines. The leaders of the foundation were not just interested in electrification, but in how to maximize the social and economic benefits gained by electrification in the rural areas concerned. An example of one of the Mirant Philippines Foundation's projects took place in five communities in the Province of Bohol, 10th largest island in the

Philippines. In Project BEACON, the foundation initiated a partnership with the Philippine Business for Social Progress (PBSP) to develop livelihood capabilities in the communities. PBSP is one of the largest non-government organizations in the country, with its membership composed of the largest companies in the Philippines. The foundation and PBSP encouraged a participative process involving the community in the five barangays that were electrified in 2002. Electricity was used to power water/irrigation systems, develop integrated farming activities, and capacitor community members in agriculture-based livelihood development. By the end of the project in 2007, productivity of the barangays had improved threefold and membership had increased in their respective people's organizations, which are kinds of self-help nongovernmental organizations.

THE AMORE PROJECT

AMORE, a rural electrification project using renewable energy, targets the poor of the conflict-ridden areas in Mindanao. As these communities are mostly located in the hinterlands, they are considered off-grid, indicating the impossibility of connecting them to existing power lines in a cost-effective manner. The electrification of these areas, therefore, can only be achieved through the use of stand-alone energy systems like those AMORE promotes. The project's non-global-warming and sustainable renewable energy systems come in three forms: photovoltaic (PV) battery charging stations; photovoltaic solar home systems; and microhydro power systems. As the project evolved, photovoltaic solar home systems emerged as the most-often used and most appropriate for the AMORE project (Winrock International, 2005).

Choice of the System

The cost of solar home systems was about twice as expensive as that of battery charging stations. Therefore, battery charging stations were developed in the first 10 participating barangays, most of which were in the island province of Tawi-Tawi. This approach entailed locating a charging station at the center of the barangay and the provision of batteries to households. A schedule was set for charging of the batteries and a fee was collected for charging time. The fee covered the wages of the battery technician and the charging station operator, as well as the cost of replacing clamps and cables (Winrock International, 2005). However, because the battery charging stations were located in the center of the barangays, no guard was around to secure them at night, resulting in pilferages that led to community conflict. In view of these and other early experiences of the program, Mirant, in consultation with the AMORE partnership and the communities, decided to shift to solar home systems.

The initial implementation of the solar home system consisted not only of 55 watt-peak solar home systems but also one 50 watt-peak community center lighting and two 75 watt-peak solar street lights. Later on in the project, due to the increase in the commercial value of the solar home systems and the termination of foreign subsidies, solar home systems for 30 households were the only components provided.

The project also tried to develop microhydro systems which have greater potentials for including wider numbers of households; however, only three were installed during the period of 2002-2005. The natural resources and local conditions turned out not to be well-suited for microhydro in the target areas (Winrock International, 2005).

Two-Pronged Approach

AMORE has a two-pronged approach to project implementation. In most target areas, there were no preexisting community-based institutions because most barangays were remote, conflict-ridden, and had been left out of the development process. Therefore, the business model required the creation of community-based institutions. Prior to installing solar power systems, the process involves "social preparation," during which a community chosen as a candidate for electrification is prepared for the installation of the systems through capacity-building activities. These activities seek to ensure the systems to be installed will be sustained. This intervention results in the establishment of a village association aptly called the Barangay Rural Electrification and Community Development Association (BRECDA).

Limited funds inhibit the electrification of all households in a barangay under the AMORE program. More specifically, only 30 households can initially be electrified in a barangay. To avoid conflicts during the selection process, transparency and fairness are sought. To qualify, a household must be able to pay an initial down payment of Php1,100 (U.S.$27.50 @ 1USD = Php40.00). If there are more than 30 remaining households which wish to be electrified, then the slots are raffled off.

Representatives from the 30 households chosen compose the membership of the BRECDA. The down payments collected initially constitute the operation and management (hereafter O&M) funds. Aside from their down payments, the 30 households are required to pay a fixed monthly amount (as agreed on by them) a percentage of which (10-20%) goes to an intensification fund, which is used for the purchase of solar power systems for the other households.

Once a BRECDA has been established, the association members are trained on basic financial management, basic operations, and maintenance for the system. After the training, the contractor (in keeping with the supply and installation contract) provides skills training and tools for basic trouble shooting in case of breakdowns. The contract stipulates that the organization of the community and the installation of the equipment should take only a year, after which AMORE is expected to make a graceful exit.

During the initial implementation of AMORE, the social preparation is done directly by AMORE staff. However, since AMORE would also like to enhance its network of nongovernmental organization (NGO) partners, the proponents decided to contract this aspect out to local NGOs.

In order to make sure that the community is well prepared to start the project successfully and to sustain it, the AMORE process entails seven tasks (Winrock International, 2005).

- **Task 1. Stakeholder dialogues:**
  At this stage, the strategies of the project are formulated though meetings with various stakeholders.

- **Task 2. Barangay electrification plan development:**
  The electrification plan for the barangays is created using secondary data and various assessments: Which barangay is to be electrified? What types of renewable energy are to be used?

- **Task 3. Community preparation activities:**
  The community assessments continue in dialogues with the communities selected. Questions raised include the following: Is the community really willing to acquire the equipment and to support the activities required for success? Can the cost be recovered? Does electrification add any value to the community, be it in productive or social terms, beyond just electrifying individual houses? The project strongly emphasizes community preparation and participation during this stage when the BRECDA is organized. A BRECDA has a minimum membership of 30 households which the project seeks to energize.

- **Task 4. Project design, procurement, and installation:**
  Winrock International, a contractor of USAID, prepares the project design, sometimes with the help of Mirant, while Mirant handles procurement.

- **Task 5. Design and development of the operations and maintenance fund:**
  The users have to assume the operation, maintenance, and replacement costs. The funds for these items must be collected by the BRECDA.

- **Task 6. Community training:**
  This task is a key elements that distinguish this project. The four main areas involved are: (1) technical training for the operation and maintenance of the energy system; (2) BRECDA operations and management, inclusive of leadership, financial management skills, and so forth; (3) business/economic development skills; and (4) livelihood training.

- **Task 7. Information, education, and communications program development and implementation:**
  Through videos, brochures, Web sites, photo exhibits, presentations, articles, and other means, the project is widely publicized among the stakeholders and potential project participants. This process is important, especially, for people who are skeptical about the intentions of the project, and of its goal of promoting peace in the region.

THE ORGANIZATION

According to the deputy executive director of Mirant Philippines Foundation, the organization running the AMORE program is quite "complicated." There are five key partners: USAID, Winrock International, Department of Energy of the Philippine government, Mirant Foundation, and the Autonomous Region in Muslim Mindanao (ARMM) government. Each has different ways of operating, different interests, and different contracts that bind them.

USAID has been aggressively involved in Mindanao in connection with its War on Terrorism. The USAID funds the social preparation phase and it makes sure that the program has been meeting the objectives of the Cooperative Agreement forged with Winrock International.

Winrock International is the U.S.-based organization that works primarily in USAID assistance projects that integrate environmental and economic sustainability. AMORE is headed by a "chief of party" of Winrock, who oversees operations, networking, and communication of AMORE. Under him, there are managers who handle functions like finance, information, education, communications, and technical. AMORE has an office

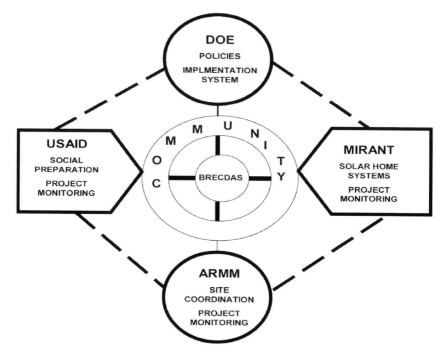

Source: Mirant Philippines Foundation (internal document).

Figure 3.2.   Organization of AMORE.

in Manila and has a field office in Mindanao. There are also three regional (site) managers located in areas where AMORE is operating.

As the policymaker, the Department of Energy determines the project implementation details and provides the list of barangays to electrify, sets the standards or systems specifications, and decides whether the installed system is suitable for final acceptance or if it requires rectification.

The Autonomous Region in Muslim Mindanao is the poorest and most difficult region to govern in the entire Philippines. The local ARMM government helps in the smooth implementation of the project.

Mirant Foundation makes sure that the specified solar power system is installed on site. Options for doing so include: (1) direct purchase/procurement and turnover of the equipment to Winrock; (2) granting of permission to Winrock to undertake procurement provided that a Mirant representative sits in the ad hoc technical working group. In both cases, if situation allows, Mirant Philippines Foundation tries to develop partnership agreements that maximize the benefits and the number of participants in the project through.

As was seen in the BEACON project, Mirant Foundation is good at bringing in many other partners. For example, numerous Filipino and multinational corporations and corporate foundations are involved in AMORE. These include ABS-CBN Foundation (recycling of used-up lead acid batteries), IBM Philippines (Computer-based early learning facilities and teacher training), Knowledge Channel Foundations (distance education facilities), SMART Communications and Globe Telecom (rural telecommunication facilities), Shell Solar Philippines and Pilipinas Shell Foundation (livelihood and health projects). Government agencies and local governments are also involved. For example, funds and/or training are provided by the Bureau of Fisheries for a seaweeds processing plant, the Bureau of Post Harvest Research for solar thermal tunnel dryers, and the Department of Science and Technology for computer training. Local government unites are responsible for program implementation and sustainability, providing political and financial supports. Likewise, foreign governments, like the British Embassy, Embassy of Japan, and so forth are involved. Other U.S. funded projects, like Growth with Equity in Mindanao, also help to provide potable water systems (AMORE, 2008a; Winrock International, 2005).

The competence of each of the program partners has helped in its success. USAID funded the social preparation side and saw to it that the major objective of the program was met. The DOE developed a viable and doable implementation policy, adjusting to the requirements of the funding agency. The ARMM Government coordinated with their constituencies who are beneficiaries of the program to assure the safe passage of labor and materials to the project sites, and Winrock International drew on its expertise in implementing renewable energy programs. Finally, Mirant made sure that the required systems were procured and installed using the highest standards of transparency and governance with special focus on sustainability of the systems.

Given that the public sector has certain constraints, the partnership of public and private sectors seems to function interesting ways, especially when operations are the difficult situations of conflict-ridden areas where

Table 3.2.   Financial Contribution to Project

Partner	Amount of Grant (in U.S.$)	Objective of Grant
USAID	10,000,000	Social preparation of support programs
MIRANT	5,000,000	Supply of solar power systems
Total project cost	15,000,000	

Source: Mirant Philippines Foundation (internal document).

law and order are fragile commodities. USAID approves a yearly work plan that Winrock submits, but once approved, USAID is strictly prohibited from "micro-managing." Winrock runs the field operation. However, according to the Mirant Foundation, USAID cannot deal, with such intricacies as perception of an unfair Chief of Party, a corrupt employee, or internal disputes. So in cases like these, it is the Mirant representative, who has no restrictions, who deals with. In short, the involvement of Mirant provides "flexibility" to deal with the environments where corruption and other abnormalities are frequent.

In one of the pilot cases of public-private collaborations with many partners, some coordination issues arose during the implementation. How to communicate who is really involved in the project and what that involvement might be became an issue. During an AMORE launching program, only the USAID-Winrock-DOE and ARMM logos were present; and in many publications, AMORE was described as an exclusively USAID Project. When those situations arose more than a few times, Mirant made it clear that it had joined the AMORE program and put in almost U.S.$5M not merely to be recognized as a supplier of solar power systems, but as a full partner in development. For more than 6 months, representatives from the partnership met to discuss how to resolve the issue of communications and other operational matters. They finally drafted a document titled, "Joint Declaration of Principles of Alliance." This document includes such items as the basis for unity among the partners, their shared vision, their common goal, and commitment to the development of a common, collaborative approach to rural electrification.

INNOVATIONS FOR SUSTAINABILITY

Many programs using renewable energy systems were implemented in the past by the Philippine government with support from foreign funding agencies. Unfortunately, many of these programs have also closed down and the systems abandoned. Because of the partners' awareness of these experiences, one of the earliest goals of the AMORE program was to establish a system establishing renewable energy that would sustain themselves into the future. (The partners might have called this a process of achieving "sustainable sustainability," but none of the interviews suggested that they used this phrase.) This section discusses some of the innovations of the AMORE project, related to sustainability for the environment, socioeconomic conditions, and peace.

SUSTAINABILITY FOR ENVIRONMENT— SOLAR HOME (PV) SYSTEMS

Establishing Solar Parts and Service Centers

To assure that the PV systems will be maintained properly by the households and community members, a supply of parts is very important. However, providing this supply proves to be a major challenge because of factors that make supply systems difficult to design and operate effectively, such as the existence of available suppliers in the area, reasonable pricing practices, and a large enough existing market to enable adequate sized operations to take place. These factors are difficult to find in AMORE communities. In the AMORE program, suppliers were required not only to put up service centers, but also to come up with 5-year warranties on service and parts (Winrock International, 2005).

This arrangement was considered to be necessary, but it also raises some issues, according to the Mirant Philippines Foundation. For a local supplier with an existing distribution network (e.g. Shell Solar Philippines) these requirements pose no problem. But, for small-scale local merchants and foreign suppliers, meeting such requirements will be very expensive. Therefore, entry barriers are high because of the need to spend substantial funds to put the necessary components in place. As a result, most of the bidding or participation in the program rarely draws more than three bidders.

Training of BRECDA Members on Operations and Maintenance of the Systems

The main units responsible for the maintenance of the systems are the BRECDAs. To make sure they have the technical capacity to meet this responsibility, they are trained by supplier technicians on how to handle the systems and how to trouble shoot in case of problems during the pre-installation period. To make sure this training occurs, this activity has been made a requirement for a supplier to qualify for the program. The proper basic tools for repairs and maintenance are also provided by the suppliers. By the time the systems arrive for installation, the BRECDA members already know how to operate and maintain the systems properly (Winrock International, 2005).

SUSTAINABILITY FOR SOCIOECONOMIC DEVELOPMENT

Training on Other Uses of PV Systems With a Focus on Improvement of Standards of Living of the Communities

Sustaining the systems will never be possible if the program does not strengthen the BRECDAs as organizations. Given the fact that the community organizing component of the program last only 1 year, strengthening the BRECDAs becomes very important during and after the 1 year intervention.

The AMORE partnership recognizes that electrification alone will not help improve the standards of living of the communities. To maximize the benefit of electrification, USAID provided funds for livelihood development programs that will help in improving the income of the BRECDA members and help in the intensification goal of the program—extending it to other households without electricity. Studies were done to establish what are the livelihood programs best suited given the profiles of the barangays. At the same time, the basic necessities of the barangays were also taken in consideration. Given these factors, livelihood programs ranging from solar seaweed dryers to floating fish pens were created. Basic services like education and health were also improved as the AMORE partnership brought in new participants like the Knowledge Channel, a local media-based NGO that provides media-based education using television and video CD players powered by solar power systems. The AMORE program also improved the water systems in the island barangays by helping them improve their respective rainwater catchments systems and training the communities on hygiene.

Later in the program, local development organizations like the Peace and Equity Foundation, provided microfinancing facilities to fund marketing activities related to livelihood programs, or even the purchase of new solar power systems for households without electricity in the barangay. Technical staff of these local organizations also linked up the BRECDAs to marketing units to help them in their livelihood programs.

Sustainability for Peace

Formation of BRECDA Federations

To strengthen the BRECDAs, the project created BRECDA federations, which are regional groupings or networks of BRECDAs. This process of creating cooperation among organizations from differing geographical locales has substantial meaning for this area, where the conflicts are deeply rooted and based on Rido, struggles between clans. Federating these BRECDAs will be the most practical and sustainable way of BRECDA empowerment. The federation will be a venue for the sharing of best practices and, at the same time, will gather together communities to work for a common goal of development rather than fighting clan wars. The BRECDAs are federated by geographical clusters and a total of 14 BRECDA Federations were established by April 2005 (Winrock International, 2005).

Leadership Training and Empowering BRECDA Federations

BRECDA members were trained on the concepts of federating and leaders were chosen to lead the Federations. Many challenges arose, such as finding sources of funds for programs and to sustain the organizations. One strategy AMORE helped develop is to enable the BRECDAs become formally recognized by the local government unit as a working people's organization within the province. In AMORE, the project area office covering Tawi-Tawi was able to develop a strong relationship with the local government. This relationship paved the way for the Tawi-Tawi BRECDA to be included in the Provincial Development Council, opening up opportunities such as gaining access to source funds for projects and for organizational development. The BRECDAs have increasingly become a part of the growth of their own province (Winrock International, 2005).

For Future Peace—
Youth Empowerment and Leadership Training

It is easy for guerillas and bandits to recruit youth. The AMORE program recognizes this phenomenon and has developed programs that will help improve the youth of the area. These programs include education, leadership development, values formation, and entrepreneurship. In Barangays Talitay and Buluan in Maguindanao, solar lights powered a community reading center that helped improve the reading and analyzing skills of local youth (Winrock International, 2005). According to Mirant, Pilipinas Shell Foundation has trained more than 1,000 young BRECDA members in entrepreneurship through their Youth Business Camps, utilizing funds sourced from the purchase of solar home systems.

Employment of the "Right" Staff

The success of the AMORE project depends heavily on choosing the right staff. It takes a different kind of development worker to survive the complexities of the conflict-torn side of Mindanao (Winrock International, 2005). Out of necessity, AMORE employed former guerillas and people who are related to the guerillas. And this mechanism functions to train them to consider peaceful mechanism for community development. (See AMORE Achievements, cases of transforming guerillas to development workers.)

A careful interview is conducted to choose AMORE community development staff. According to the Mirant Foundation officers, in the interview, two things are checked. One is the language. The staff should know the regional language or local dialect of that particular area: Visayan and Cebuano as the basic language, and also Tausug as a second language. Second is the candidate's network in the area, or rather "security" connections. It should be noted that connections in both the legal local authorities as well as the rebels are considered important. During the interview, AMORE officers ask candidates questions like "Who do you know in the area?", "Do you have your own gun?", and "Do you have friends in the military, how about the rebel groups?"

The ideal profile of AMORE staff can be Samba, a female community development worker in Sulu. She has done the Haj (annual pilgrimage of all Muslims to the Holy Site in Mecca, Saudi Arabia) twice in her lifetime. She is a recognized community leader well respected by both military and rebel sides. Therefore, she can go to the most remote areas of the ARMM without fear of harm.

AMORE ACHIEVEMENTS

By the end of 2007, more than 10,000 households in 400 barangays enjoyed solar power systems by virtue of the AMORE program. According to the Mirant Philippines Foundation, an assessment/planning session in September of 2007 revealed that since the program's inception in 2002, 314 or 43.9%, of the 716 barangays electrified through solar power systems were electrified by the AMORE program.

Did AMORE truly succeed in creating environmental, social, economic, and political sustainability? Did AMORE really hit the four birds with one stone? The answer appears to be yes. Following are the achievements.

Environmental Achievements

In terms of environmental achievement, there are no data dedicated solely to AMORE. However, enough data exist to suggest strongly that the program reduced the area's on impact to the earth's ozone layer. The following explanation and calculation were given by the Mirant Philippines Foundation.

**Table 3.3.   AMORE's Contribution to
Electrification at the ARMM, 2002-2007**

Year	Barangays Energized by AMORE	New Barangays Energized	% Contribution
2002	10	120	8.3
2003	84	188	44.7
2004	55	115	47.8
2005	35	54	64.8
2006	37	133	27.8
2007	93	106	87.7
Total	314	716	43.9

Source: Mirant Philippines Foundation (internal document).

Kerosene is one of the most frequently used fossil fuels to provide heat and light to a household bereft of electricity. Kerosene's uses range from lighting lamps to cooking. Based on the standards for assessing carbon mitigation for projects under the Kyoto Protocol, the combined solar power projects of BEACON and AMORE displaced a total of 660,000 kerosene lamps at the rate of 40 liters of kerosene consumed per year per household for 5 years. Most renewable energy projects are under AMORE. With a computed carbon dioxide (CO_2) emission rate of 0.10355t CO_2/yr per lamp, a total of 2,321.60t CO_2 was mitigated by Projects BEACON and AMORE.

Socioeconomic Achievements

Establishing BRECDAs and BRECDA Federations has helped to mend the war-torn social fabrics of the communities in the region. By April 2007, 386 BRECDAs were established in the 5 years since the inception of AMORE in 2002, and 14 BRECDA Federations were created, most of which still exist often metamorphosing into full development organizations (AMORE, 2008b). The Mirant Foundation officers think that 70-80 percent of current BRECDAs will survive or even evolve into core organizations for the development of respective communities.

AMORE did not focus on only providing solar home systems. Rather, relying on the additional support provided by the DOE and USAID, plus other development agencies, the program helped enhance the standards of living of the communities. Philippine-based solar wafer manufacturer Sun Power, Philippine nongovernment organization Peace and Equity

Foundation, ABS-CBN Foundation, media-based education stalwart Knowledge Channel, Pilipinas Shell Foundation, and others were able to bring in programs. According to Mirant Philippines Foundation, AMORE thus far has provided more than 400 barangays or more than 10,000 households access to safe water, given almost 34,000 students in more than 160 schools in the ARMM access to distance or improved education, and given more than 14,000 households or more than 70,000 individuals access to telecommunications facilities. In terms of health, although further research needs to be conducted, it can be said that respiratory disorders among the household members decreased when they switched from kerosene to solar home systems.

Education Enhancement

Students from Kabuling Elementary School received gold and silver medals in an academic districtwide mathematics and science competition. They credited this feat to electricity from the AMORE-installed solar panel on their school, which facilitated the launch of the multimedia or the e-media project simultaneously with the school's electrification. Teachers now use CDs of educational television programs as instruction aids, playing them on a solar-powered DVD player and television. AMORE benefited over 100 schools with over 51,000 students (AMORE, 2008c).

Clean Water

In the Autonomous Region in Muslim Mindanao (ARMM), only 24% of the population has access to clean water. Safe water is precious. Villagers of Sibak-Latud tried to get water by drilling over 100 unsafe hand-pumped wells, while the women fetched water from far distant rocky terrain. The children also hauled heavy buckets of dirty water. The unsafe water caused water-borne diseases.

Then AMORE ventured into a project to address the need for clean and safe water, with support from the British government. By July 2007, the community-managed potable water system benefitted at least 680 homes. Villagers contributed to funding the operation and maintenance of the water system, and to protecting and developing the Sibak-Latud watershed. The participation of the community empowered local people and created a sense of ownership, commitment and responsibility. With less time spent fetching water, mothers have more time to go into income-generating activities and to look after their children, and daughters can now attend school (AMORE, 2008d).

A High-Value Vegetable Project

Kalumenga, a mountainous barangay was a center of fierce military encounters, with a warring Datu (chief) and a Sultan seeking to take control of it. To avoid crossfire between the warring parties, the people frequently had to leave their farms. Eventually, they banded together to protect their community by arms.

When AMORE became involved in the community, it organized household beneficiaries in Kalumenga into the Kalumenga BRECDA (KaBRECDA). Through KaBRECDA, the village residents have begun doing environmental scanning to determine community resources that may be tapped to improve living conditions. One such undertaking, with assistance of AMORE, is a high-value vegetable project (AMORE, 2008e).

Achievements Concerning Peace

Finally, the project helped narrow the psychological gap between the Christian population, the U.S. and Islam populations. Given that the USAID is a U.S. government agency and Mirant Philippines Foundation is part of Mirant Corporation, an American company; and given the acknowledged animosity between many Muslims and Americans, many would predict that this program cannot be implemented without posing large security risks for the program personnel. According to a Mirant officer, Dr. Abas Candao, then executive director of the Bangsa Moro Development Agency, the MILF guerilla's implementing arm for development projects related to the peace process, visited Manila in April 2005, and said, "Mirant and the USAID are our natural enemies if you look at it from a fundamentalist point of view. But from a development point of view—when you go home, look around you, what do you see? Lights where there was once darkness. They extended their hands out to help; therefore, they are our friends."

Stopping Conflicts

Barangay Mandulan's captain and his wife were brutally killed in late 2003. According to their custom of Rido (clan wars), some family members organized to avenge their deaths. In further retaliation, they planned to steal the AMORE installed communal solar battery charging stations, the solar-powered streetlights, and the solar home system installed in the community center.

In December 2003, AMORE organized an BRECDA federation for all BRECDAs in Bongao, with a former police colonel as chairman of the federation. Barangay Mandulan was included in the federation. The chairman heard of the plan and immediately met with the captains of the 10 neighboring barangays. With the assistance of these key people, the former police colonel arranged for a dialogue with the leader of the avenging group. He sought their cooperation in the protection of the renewable energy system in Mandulan. The avenging group eventually agreed. By mid-February 2004, local police arrested the suspected murderers (AMORE, 2008f).

Transforming Guerillas Into Development Workers

In the 1970s, military officers and soldiers, big businessmen, and politicians feared Kumander Gubat ("Commander Forest"), then commander of the biggest zone of the military arm of the Moro National Liberation Front. Today Kumander Gubat is a development worker who, in the sphere of social development, has brought back his real identity as Mohamad Mambatawan. He believes peace and order is essential for more projects to come to the communities (AMORE, 2008g).

Another example is Neneng Muarip, a community development worker who has worked with many poor, remote, conflict-affected communities in Muslim Mindanao. While growing up in Tubugan, Basilan, she witnessed the brutal killing of relatives during the military offensive against the Moro National Liberation Front during the martial law era. These memories led to her hatred for all Christians. She joined the MNLF and was sent to Libya for 7 years for training in guerilla warfare. But time, age, and love diminished some of her hatred toward Christians. Now married, she is a catalyst for development through her work as a community development worker for AMORE (AMORE, 2008h).

CHALLENGES

In spite of its publicized success, AMORE encountered many problems in implementing the program: war and disorder, the topography of the land, culture, and many others. Three significant challenges that concern the Mirant Philippines Foundation relate to peace and order, battery replacement, extreme poverty, and the need for innovation for the future.

Peace and Order

The most serious obstacle so far for AMORE is the lack peace and order. Until a peace agreement is signed and the armed banditry of the Abu-Sayyaf, which some say is backed by al-Qaeda, has been checked, the lack of peace and order will be a major challenge. The following incidences were reported.

- In the Province of Maguindanao, the population is divided between Muslims and Christians. Even among the Christians, armed fighting to settle such issues as land disputes, business control, and even politics is rampant. On many occasions, Muslim population near these conflict-ridden Christian areas are brought into the mess as part of the warring factions "private armies." AMORE, having been created to help communities in these areas, was expecting to meet these conflicts in the field. AMORE staff were threatened with harm, refused entry into the barangay, and even ignored.

- One AMORE staff was killed by armed conflict.
- Nine barangays were delayed due to clan wars in 2006.
- In some AMORE areas, even the communist-backed rebel groups suspicious of the U.S. government's intentions in Mindanao threatened the AMORE staff.
- Political rivalries and clan wars, facilitated by widespread access to military-type assault weapons, resulted in murders and mass evacuations. A BRECDA member and his son were killed.
- Thirty-six photovoltaic panels were lost and only two were recovered.
- Illegal drug trafficking in some barangays prompted a shooting spree and thereafter the pilfering of O&M Funds.
- In 2006, five barangays under the AMORE program were burned down as a result of clan wars. (Fortunately, the panels were safely hidden by the beneficiaries and when hostilities ceased, they went back and set up new houses with the same solar home systems.)

Battery Replacement

One major component of the PV system is the battery, similar to a car battery but with special features designed for a solar power system. The cost of one battery is expensive and an AMORE community cannot afford to purchase the battery outright given their marginalized status. Without the battery, the solar panels and wirings are useless. Therefore, the effective sustainability period of the whole PV system is dependent on the life of the battery and the coast off a replacement.

The life of the battery depends on the efficiency and extent of its utilization. In many cases among AMORE beneficiaries, the life of the battery reaches 4 years. But these situations are in communities where the households use it strictly for lighting purposes and for only 4 to 6 hours a day. In areas where solar power units are used for such appliances as television, the life of the battery is shorter. As this chapter is being written, most of the batteries are still okay. In 2009, when some of the batteries would have reached 4-7 years, the impact on the project of this inevitable occurrence will be felt. So far it is unclear how to prolong the life of the batteries or how to help the communities reach that level that they can afford to purchase new ones.

Extreme Poverty and Innovation for the Future

Recently, AMORE adopted the market development approach to rural electrification, a new mechanism where funding would be provided for communal facilities, while housing electrification would be undertaken by the contractor on a commercial basis. Unfortunately, the profiles of the majority of the communities indicated that the people there were experiencing extremely poor situations and, could not afford even to develop marketing activities because the communities could barely afford to buy the basic necessities in the first place.

Based on the experience derived from developing AMORE in poverty-stricken areas over the past 5 years, MIRANT Foundation decided that future programs in rural electrification should differentiate across three participation categories: those who could afford electricity, those who could partially afford it, and those who could not afford it. The matrix in Figure 3.3 describes the profile, objectives, and recommended intervention for each category.

Essentially, those who could not afford should be helped in livelihood development because they are too poor to even implement microfinance schemes. On the other hand, those who could, at least, partially afford electricity should be introduced to microfinance schemes. This particular intervention emphasized the requisite leadership training for BRECDAs in the belief that if BRECDAs could be strengthened by good leaders, they could overcome several difficulties and come up with much more productive results as a result of electrification.

In the Philippines, approximately 1,400 barangays remain without electricity, according to Mirant. These barangays are farthest from the grid and probably the poorest in socioeconomic terms. Given their profiles, these communities may be hard put to move out of the dole-out system of rural electrification. Therefore, by subdividing the market as described earlier, chances of attaining project objectives are better.

It is evident that the BRECDAS developed the technical capacities to maintain the systems. Although social preparations were made to ensure that the BRECDAs could manage and sustain the solar home systems, gaps in capabilities remained in terms needing to strengthen the BRECDA organization itself. Two evaluations of the social preparation strategy of AMORE revealed that sometimes it was too technical and that some BRECDAs would become inactive once AMORE left the area. To

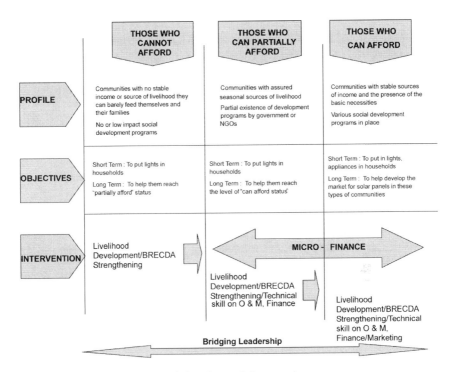

Source: Mirant Philippines Foundation (internal document).

Figure 3.3.   Segmentation of beneficiaries.

address this propensity, another program being funded by Mirant called the Bridging Leadership Program was brought into the equation. The Bridging Leadership program was expected to help strengthen the BRECDAs because their leaders would be trained to transcend gaps and influence everyone to work for development.

CONCLUSIONS

This chapter discussed AMORE project, a rural electrification project conducted in the conflict-affected area of Mindanao, Philippines. Mirant Philippines joined AMORE as part of its corporate social responsibility commitment. AMORE is one of the projects that USAID conducted successfully under its Global Development Alliance initiative, a public-private partnership for the development. The project has many alliance partners of different mandates and characteristics. The coordination was not easy, but they managed to utilize their diversity to push implementation of the project.

The project is targeted in the area where people are extremely poor and where terrorist activities are reported. The electrification project's primary goal is not simply to supply electric power in the areas. Rather, it seeks to be a community development project meant to empower the communities so that they can start their own projects for economic growth. The heart of the project is the organization of key people in the communities for peace and development.

The project is innovative in many ways, and provides various lessons. This chapter addresses innovations to achieve sustainability in four aspects of this project: environmental, economic, societal, and political. Innovation is especially important because the target areas are so poor and so unsafe. Although AMORE is an innovative project, it calls for further innovation and refinement of the program. Further segmentation of people and communities seems to be needed for the further sustainability.

NOTE

1.   The author is thankful to the great assistance made by Roderick De Castro of Mirant Philippines Foundation.

REFERENCES

Alliance for Mindanao Off-Grid Renewable Energy. (2008a). *AMORE partners.* Retrieved June 23, 2008, from http://www.amore.org.ph/html/partners/partners_others.html

Alliance for Mindanao Off-Grid Renewable Energy. (2008b). *Accomplishments.* Retrieved June 23, 2008, from http://www.amore.org.ph/html/whatwevdone/whatwevdone_main.html

Alliance for Mindanao Off-Grid Renewable Energy. (2008c). *Young students in the south excel.* Retrieved June 23, 2008, from http://www.amore.org.ph/html/ss/ss_32.html

Alliance for Mindanao Off-Grid Renewable Energy. (2008d). *Water facility change lives of Muslims in southern Philippine town.* Retrieved June 23, 2008, from http://www.amore.org.ph/html/ss/ss_31.html

Alliance for Mindanao Off-Grid Renewable Energy. (2008e). *Sense of permanence settles in war-ravaged Maguindanao community.* Retrieved June 23, 2008, from http://www.amore.org.ph/html/ss/ss_20.html

Alliance for Mindanao Off-Grid Renewable Energy. (2008f). *Peace now reigns in war-prone community.* Retrieved June 23, 2008, from http://www.amore.org.ph/html/ss/ss_23.html

Alliance for Mindanao Off-Grid Renewable Energy. (2008g). *From rebel to peace-keeper.* Retrieved June 23, 2008, from http://www.amore.org.ph/html/ss/ss_18 .html

Alliance for Mindanao Off-Grid Renewable Energy. (2008h). *Love ("AMORE") con-quers all.* Retrieved June 23, 2008, from http://www.amore.org.ph/html/ss/ ss_15.html

Central Intelligence Agency. (2008). *The world factbook.* Retrieved June 23, 2008, from https://www.cia.gov/library/publications/the-world-factbook/geos/rp .html#top

Collier, K. (2006). Terrorism: Evolving regional alliances and state failure in Min-danao. In D. Singh & L. C. Salazar (Eds.), *Southeast Asian affairs 2006* (pp. 26-38). Singapore: Institute of Southeast Asian Studies.

Human Development Network, United Nations Development Program, & New Zealand Agency for International Development. (2005). *Philippine human development report 2005: Peace, human security and human development in the Phil-ippines.* Manila, Philippines: 2005 Human Development Network.

Kamlian, J. A. (2005). *Incidences of clan conflict and conflict management: Survey of feuding families and clans in selected provinces of Mindanao.* Retrieved June 23, 2008, from http://asiafoundation.org/pdf/PH_conflict/ MSU_IIT_Exec_Summary4.pdf

National Statistic Office. (2003). *Autonomous region in Muslim Mindanao: Nine in every ten persons were Muslims.* Retrieved June 23, 2008, from http://www.census .gov.ph/data/pressrelease/2003/pr0301tx.html

Philippine Institute for Development Studies. (2008a). *Economic and social data-base: Functional literacy rate.* Retrieved June 23, 2008, from http://econdb.pids .gov.ph/index.php?option=com_dirp&tab2=323&class_id=&sort_id= Place_ID&disp_flag=&dat_class=152

Philippine Institute for Development Studies. (2008b). *Economic and social data-base: Infant mortality rate.* Retrieved June 23, 2008, from http://econdb.pids .gov.ph/index.php?option=com_dirp&tab2=244&class_id=&sort_id= Place_ID&disp_flag=&dat_class=147

Philippine Institute for Development Studies. (2008c). Economic and social data-base: Poverty incidences families. Retrieved June 23, 2008, from http:// econdb.pids.gov.ph/index.php?option=com_dirp&tab2=33&class_id= &sort_id=Place_ID&disp_flag=&dat_class=150

Schiavo-Campo, S., & Judd, M. (2005, February). *The Mindanao conflict in the Phil-ippines: Roots, costs, and potential peace dividend* (Paper No. 24). Washington, DC: Social Development Department, The World Bank.

Sharma, D., Madamba, S. E., & Chan, M. A. (2004). Electricity industry reform in the Philippines. *Energy Policy, 32*(13), 1487-1497.

Stark, J. (2003). Muslims in the Philippines. *Journal of Muslim Minority Affairs, 23*(1), 195-209.

Toba, N. (2007). Welfare impacts of electricity generation sector reform in the Philippines. *Energy Policy, 35* (12), 6145-6162.

U.S. Agency for International Development. (2008). *Alliance for Mindanao Off-Grid Renewable Energy: The challenge.* Retrieved June 23, 2008, from http:// www.usaid.gov/our_work/global_partnerships/gda/resources/mindanao.pdf

Winrock International. (2005). *Alliance for Mindanao Off-grid Renewable Energy Project. Final performance report*. Arlington, VA: Winrock International.

World Bank. (2002). *Rural electrification and development in the Philippines: Measuring the social and economic benefits*. Washington, DC: Author.

World Bank. (2003). *Human development for peace and prosperity in the Autonomous Region in Muslim Mindanao*. Washington, DC: World Bank.

CHAPTER 4

LEARNING TO COOPERATE

A Model at the Nexus of Business and Society and Its Impact Around the World

Bonnie Richley

This paper is a study of what is widely recognized as the most successful cooperative in history, Mondragón Corporacion Cooperativa (MCC) and its significant influence throughout the world as a social innovation. A cases-within-a-case study approach has been utilized to understand two important aspects of the project: (1) attributes of MCC that define it as a social innovation and (2) the impact of MCC as a business/social model. Nine secondary cases situated within the primary site serve as a starting point for understanding how such a model has been adopted throughout the world. The study aims to demonstrate what is being learned by individuals going to MCC and how they successfully implemented elements of the experience in their own work. The study employs existing knowledge about the diffusion of innovation as a way to develop a practical theory that will clarify how to enjoin the often disparate agendas of both business and social agents through the adoption of a value-based innovation.

Global Sustainability Initiatives: New Models and New Approaches
pp. 61–84

61

INTRODUCTION

We think that management should be a noble profession, that it should have some higher aspiration. In law, the value aspiration is justice. In medicine, it is the absence of disease. In management, it is to help enlarge humanity's cooperative capacity.

—David Cooperrider
Founder, Center for Business as an Agent of World Benefit

Without question the areas of innovation and social entrepreneurship are two of the most promising areas in organizational studies. In part this is because we are struggling to manage unprecedented challenges in every aspect of life crucial to our existence. Business enthusiasts and social champions alike wonder how to survive and thrive amidst increasing competition and seemingly insurmountable challenges. But these topics are not only prominent because of our need to solve our present-day problems. Our desire to push toward new horizons is a part of our intellectual and emotional DNA. We share a collective longing to develop, to flourish, and to satisfy an innate curiosity. One need not stretch very far for evidence of this assertion. The successful flare of the first fire, the slow but constant movement of the initial assembly line, or the instantaneous search capacity of Google all demonstrate how our creativity has led to innovations that have irrevocably altered the world.

These innovations and countless others shift our vision toward new possibilities and at the same time provide the impetus for the next wave of inventors. In this way the process of innovation can be likened to a strand of genetic code. While it is not readily visible it is present wherever human life can be found and it is what enables future generations. Similarly, it is through innovation that we have the ability to create a better world.

Most often innovation means rediscovering new ways of seeing the old but altering its meaning or use within relevant contexts. Through the lens of innovation much can be learned from reconsidering organizational models that are less conventional than traditional forms and may be regarded as old-fashioned, idealistic, or even obsolete. Unless we look at radically different forms of organizing we have little chance to innovate. "Work is socially constructed and unless the old work concept is formally buried and a new work concept developed and formally introduced as a replacement, organizations cannot escape the social bonds binding them to old practices" (Chaharbaghi & Newman, 1996, p. 6).

One model with the potential to create such a paradigm shift is cooperatives or worker-owned organizations. In comparing a traditional organization to that of a cooperative it is clear that they differ in several key ways (Table 4.1).

Table 4.1.   Comparison of a
Traditional Organization to That of a Cooperative

Characteristics	Traditional Organization (i.e., for-profit or nonprofit)	Cooperative
Workforce membership	• Members are employees.	• Members are worker-owners
Participation and decision-making processes	• Concentration of power at top of hierarchy. • Top-down decision making.	• Democratic (i.e., one-person one-vote rule); worker-owner participation in management
Economic participation	• Hourly or salaried remuneration. • Separation of capital investors and employees.	• Profit-sharing by worker-owners
Access to information, education, and training	• Restricted flow of information and limited provisions for education and training.	• Equal and open access to education and information; seen as critical to promote democratic participation
Primary objective	• Focus on ROI to benefit investors.	• Tripartite focus on the individual, organization, and community.

Cooperatives are widely regarded as having both a business and social mission with an emphasis on the human side of enterprise. Rarely, however, are they considered to be representative of an efficient and savvy business model. Contrary to these assumptions, the Mondragón Corporacion Cooperativa (MCC) located in the Basque country of Spain, is an exemplar of a social innovation that represents the positive possibilities at the intersection of business and society. MCC is considered to be the most successful worker-owned enterprise in the world with businesses located across the globe. Since its inception MCC has functioned as a for-profit business guided by its unique vision based on social and economic justice, the dignity of human persons and their work and solidarity, values derived from Catholic social thought (CST) (Herrera, 2004).

The focus of the chapter is a study of MCC and its impact as an organizational role model, or a "social invention" (Whyte, 1982). To highlight the extent of MCC's influence, "In 2003, over 1,200 people (globally) visited MCC's education and training center, Otalora, to find out about the Mondragón Cooperative movement in situ" (Mondragón Corporacion Cooperativa [MCC], 2003). The fundamental question in this chapter is to understand what and how people around the world are learning and adopting from a unique organizational model with a distinct business structure and social vision. MCC provides a way to surface the dynamics of how a social innovation is adapted through "the linking of people, ideas, and objects together to form effective and lasting communities or technologies" (Hargadon, 2003, p. 6).

MCC provides a context to further understand the interrelationships between the person, organizational structure (i.e., workplace democracy), and the intersection of business and society not only within MCC but across geographical boundaries toward developing sustainable and rejuvenated communities around which corporations are embedded. This chapter does not intend to argue solely in favor of cooperatives but rather to demonstrate how such an exemplary model has been adapted by social entrepreneurs in order to create positive sustainable initiatives at the organizational, local, and regional levels.

MONDRAGÓN CORPORACION COOPERATIVA

The Mondragón case is a great confirmation for those who believe that the only rational goal for business and technology is worker as well as community improvement.

—Father Gregory MacLeod (1997)
In *From Mondragón to America:*
Experiments in Community Economic Development

MCC's mission combines the basic objectives of a business organisation competing in international markets with the use of democratic methods in its organisation, job creation, promotion of its workers in human and professional terms and commitment to the development of its social environment.

—Jesús Catania
Chairman of the General Council, MCC

MCC, located in the local Basque country of Spain is a for-profit organization, created in 1956 in an effort to address the job shortage in the local Basque community. What began as an experiment with only a handful of people is today an international corporation with a total work force of 78,455. MCC is comprised of 264 enterprises including MCC Worldwide (MCC, 2003) (i.e., 7 corporate offices and 38 plants) and an annual revenue of $8 billion (MCC, 2003). Founded on Catholic social thought, MCC expresses this philosophy and ideology through its corporate mission, values (Figure 4.1), and its 10 basic principles (Table 4.2). Together, they form the foundation that guides MCC's cooperative structure and serve to "balance individual, organizational and community needs" (Herrera,

MCC'S MISSION

MCC's mission encompasses those basic objectives of a business organization that competes on markets worldwide, together with the use of democratic methods in its corporate organization, the creation of employment, the personal and professional development of its workers and a pledge to develop its social milieu.

Source: Mondragon Corporacion Cooperativa,2005 Annual Report, MCC, www.mcc.es

Corporate Values at MCC

The Corporate Values are the heart of MCC's business culture, providing a sense of direction for all worker-members and a set of general guidelines for the everyday working of each company. They represent the fundamental nature of the organization and create a specific sense of identity. The last Congress meeting, held in May 1999, reduced the list of Corporate Values to just four in an effort to facilitate their communication, absorption and application.

CO-OPERATION	PARTICIPATION	SOCIAL COMMITMENT	INNOVATION
"Owners and protagonists"	"Commitment to management"	"Distribution of wealth based on solidarity"	"Constant renewal"

[Source: Mondragon Corporacion Cooperativa, 2003 Annual Report, MCC, www.mcc.es]

Figure 4.1.   MCC corporate mission and values.

2004, p. 57) through a sociobusiness approach to the organization and its governance (MCC, 2003). "The goal of cooperative entrepreneurship is not simply economic prosperity but social success" as expressed through a shared distribution of power among worker-members (i.e., owners of the company) (Morrison, 1991, p. 135).

As the cooperative structure grew in scope and number it was agreed that it should be incorporated with the intent to leverage synergies among the members. "The corporation does not own the cooperatives" but provides a management structure (see Figure 4.2) to serve and enable the functioning among the various cooperatives (http://www.Mondragón.mcc.es) while adhering to the guiding ideology. MCC is structured on a participative and democratic basis with the majority of ownership held by worker-owners. The management model consists of three dominant areas: enablers, strategy, and results (see Figure 4.3). The enablers represent the guiding forces for management practices, the strategy determines what is essential to reach MCC's targets, and the results indicate measures for suc-

Table 4.2.   Ten Basic Principles of Mondragon

Principle	Definition
1. Open admission	Mondragon is open to all persons who are capable of carrying out the available jobs. There is no discrimination based on religious or political grounds, nor due to race, gender, age, or socioeconomic levels. The only requirement is the acceptance of these basic principles.
2. Democratic organization	Workers are owners, and owners are workers. Each cooperative is managed by a system of "one person-one vote."
3. Sovereignty of employee's work over capital	Workers join Mondragon and become owners after making a capital contribution at the end of a trial period. All workers are entitled to an equitable distribution of profits. The return on saved or invested capital is just but limited, and it is not tied up to the surpluses or losses of the cooperatives.
4. Subordinate character of capital	Capital is a means to an end, not an end in itself. Available capital is used primarily to create more jobs.
5. Participatory management	Worker-owners participate in decision making and the management of the cooperatives. This implies development of self-management skills. Formal education and adequate information is provided to improve worker-owners' ability to participate competently in decision making.
6. Payment solidarity	Remuneration is regulated internally and externally. Internally, an agreed differential between the highest and lowest paid job is applied. Externally, a remuneration level is maintained in relationship with similar local industries.
7. Intercooperation	Cooperatives form groups to pool profits, to absorb worker-owner transfers when necessary, and to attain synergies. These groups associate with each other to support corporate institutions. Mondragon associates with other Basque cooperative organizations to promote the cooperative model.
8. Social transformation	Mondragon cooperatives invest a majority of their profits in the creation of new jobs. Funds are also used in the community projects and in institutions that promote the Basque culture and language.
9. Universal nature	Mondragon proclaims its solidarity with other cooperative movements, with those working for economic democracy and with those who champion the objectives of peace, justice and human dignity. Mondragon proclaims its solidarity especially with people in developing countries.
10. Education	Mondragon cooperatives commit the required human and economic resources to basic, professional and cooperative education in order to have worker-owners capable of applying all basic principles mentioned above.

Source: Adapted from Ormaechea (1993).

cess toward established goals including that a balance is achieved in each of the key areas: customer satisfaction, profitability, internationalization, development, social involvement and innovation. Both critics and supporters of MCC seem to agree on one thing: the actual structure and internal processes of the cooperative is one of its most unique features and seems to be a fluid dynamic involving a paradox of stability and change, tradition and innovation. The unusual nature, and subsequent success, of the system are what many refer to as the "mystery" of Mondragón.

Because MCC is an exemplary organization, and one from which much can be learned, it is helpful to understand its history. Many references to MCC credit the early visionary leadership of Father Jose Maria Arizmendiarrieta with creating "the experience" (i.e., the cooperative). However, others caution that innovations are never created by a single person (Hargadon, 2003; MacLeod, 1997) but are the result of a series of events, conditions, existing bodies of knowledge and the actions and insights of a collective. A closer look at the early inception of MCC reveals that it was a combination of all of these factors that created this unique social innovation. Without doubt Father Jose Maria Arizmendiarrieta planted the visionary seed of MCC but it was a true collective effort that allowed it to grow and flourish. It is important to note that both supporters and critics of MCC most often agree that the tight culture among the Basque community should be accounted for in any mention of its success. There is an ongoing argument, and a belief held by many, that MCC is so unique that

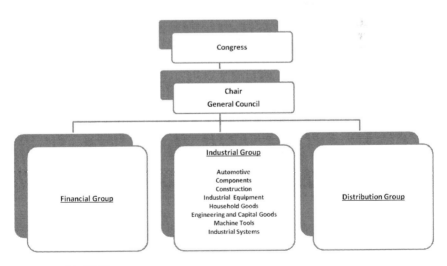

Source: MCC (2005).

Figure 4.2 MCC organizational structure 2005.

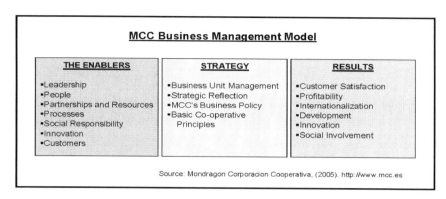

Figure 4.3.   2005 MCC management model.

it cannot be replicated beyond the Basque country because the culture is tightly bound by their value for solidarity.

Because of the unique achievements of the cooperative, scholars from around the world have made their way to MCC to understand its many dimensions. Researchers have studied MCC through the lens of the structure and effects of workplace democracy (Greenwood & Gonzalez Santos, 1991; Herrera, 2004; MacLeod, 1997; Morrison, 1991; Oakeshott, 1978; Vanek, 1971; Zirakzadeh, 1990; Zwerdling, 1978), others have offered a critical analysis of its idealistic structure (Kasmir, 1996), the nature of MCC's organizational communication (Cheney, 1997), controversy over internationalization and cooperative practices (Bakaikoa, Errasti, & Begiristain, 2004; Clamp, 2000; Errasti, Heras, Bakaikoa, & Elgoibar, 2002); Basque patriarchy as analyzed through feminist critique (Echeverria, 2001; Hacker & Elcorobairutia, 1987); among many others. In summary, most research on MCC focuses on its internal structure, the strengths and weaknesses of the cooperative, applied economic theory and current challenges from the environment. Yet while MCC is widely recognized as a social invention (Whyte, 1982) most studies have highlighted MCC's economic perspective and its structure. However, in my conversations with members across levels in the organization during my visits they resonated with my proposal that MCC should be studied from a values systems perspective. This chapter represents a fresh perspective on a key factor central to the functioning and success of MCC. MacLeod (1997) supports this observation:

Observers of Mondragón usually search for the secret formula. Thinking in terms of a mechanistic technique or some financial support system, they usually analyze at the wrong level. The answer is found in a category which should be classed as value systems. It concerns how we understand ourselves and our society. It is about choosing one way of life over another. (p. 37)

This study offers an analysis of the impact of MCC as a role model for individuals wanting to extend such an innovation around the world or how such adaptations are manifested globally.

Innovation and Diffusion of Innovation

Interest about innovation may reflect the bifurcation between business and society in the lived world. Business people typically want innovations that focus on "new delivery mechanisms, customer service strategies, and business models" or are new products born in R&D laboratories (Christensen, Anthony, & Roth, 2004, p. 293). Business innovations must contribute to the bottom-line. Conversely, social agents (e.g., nonprofit managers, philanthropists, activists) want innovations that solve societal problems. Social innovations must contribute to humanity. Yet, this line is becoming increasingly blurred as businesses try to learn how to enact socially responsible practices and nonprofit agents enroll in management schools to learn how to exploit business knowledge.

Two common factors exist between the interest in, and the need for, innovation among the two sectors: (1) people and (2) learning. Both business and social agendas need people and knowledge to foster and implement innovation. In this regard the innovation process can best be understood as a network of relationships "among people, ideas and objects" (Hargadon, 2003, p. 8) and as a learning process (Van de Ven, Polley, Garud, & Venkataraman, 1999). If the aim is to understand how to enjoin business and social objectives then it is necessary to trace the diffusion of the innovation process of successful initiatives in a way that highlights the role of both people and learning.

Broadly defined innovation is that which "create[s] new resources, processes, or values or improves a company's existing resources, processes or values (Christensen et al., 2004, p. 293). More specifically, innovation is also considered a technology whose function is to transfer knowledge. "In this sense, technology transfer amounts to communicating information about tools for achieving a desired goal both within and between organizations" (Van de Ven & Rogers, 1988, p. 634). The process of transferring innovation related information is referred to as diffusion (Rogers, 2003). Rogers states that "diffusion is a special type of communication in which the messages are about a new idea ... some degree of uncertainty is involved [and] alteration occurs in the structure and function of a social system" (Rogers, 2003, p. 6). "Diffusion is defined as the process by which (1) an innovation (2) is communicated through certain channels (3) over time (4) among the members of a social system ... these elements are identifiable in every diffusion research study and in every diffusion campaign or program" (Rogers, 2003, p. 11). While the study of innovation is a well established area in management, and is viewed as significant to the corporate sector, it is also critical to other realms that may garner less attention, or as Mumford aptly describes as "one of these 'lost' domains ... social innovation" (Mumford, 2002, p. 253). This chapter attempts to join these by exploring the process that fosters the diffusion of innovation at the intersection of business and social good. The main objective of this inquiry is to surface the dynamics of the process that leads to the diffusion of an exemplary model with a tripartite mission focused on people, profit and community such as MCC.

METHODOLOGY

The chapter presents an initial study to develop an understanding about the lived experience of individuals visiting MCC and to understand how they applied this information toward a successful or positive outcome at the intersection of business and society. A qualitative approach was used to support the exploratory nature of the inquiry and because it would allow for the collection of descriptive data. Further, this method is appropriate because it "can be used to uncover and understand what lies behind any phenomenon about which little is yet known" (Strauss & Corbin, 1990, p. 19). Appreciative inquiry (AI) and the emergent field of positive organizational scholarship (POS) serve as the philosophical frameworks guiding the research and the methodological approach. Unlike dominant and traditional approaches to studying organizational change that focus on problem solving, negative attributes and consequences, AI and POS seek to bring forth the best in people and practices by "emphasizing theories of excellence, transcendence, positive deviance, extraordinary performance, and positive spirals of flourishing" (Cameron, Dutton, & Quinn, 2003, p. 1).

Enjoining AI and POS offers a new way to understand the social processes and qualities that lead to positive outcomes for both people and organizations and to build a body of scholarship toward a more humanistic way of organizing. AI and POS are jointly employed to target the factors that contributed to the participants' initial desire to learn from MCC, highlight peak learning experiences and to understand what and how this was adopted in their work.

Participants

Because the intent of this project was to uncover the process of the diffusion of social innovation participants needed to have been engaged in learning about the primary site, be able to articulate MCC's influence, and to demonstrate the successful application of this experience in their own work. For purposes of this project a successful outcome is defined as one where learning about MCC has occurred and that knowledge gained from the cooperative has been transferred and applied in a demonstrable way to the participants' work and also directly attributed to MCC's model. Selection criteria were developed for the study as follows: (1) attended Otalora or visited MCC with a desire to learn from the model; (2) articulate how and what they learned from the experience, and (3) represent how this has been replicated in their work.

Studying the diffusion of an innovation is a complex matter for several reasons. First, diffusions occur slowly over time making it difficult to locate a person familiar with the onset of the diffusion process. Second, it is a challenge to find individuals influenced by the same innovation source since this information is not often made explicit. Therefore, tracking down qualified study participants was an involved process that unfolded in three steps. Step one involved asking key organization members at MCC for the names and contact information about potential participants during my second visit to Basque country. This was done via six informal interviews conducted over the course of two days including multiple conversations where I recorded mention of any possible leads through anecdotal references. I then employed purposive sampling which is appropriate when a researcher wants to "select unique cases that are especially informative … [involve a] difficult-to-reach specialized population … [and] to identify particular types of cases for in-depth investigation" (Neuman, 1997, p. 206).

Step two required an extensive vetting process working with members of MCC via reflective conversations about site visits to the cooperative, a Web search to locate potential contacts and concluded with a review of records of visitors dating from 2002 through 2004. The result of these efforts was a list of contacts for further follow up.

The third step to locate participants was conducted independently by me. I continued to search for individuals using the internet. Participants were initially screened by locating references in their work accrediting MCC. Based on the criteria established for the study, a total of 11 individuals qualified and nine agreed to be interviewed. Details about each of the participants are shown in Table 4.3.

This research is specifically focused on those individuals or groups coming to MCC to learn about the cooperative and as a way to enact all or

Table 4.3.   Details of Participant Information*

Name	Title	Structure	Sector	Country
Participant A	Business counselor, restaurateur	Cooperative	Community economic development organization	North America
Participant B	Attorney, founder, consulate member	Cooperative	Immigration	Spain
Participant C	Founder and president	Principal and network based	International consulting firm	North America
Participant D	Visiting scholar and Economist	Independent	Economics/ education	North America
Participant E	Executive director	Foundation	Trust-owned investment fund	Scotland
Participant F	Cofounder and CEO	Employee owned	Building and design company	North America
Participant G	Cofounder, consultant, attorney	Cooperative	Bakeries and technical assistance	North America
Participant H	Professor	University	Education	United Kingdom
Participant I	Reverend, social activist	Foundation	Regional development	South Africa

Note: *Participants visited MCC anywhere from a week to multiple times over the course of several years.

part of its social vision. Because MCC is also a remarkably successful business organization, people may come to learn about specific aspects of production or efficiency as related to one of its divisions (e.g., automotives, household appliances). The sample for this study, however, are only those people coming to MCC who expressed their intent to use the cooperative as an organizational "role model" toward creating some aspect of positive social change.

Procedure

The interview protocol was developed based on AI and POS philosophy and methodology to capture, in essence, the positive aspects and high point stories that emerged as participants were engaged in the diffusion of a social innovation. The interview protocol was designed in three parts. In Part I asked questions about the participants' life and career experiences. Part II was focused on questions about their experience with MCC and Part III were questions about the impact of MCC in their work. The interviews were designed as semistructured to allow for additional questions and to encourage participants to add information they considered to be significant. The participants were interviewed by telephone and all interviews were taped recorded and transcribed. The tape recorded interviews were listened to twice: once for the initial transcription and a second time while reading the transcripts and correcting any errors. I also added my own notes during this time to assist in the initial open coding process. The interviews lasted between 1 to 1-1/2 hours each.

Data captured from the interviews was analyzed as cases-within-a-case study to identify common themes based on each interview that highlight the process of the diffusion of a social innovation. A grounded theory approach to data analysis is employed according to the methodology outlined by Glaser and Strauss (1967). My interest is not to test theory but to focus on the emergent themes directly from the data using an inductive approach. The themes that emerged from this data were contrasted against existing research about the diffusion of innovation.

DIFFUSION OF AN INNOVATION AT THE NEXUS OF BUSINESS AND SOCIETY

The findings of this study are based on the interviews of nine individuals in various stages of diffusing an innovation adopted from the primary site of the study, namely MCC. The results from the cases-within-a-case study permit a deeper analysis of the data as well as providing a vantage point from which to understand individual and shared experiences.

This research began with several simple questions. Why do people go to MCC and what do they hope to learn? How have they used this experience in their work? The findings in this study reveal five codes and seven themes resulting in the adoption of an innovation at the nexus of business and society at three levels to include organizational, inter-organizational and local/regional levels (see Figure 4.4).

Detail for each code and theme is shown in Table 4.4. In every case the participant was strongly influenced by some aspects of their environment to include family life, historical and social contexts and educational experience. The participants, over time, developed an awareness of a social and economic caste system that privileged a limited number of elites at the top of the hierarchy and disadvantaged a greater proportion of indi-

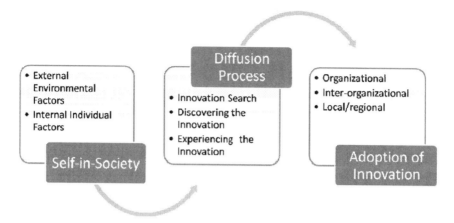

Figure 4.4.   Five primary codes with seven nested themes and levels of adoption.

viduals, communities and countries. This culminated in a desire for them to want to enact some element of social change to readdress this imbalance. I label this precursor to the diffusion process as Self-in-Society which is the collective experience of two emergent themes, external environmental factors and internal individual factors. Both external and internal conditions contributed to an awareness of one's relationship compared to others in different social strata. External Factors include the following: Personal experiences (family or work related); Social/Historical contexts (cultural, economic or political based); and Educational experience (formal education that may be from primary to graduate school). A related theme to emerge from the data is labeled Internal Individual Factors. Through their stories participants explained how their values and lived values (i.e., intentional actions based on their belief systems) were formed as the direct result of external influences as previously indicated. These experiences provided the inspiration and guide for determining a course of action to initiative positive social change through economic/business development in alignment with their values or principles.

The diffusion process is noted by three interrelated codes that provide a sensemaking experience incorporating both value congruence and knowledge transfer resulting in the desired adoption of innovation. The onset of this experience is labeled innovation search process. In each story participants discussed in detail how they actively sought out an innovation that aligned with their key values or principles. Individuals embarked on both informal and formal learning experiences (i.e., reading, discussions) to locate information about a model or process to enable them to express their lived values via a business/social initiative. Upon locating initial

Table 4.4. Details of Codes and Themes

Phase One: Precursors: Self-in-Society

Code 1	External Environmental Factors	Quotes From Data
Themes	Personal experience	"I would always identify myself as a community organizer. I grew up in suburban Cleveland and even in grade school and in high school I did a lot of community work back in the sixties, so I think I have always kind of gravitated towards that. A lot of it is probably my parents' upbringing and influence, but certainly the school system that I was in really pushed me in that direction as well."
		"I was born into a family that owned a paper mill so we were very well off…and I noted from a young age that the people I went to school with in some cases were very poor and secondly we used to go around and see the way that people work…. in order to provide my family with a very fine standard of living and that sounds quite unfair, that the people who were doing the actual work were getting much less benefit from the whole than most of us who were doing nothing for it. So throughout the things that I have done over the years, there is a theme of trying to readdress the balance of it, trying to improve the system so that people who do the work and do create wealth have a share in that wealth."
	Social/historical context	"My early formative years were spent living in Glasgow just west of Scotland. And Glasgow continues to be a fascinating and interesting city that everybody loves but that same city has some of the worst poverty and some of the worst profile of ill health even today as much as it had 50 years ago … so it is this context which has a kind of rich exciting background of ship building and all these interesting innovations in that same city there is relative poverty, deprivation and disadvantage."
		"They (values) come from my family and the history I went through … Martin Luther King and Robert Kennedy were assassinated during the year I was in high school. It was tragic … getting a sense that these courageous people were being killed."
	Educational experience	"I went to a North American school with catholic nuns and they were saying that we were living in a place that was surrounded by poverty, and well, they helped us to look at that and try to do something about it."
		"My background is mostly as a philosopher; my undergraduate degree and first graduate degree were in philosophy. And then I switched to economics. This was certainly in the late 50s and there was this question of Vietnam war and the rest. And basically the sort of ethical theory that I developed then was one that very much moved towards democracy in the workplace, where people owned what they would produce and would not be used up, in other words, to be member of the firm. As I learnt more about different types of firms and cooperatives, workers cooperatives were the ones which exemplified those structures."

(Table continues on next page)

Table 4.4. (Continued)

Code 2	Internal Individual Factors	Quotes From Data
Themes	Value/principles	"I think creating democracy opportunities or more flexibility … in workplaces for ownership and a voice and decision making has been really a core value of mine."
		"And it's not so much a question of values but a question of the principles involved in the legal structure of the company where the people in the company are members of that organization … outside resources are hired or rented by them, by the company. So the cooperatives were the forms that basically realized that principle."
	Actions (i.e., lived values)	"One of my purposes is to serve because it is one of the most gratifying things in the world. I serve my Peruvian fellows and the joy that I take out of serving them and helping them out in their new life in Spain is what drives me the most."
		"Not just writing papers about (workplace democracy), I (wanted) to try to go and do it and I was thrilled to be able to help … I actually got a fellowship for a couple of years that was paying a salary for me and giving me a break from my doctoral program so that I was able to work for them for free; to work for this new emerging entity that was called the industrial cooperative association and so I had joined the train, you know, and I worked with that entity, ICA, until 1987 and in 1987 I left ICA to start ownership associates."
		Phase Two: Diffusion Process
Code 3	Innovation Search Process	"(We were) trying to figure out how to start a cooperative business. I would say from a governance perspective that was probably the initial attractor. Looking at how to communicate more effectively in terms of cooperation, you know, just to see what it meant just to chart the vision of what the cooperative was going to be in the early days."
		"It was maybe the middle to late 70′s when finally I learnt about Mondragon as one of the better examples of where a sort of structure had been developed. And there were certain problems in the legal structure of cooperatives that we had worked out roughly here in the United States and we found out that in the mid-70s Mondragon already had a semi-type structure. So that was all part of the principles that I tried to develop in my theoretical work and then Mondragon was one of the practical examples of that."

Code 4	Discovering the Innovation	"For me the appeal was, here's the model with some of the similar challenges that we have faced in the Appalachia area… a lot of people have lost jobs and have been downsized…and to see the tremendous economic transformation really of the Basque region of Spain."
		"I learned about them in the late seventies, I learned about them from the first articles of Robert Oakeshott who wrote the first English articles…given that this was what I wanted to do and since I took a real strong interest in Mondragon as a concrete example for where it did work…and that kind of gave me further hope that these ideas had a future and I read everything I could about it and got over there."
Code 5	Experiencing the Innovation	
Themes	Seeing the innovation	"I came to Mondragon and then I talked with them for a few days, and that was directly influential in giving me the courage I suppose to go ahead and do something which I think sounded odd in the Scottish capital of that time. So I did benefit a great deal and in a practical way from the visits to Mondragon."
		"It was the holistic part of Mondragon that really caught the imagination for the three of us who went there. If you look at the holistic needs of a community and constrain them into an organizational need and an organizational patent for processes, we've seen that Mondragon has helped to do some incredible change and we see that the model is adaptable to be able to work from the grass roots to the treetops."
	Concrete examples of success and what participants wanted to learn how to adopt	"I wanted to learn everything I could. I was interested in the education and training work that was done. I was interested in R&D work."
		"What we thought we learned from Mondragon was that education was very important, that you need to grow from your successes, in terms of when one business develops a line of work that can be spun off as a cooperative that that is something to pursue rather than starting over from scratch each time. That you need to take the resources that you have developed with regard to business knowledge and finance and that you need to reinvest them and to start new cooperative jobs and structures and that is not just a random thing. And eventually to aim toward creating a comprehensive system."

information about MCC, participants then sought confirmatory evidence to identify specific shared values between them and the organization. This experience is labeled Discovering the Innovation where participants ascertain and verify shared values which provides the impetus for them to move forward to the next step in the process, namely, experiencing the innovation.

Participants expressed two key factors involved in experiencing the innovation categorized by the codes, seeing and how to. Seeing the innovation provided participants with an additional source of inspiration and the reality that such a model is possible. Throughout the "experience" participants transfer an "ideal" type (i.e., a conceptual model of an exemplar) into a concrete "reality" as they begin to make sense of how such a model could be adapted to their particular situation (i.e., context) and objectives (i.e., expression of their lived values). Integrated into this experience are concrete examples of "how to," specifically the transfer of lessons learned from MCC. Lessons include the framework for initiating a cooperative economic model, transitioning a cooperative mission and vision into organizational practices and processes, the importance and development of an internal capital structure, knowledge transfer and sustaining a sociobusiness model over time. The outcome of this experience is the adoption/adaptation of the exemplary innovation into the participants' specific contexts.

Highlighted in these stories is the description of how MCC was an exemplary role model that demonstrated how to unite their desired business and social objectives and one from which they could realize their own innovation. MCC not only provided a grounded example that is both feasible and successful, but also helped them engage in a sensemaking process to become aware of innovations within this innovation that could be adopted in their society. Embedded in this sensemaking process is the awareness of their own self-in-society focus before, during and even after discovery of MCC as the role model for their innovation.

A critical aspect of this process is the actual visiting of MCC to provide a grounded reality—seeing is believing—and also a way to understand the "how-to" to equip them with the knowledge and skills to develop their own innovations based on the MCC model. I label this process, "the diffusion of an innovation at the nexus of business and society" that culminates in the distinct and unique innovations that were spin-offs from the MCC model.

The information garnered from the stories and the codes that emerged from the analysis show that the diffusion of an innovation at the nexus of business and society is a two-phase conceptual model as shown in Figure 4.5, phase one centers on the individual's self-awareness in terms of development of their core values based on their internal and environmen-

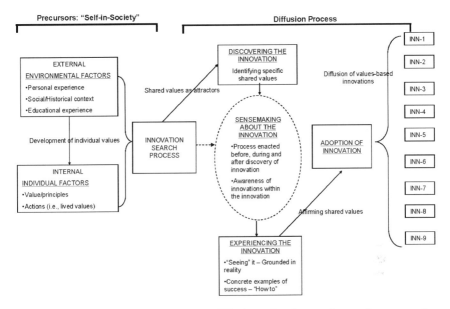

Figure 4.5.   Conceptual model of the diffusion of an innovation at the nexus of business and society.

tal factors. Their values provide the initial impetus to pursue some sort of positive change at the intersection of business and society.

In phase two, the search for and discovery of an exemplary model is value-based and it is this alignment of shared values between the individual and the exemplary organization that serves as attractors to spin off the diffusion dynamic in the process. Physically visiting the exemplary organization was identified as a key element in the process as it enables individuals to engage with the values and the successful philosophical and methodological approaches used in the organization. Finally, the variations of the adaptations (i.e., spin-offs) that emerged in this study is a function of the affirmation of shared values and the intent (or goal) of the individual.

Spin-offs of the initial model are noted at three distinct levels to include: organizational, interorganizational and local/regional (Figure 4.6). Each adaptation reflects a shared mission of creating economic wealth and social good through democratic principles within an organizational context but designed to benefit the individual and localities where these entities reside. The organizational level highlights two adaptations of the MCC model. In one case the president of a privately-owned architectural firm transformed the organization into a cooperative model

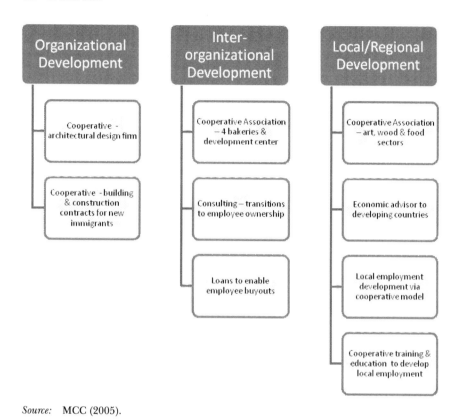

Source: MCC (2005).

Figure 4.6.   Adoption of innovation and levels of development.

where today, more than half of the 30 members are worker owners. The organization is actively involved in development at the community level to include addressing issues of affordable housing and environmental sustainability. The second case reflects the development of a cooperative organization in its beginning stage which is designed to provide employment for immigrants coming to Spain in order to work as contracted employees throughout the area ensuring fair wages and benefits. The cooperative structure will allow the worker-owners to secure the appropriate work visas for employment in the European Union which is otherwise the primary barrier for immigrants throughout Spain and Europe.

An example of the interorganizational spin-off is a cooperative bakery that was developed based on the principles of MCC and its success has led to the actualization of three other cooperatives in the area. Together they have formed an association designed to spin-off other cooperatives. One of their objectives is to create jobs within communities that are locally owned and rooted. Additionally at the interorganizational level, two participants formed consulting companies that provide assistance for organizations transitioning to an employee ownership model or to enable employee buyouts.

Spin-offs at the local/regional level include an agricultural cooperative designed to rejuvenate a failing region of farmland in the Appalachia area. Today, this region is known for its agricultural focus and success based on the cooperative model of MCC. Three additional adaptations at this level represent using lessons learned from the MCC model to assist regions in various countries address issues of poverty, unemployment and education.

DISCUSSION AND IMPLICATIONS

Based on the findings in this study the diffusion of an innovation at the nexus of business and society include aspects that support existing work on the diffusion of innovation while also highlighting some unique characteristics that suggest new areas for further exploration. Rogers states that "diffusion is a special type of communication in which the messages are about a new idea … some degree of uncertainty is involved [and] alteration occurs in the structure and function of a social system" (Rogers, 2003, p. 6). "Diffusion is defined as the process by which (1) an innovation (2) is communicated through certain channels (3) over time (4) among the members of a social system … these elements are identifiable in every diffusion research study and in every diffusion campaign or program" (Rogers, 2003, p. 11). These four elements focus on the knowledge, ideological, temporal and problem solving aspects—largely cognitive or structural—without highlighting the emotional or value driven aspects that were surfaced in this study.

Rogers (1995) differentiates the adoption process as distinct from the diffusion process and defines it as "the mental process through which an individual passes from first hearing about an innovation to final adoption" (p. 35). The adoption process is marked by five stages: (1) awareness—the individual is exposed to the innovation but lacks complete information about it; (2) interest—the individual becomes interested in the new idea and seeks additional information about it; (3) evaluation—individual mentally applies the innovation to his present and anticipated future situation, and then decides whether or not to try it; (4) trial—the individual makes full use of the innovation; and (5) adoption—the individual decides to continue the full use of the innovation (Rogers, 1995).

Although this study supports Rogers work on diffusion and adoption of innovations, it points to an overlooked area in the literature, namely the critical role of values throughout the process. Values are the expression of our beliefs and are made manifest by our actions (Richley, 2007). Our values are present in every choice we make and shape our world. Yet this central belief system has remained on the fringe of scholarship and practice. This research reveals how a specific set of values has created positive change at what was once thought to be the impenetrable divide between business and social good. In fact, the values central to this study demonstrate how an exemplary organization defined by its belief system has led the way for others around the world to enact such change. Values are the central and enduring factor at each step of the diffusion process of an innovation at the nexus of business and society. These values are embedded throughout the diffusion process and identifiable in the resultant spin-off or adapted innovation.

This research further suggests that innovations are not merely adopted in their entirety but may more likely be adapted to fit within a specific context and to meet particular needs. Social entrepreneurs may be less likely to, as Roger's states, "make full use of the innovation" (1995, p. 35) and instead engage in a continuous and complex process of adapting and reinventing to meet their specific objectives. This adaptation process is the key factor in creating innovations that are sustainable because they are grounded in the resources and in the needs of each environment. This study suggests that our knowledge about the diffusion of innovation can be applied to understanding how successful exemplars of such businesses can serve as practical guides for other organizations and offers insight into how core values can lead to successful human and profit driven enterprises.

Finally, this research sheds new perspectives on how knowledge about the process of innovation can be more broadly used by social entrepreneurs or organizations looking to enact new models with a primacy on enjoining business and social good. While this chapter offers only a brief overview of a working theory, it highlights the significance of new organization role models who readily share information across borders and boundaries to help foster future innovations. In the way that MCC generates new cooperatives in their spin-off model, they are assisting social entrepreneurs in creating new innovations adapted to succeed in other parts of the world. The working model in this chapter offers a template for understanding the foundation on which this sort of innovation process may be initiated and hopefully provides inspiration for those hoping to embark on such a journey.

A limitation of this study is inherent in the fact that this is the first of many studies to follow. Studying MCC and its spin-offs has provided the beginning of a practical theory that focuses on enjoining human values and technical savvy at the intersection of business and society. Expanding this search to include other spin-offs that succeeded and failed would help us understand the characteristics that helped or hindered the process of diffusion of a business social innovation. Also, other exemplary models that exist should be identified and studied so as to support or refine this existing model; to help develop a more robust theory; surface new models and new approaches so as to support and contribute to critical sustainability initiatives.

REFERENCES

Bakaikoa, B., Errasti, A., & Begiristain, A. (2004). Governance of the Mondragón Corporacion Cooperativa. *Annals of Public and Cooperative Economics, 75*(1), 61-87.

Cameron, K. S., Dutton, J. E., & Quinn, R. E. (Eds.). (2003). Foundations of positive organizational scholarship. In *Positive organizational scholarship: Foundations of a new discipline* (pp. 4-13). San Francisco: Berrett-Koehler.

Chaharbaghi, K., & Newman, V. (1996). Innovating: Towards an integrated learning model. *Management Decision, 34*(4), 5-13.

Cheney, G. (1997). The many meanings of "solidarity": The negotiation of values in the Mondragón worker-cooperative complex under pressure. In B. D. Sypher (Ed.), *Case studies in organizational communication 2: Perspectives on contemporary work life* (pp. 68-83). New York: The Guilford Press.

Christensen, C. M., Anthony, S. D., & Roth, E. A. (2004). *Seeing what's next: Using the theories of innovation to predict industry change.* Boston: Harvard Business School Press.

Clamp, C. A. (2000). The internationalization of Mondragón. *Annals of Public and Cooperative Economics, 71*(4), 557-577.

Echeverria, B. (2001). Privileging masculinity in the social construction of Basque identity. *Nations and Nationalism, 7*(3), 339-363.

Errasti, A. M., Heras, I., Bakaikoa, B., & Elgoibar, P. (2002). The internationalisation of cooperatives: The case of the Mondragón Cooperative Corporation. *Annals of Public and Cooperative Economics, 74*(4), 553-584.

Glaser, B. G., & Strauss, A. L. (1967). *Discovery of grounded theory: Strategies for qualitative research.* Chicago: Aldine.

Greenwood, D. J., & Gonzalez Santos, J. L. (Eds.). (1991). *Industrial democracy as process: Participatory action research in the Fagor Cooperative of Mondragón.* Assen/Maastricht, The Netherlands: Van Gorcum.

Hacker, S. L., & Elcorobairutia, C. (1987). Women workers in the Mondragón system of industrial cooperatives. *Gender & Society, 1*(4), 358-379.

Hargadon, A. (2003). *How breakthroughs happen: The surprising truth about how companies innovate.* Boston: Harvard Business School.

Herrera, D. (2004). Mondragón: A for-profit organization that embodies Catholic social thought. *Review of Business, 25*(1), 56-68.

Kasmir, S. (1996). *The myth of Mondragón: Cooperatives, politics, and working-class life in a Basque town.* Albany: State University of New York Press.

MacLeod, G. (1997). *From Mondragón to America: Experiments in community economic development*. Syndney, Nova Scotia: University College of Cape Breton Press.

Mondragón Corporacion Cooperativa. (2003). *2003 annual report*. Retrieved June 14, 2008, from http://www.mcc.es

Mondragón Corporacion Cooperativa. (2005). *2005 annual report*. Retrieved June 14, 2008, from http://www.mcc.es

Morrison, R. (1991). *We build the road as we travel*. Philadelphia: New Society.

Mumford, M. D. (2002). Social innovation: Ten cases from Benjamin Franklin. *Creativity Research Journal, 14*(2), 253-266.

Neuman, W. L. (1997). *Social research methods: Qualitative and quantitative methods* (3rd ed.). Needham Heights, MA: Allyn & Bacon.

Oakeshott, R. (1978). *The case for worker's co-ops*. Boston: Routledge & Kegan Paul.

Ormaechea, J. M. (1993). *The Mondragón cooperative experience*. Mondragón, Spain: Lit Danona, S.Coop.

Richley, B. A. (2007). Corporate values. In S. Clegg & J. R. Bailey (Eds.), *International encyclopedia of organizational studies* (Vol. 1, pp. 305-308). Thousand Oaks, CA: SAGE.

Rogers, E. M. (1995). *Diffusion of innovations* (4th ed.). New York: Free Press.

Rogers, E. M. (2003). *Diffusion of innovations* (5th ed.). New York: Free Press.

Strauss, A., & Corbin, J. (1990). *Basics of qualitative research: Grounded theory procedures and techniques*. Newbury Park, CA: SAGE.

Van de Ven, A. H., Polley, D. E., Garud, R., & Venkataraman, S. (1999). *The innovation journey*. New York: Oxford University Press.

Van de Ven, A. H., & Rogers, E. M. (1988). Innovations and critical perspectives. *Communications Research, 15*(5), 632-651.

Vanek, J. (1971). *The participatory economy: An evolutionary hypothesis and a strategy for development*. Ithaca, NY: Cornell University Press.

Whyte, W. F. (1982). Social inventions for solving human problems. *American Sociological Review, 47*(February), 1-13.

Zirakzadeh, C. E. (1990). Theorizing about workplace democracy: Robert Dahl and the cooperatives of Mondragón. *Journal of Theoretical Politics, 2*(1), 109-126.

Zwerdling, D. (1978). *Workplace democracy: A guide to workplace ownership, participation, and self-management experiments in the United States and Europe*. New York: Harper & Row.

PART II

**BUILDING BUSINESS AND UNIVERSITY SUPPORT FOR
GLOBAL SUSTAINABILITY INITIATIVES**

CHAPTER 5

CONVERGENCE OF FOR-PROFIT AND NOT-FOR-PROFIT ORGANIZATIONAL PRACTICES FOR GLOBAL SUSTAINABILITY AND FINANCIAL SUCCESS

Martin Stack, Laura Fitzpatrick, and Tim Keane

This chapter examines the growing convergence between for-profit firms and not-for-profit organizations. Historically, many observers regarded for-profit firms as being driven primarily by narrow goals such as maximizing shareholder value while not-for-profits were regarded as well intentioned but not particularly savvy institutions. Drawing on two related though distinct streams of literature, we argue that on several key dimensions, for-profit and not-for-profit organizations are beginning to converge. For example, many for-profit firms are explicitly emphasizing the importance of stakeholder as opposed to shareholder concerns. At the same time, many not-for-profit institutions recognize that in order to deliver better results, they need to improve their internal efficiencies in order to deliver more and perform better. To highlight this convergence, we examine the experiences of two institutions: WaterPartners, an innovative not-for-profit dedicated to providing clean drinking water in developing world countries, and Fertiga-

Global Sustainability Initiatives: New Models and New Approaches
pp. 87–102

tor, a for-profit company whose actions demonstrate that commercial enterprises can do well by doing good.

In the United States, we have long been accustomed to two types of organizations: for-profit businesses and nonprofit organizations. At the risk of oversimplification, for-profit businesses have often been associated with rather narrow purposes such as "maximizing shareholder value" while not-for-profits are often portrayed as trying to serve a broader social purpose and are often not regarded as "business savvy" or driven by bottom line quests regarding financial performance. While this view is superficially attractive, it has long been clear that many businesses have tried to balance a number of competing goals that vie with shareholder return. And, for anyone who has worked in a large not-for-profit organization, such as ones in healthcare or education, it is patently apparent that large hospitals and universities are tremendously sophisticated operations which are often at least as efficient, if not more so, than their private sector counterparts. Yet, despite many clear counterexamples, these stereotypes persist. The goal of this chapter is to provide another way to view the relationship between for-profits and not-for-profits, one that highlights how these two groups often borrow from each other in terms of underlying motivations and operational acumen.

Historically, for-profits (FPOs) and not-for-profits (nonprofits—NPOs) are often counterposed as representing opposite sides of a continuum stretching from one side which consists of organizations motivated purely by narrow, profit maximization concerns to the other side consisting of "less sophisticated" NPOs thought to be motivated by a more noble mix of various stakeholder concerns. Yet, the reality is considerably more complicated. While NPOs may not be motivated by profit maximization goals, they often seek to realize other, closely related objectives which balance a range of internal and external concerns. NPOs that rely extensively on outside funding must often meet their funders' requests by ensuring efficient operations, delivering high quality goods or services, and providing challenging but rewarding work environments for their employees (McGuigan & Moyer, 1989). More self-sustaining NPOs can focus on their own self-identified goals, as they may not be as beholden to outside contributors, but they too will be motivated to pursue efficient operations. NPOs falling into this category will seek to maximize benefits for a given level of costs, minimize costs for a set level of benefits, or maximize net benefits (McGuigan & Moyer, 1989). Ultimately, these goals are not that different from those of for-profit firms: all organizations seek operational efficiency and have to address the concerns of their constituents, be they customers or end users. While NPOs may not have to answer to shareholders, they depend to varying degrees on donors or other outside groups for funds, expertise, and stewardship.

The other part of our story concerns how FPOs have developed broader perspectives regarding their ultimate goals and responsibilities. Milton Friedman (1970) presented a provocative, but ultimately unsatisfying, version of FPOs responsibilities in his well known 1970 essay in *The New York Times Magazine* titled, "The Social Responsibility of Business is to Increase Its Profits." In this essay, he asserted that "In a free-enterprise, private-property system, a corporate executive is an employee of the owners of the business. He has direct responsibility to his employers. That responsibility is to conduct the business in accordance with their desires, which generally will be to make as much money as possible while conforming to their basic rules of the society, both those embodied in law and those embodied in ethical custom." Or, as he emphasizes at the end of the essay, the single social responsibility of business is to "increase its profits" provided it does so legally. Since this essay, an array of management and business scholars and practitioners has challenged this fundamental premise that the shareholder is supreme, though there is a wide range of positions regarding how they modify Friedman's thesis. Here, we will focus on two in particular, those of Michael Porter (Porter & Kramer, 2002) and Charles Handy (2002).

Porter is perhaps best known for his work on strategy, so the title of his essay "The Competitive Advantage of Corporate Philanthropy" manifests his interest in linking strategy and social responsibility. Porter seeks to modify, perhaps soften Friedman's extreme position. According to Porter, FPOs can and should engage in activities that may fall beyond the narrowly defined goal of maximizing shareholder value, yet they should do so only when these activities help promote specific competitive goals:

> Corporations can use their charitable efforts to improve their competitive context—the quality of the business environment in the location or locations where they operate. Using philanthropy to enhance context brings social and economic goals into alignment and improves a company's long-term business prospects—thus contradicting Friedman's first assumption. In addition, addressing context enables a company not only to give money but also to leverage its capabilities and relationships in support of charitable causes. Doing so produces social benefits far exceeding those provided by individual donors, foundations, or even governments. Context-focused giving thus contradicts Friedman's second assumption as well. (Porter & Kramer, 2002, pp. 58-59)

Porter examines several examples of how companies have helped their competitive position through investing in their communities. He discusses how Cisco Systems set up the Cisco Networking Academy, an initiative which benefited both Cisco itself and the communities near which it operated along. The program was the result of two developments. Cisco initially donated equipment to schools near its headquarters. Several Cisco employees helped train staff and teachers at these schools how to build and maintain computer networks. Then, Cisco realized that it could help students at those schools while also helping itself in the process: at the time this initiative began in the 1990s, there was a scarcity of network administrators, a key skill set for the industry in general and for itself in particular. The Cisco Network Academy was formed to train secondary and postsecondary students in network and other Internet related skill sets. Some of the graduates went to work for Cisco, while many others took their skills to other firms in the market. What is key for Porter is that Cisco was not engaging in philanthropy for the sake of philanthropy, but that it invested in its community in a way from which it could benefit.

Yet, while this position represents an evolution from Friedman's thesis, it is also clear that the business comes first and that helping the community, to the extent this becomes a consideration, should be done strategically. The last expert considered in this context is the British management author Charles Handy (2002). Writing in the same issue of the *Harvard Business Review* as Porter and Kramer's essay above, Handy addresses the central question in the title of his article, "What's a Business For?" Handy approaches this question much more broadly than either Friedman or Porter. According to Handy,

> The purpose of a business, in other words, is not to make a profit, full stop. It is to make a profit so that the business can do something more or better. That "something" becomes the real justification for the business. Owners know this. Investors needn't care. (Handy, 2002, p. 51).

To reinforce his position, Handy quotes from David Packard:

> I think many people assume, wrongly, that a company exists simply to make money. While this is an important result of a company's existence, we have to go deeper and find the real reasons for our being ... we inevitably come to the conclusion that a group of people get together and exist as an institution that we call a company so that they are able to accomplish something collectively that they could not accomplish separately—they make a contribution to society, a phrase which sounds trite but is fundamental. (Handy, 2002, p. 51).

Handy's view is an important corrective to Friedman, and even to Porter, as it repositions what the ultimate goal of the firm is: society does not exist to help the firm, the firm exists to help society. Work such as Andres Savitz's and Karl Weber's *The Triple Bottom Line* (2006) is a direct descendant of Handy's position, as it emphasizes that profits must be evaluated along with environmental and social performance. According to Savitz and Weber, "The truly sustainable company would have no need to write checks to charity or 'give back' to the local community, because the company's daily operations would not deprive the community, but would enrich it" (p. 21). In a sense, this position builds on Porter's notion of competitive philanthropy, but it changes the emphasis from the firm to the community while keeping the idea that both firm and community can benefit from well thought out initiatives.

Thus far, we have highlighted two basic though fundamental trends: that many NPOs have, over time, introduced a number of efficiency and operational ideas from FPOs, and that many FPOs have increasingly replaced narrow Friedman-esque shareholder analysis with a broader Handy-esque stakeholder approach. In a sense, we can view this as two polar opposites beginning to find more common ground.

Figure 5.1 illustrates how we see two ends of a continuum beginning to intermingle. Traditionally, FPOs and NPOs have been thought of as being motivated by different goals, a difference that in turn was manifest in how the organizations themselves were run. It is our contention that FPOs, far from being the profit maximizing automatons envisioned by Friedman, are becoming increasingly motivated by the goals and concerns articulated above by Handy, Packard, and Savitz. In this way, FPOs are becoming more similar to NPOs which have always been motivated by more than simply maximizing profits. In turn, NPOs are increasingly turning to the for-profit world for ideas regarding how they can improve their efficiencies and productiveness. This is not to say that they are changing their fundamental mission, but it does argue that there is a growing recognition among NPOs that good intentions are not enough: if the goal is to promote a cause, be it healthcare, education, or some other endeavor, then it may be necessary to step back and ask how can we as an organization deliver more and perform better. To this end, there is recognition

FPOs   NPOs

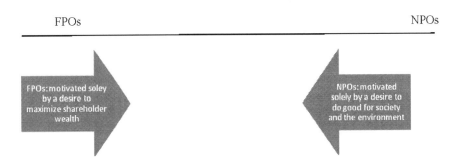

Figure 5.1.   Convergence of FPO and NPOs.

that there are many long standing principles embodied in the FPO domain that may be appropriate to the world of not-for-profits.

Thus, we see in Figure 5.1 a trend in which NPOs are increasingly borrowing from the FPO world ideas and principles to help them function and operate more effectively while FPOs are increasingly looking at NPOs for inspiration regarding how to expand beyond the ultimately unsatisfying world of pure, unadulterated profit maximization. To help illustrate our thesis, we present two brief case studies. The first concerns the NPO, WaterPartners (WaterPartners, 2008). WaterPartners began as and remains a not-for-profit organization. But, as our case illustrates, over time, it has realized that in order to fulfill its basic mission more effectively, it needed to begin to experiment with ideas that to some seem more representative of the for-profit world. Changes such as these are never easy, as they reflect a desire to bring into one world, the NPO continuum, ideas from another world, the FPO continuum. The second case examines a for-profit company, Fertigator (Fertigator, 2008). This case very much illustrates the basic points being suggested by Handy and Savitz, that commercial enterprises can do good by doing well. In the language of Figure 5.1, it shows how FPOs can effectively borrow from notions and ideas long associated with organizations on the opposite end of the continuum.

WATER PARTNERS

The motivation that drives the not-for-profit, WaterPartners International, is immediately clear from just a sampling of data they cite in their literature (WaterPartners, 2008) on the global water crisis

> More than one billion people lack access to a safe supply of drinking water. Water-related diseases are one of the leading causes of disease and death in the world. At any given time, half of the world's hospital beds are occupied by patients suffering from a water-related disease. Compounding the problem is the fact that approximately 50 percent of the water supply projects in the developing world fail.

For an even clearer and admittedly more shocking view of the crisis, more specific data are included in their literature. These include:

- 2.6 billion people in the world lack access to improved sanitation;
- Less than 1% of the world's fresh water (or about .007% of all water on earth) is readily accessible for direct human use;
- Every 15 seconds, a child dies from water-related disease;

- For children under age 5, water-related diseases are the leading cause of death;
- Close to half of all people in developing countries are suffering at any given time from a health problem caused by water and sanitation effects.
- The water and sanitation crisis claims more lives through disease than any war claims through guns. (WaterPartners, 2008)

Confronted with these types of data and the awareness that so many attempts to address the crisis at some level fail, WaterPartners was formed to make a difference not only in how water issues were addressed, but also in the lives of the sixth of the world's population that was affected by the crisis.

Typical water programs through not-for-profit organizations were grant-funded by individual and philanthropic foundation grants to those targeted for water improvement projects. Like many other traditional development projects of all sizes and foci in the previous decades, the common model was that funding for a project was raised and a project implemented or largely "gifted" to those targeted in the hope that the project would contribute to the elimination of some of the impediments to development the targeted population was experiencing. This model comes largely from the economic development theory that perceives the process of development as one that is available to all and what is required for success is the securing of the necessary tools and resources to begin and continue the process of economic development. Economic development itself is perceived as the means through which poverty and all of its attendant problems will be relieved. The magnitude of funds, resources and goodwill directed at this process of development has been enormous, yet the persistence of the fundamental inability for so much of the world's population to meet even the most basic of needs such as water, food, shelter, and basic medical care has led many to question the means by which these problems are addressed.

Gary White began fundraising for water projects in 1990, but the official formation of WaterPartners International 5013C organization took place in 1993. At that point primary fundraising came from individual donors and smaller foundations. As more people became more aware of the magnitude of the water crisis, celebrity fundraising and larger foundations became funders of water programs. By 2001/2002 businesses also became part of the donor base for WaterPartners. In the first decade of WaterPartners, it remained a traditional donor-driven nonprofit which raised funds to distribute to needed communities in poor countries. Some of their earliest projects, such as those in Honduras, involved provision for protection of springs with gravity distribution systems. WaterPartners projects required community commitment and some in kind and/or in cash contributions for system development, and a fee structure was set up to help pay operating and maintenance costs, all with an eye on providing a sustainable water project. This approach set WaterPartners apart from many other NPOs in the water project arena because it incorporated both community and financial support and contribution. The community involvement gave the community a stake in the project, a stake that contributed to the sustainability of the project. Although WaterPartners experienced success with their approach to the water crisis, they also realized that there remained many poor who could be helped if resources could be marshaled differently.

To help further its goal of aiding more communities in need, Water-Partners realized that drawing only on the examples of and lessons learned from other NPOs might not be sufficient: they, like a number of other not-for-profits began to review more systematically examples and ideas from the FPO literature. The goal was a simple but ultimately very important one: how to serve more people in need more effectively. In 2004/2005, WaterPartners began a significantly new initiative. Among the factors contributing to this initiative were:

1. WaterPartners' success in providing sustainable water projects that relied on community contribution and support;
2. WaterPartners' growing commitment to providing not just water, but also sanitation and hygiene education as part of their projects for long-term sustainable results;
3. WaterPartners' experience that many of the poor can contribute financially to the provision of water/sanitation and hygiene education projects;
4. The growing success of the Gramene Bank and other similar microcredit based development projects;

WaterPartners began this new approach—called the WaterCredit Initiative—as a means to address the water crisis on a case by case basis. The success of this new initiative was based on points 3 and 4 above, that the poor already pay (and pay dearly) for their water, and that microcredit can be a very successful development vehicle.

While it may not be immediately apparent to many given the excessive amount of water a typical American uses (approximately 100-176 gallons per day), we do in fact pay for our water. It is no different elsewhere. In poor countries however the cost is calculated in a number of ways. First there are the explicit cash payments for water. WaterPartners has found many residents in urban areas spend 25% or more of their income on water that is often contaminated. Further, even slum dwellers have demonstrated their ability to pay for water, as they spend about 5-10 times more for water from private vendors than middle-class residents who have access to municipal water supply systems. (WaterPartners, 2008)

Exacerbating this situation are the ways typical water provision rests more heavily on some, ultimately leading to the exclusion of many from accessible water.

Even in slums, poor people are not uniformly poor—poor people in some slums have 10 or 20 times the income of those in other slums, yet because almost all water projects are grant-driven, those with greater resources are not sharing in the capital costs of the projects. The net result is that some communities who could afford to pay for projects get them for free while millions of extremely poor people go unserved. (WaterPartners, 2008)

There are also costs paid for water that are measured in time, time that if not spent searching for and carrying water, could be spent in other ways. "Millions of women and children spend several hours a day collecting water from distant, often polluted sources" (WaterPartners, 2008).

What was clear to WaterPartners is that the poor are clearly paying for water already and their lives would benefit immeasurably if they could have greater and more affordable access to clean water (and the provision of sanitation, which must also accompany clean water). Affordable clean water and sanitation would free up income currently spent on exorbitant water prices, time spent in the search for and carrying of water, and provide healthier lives for those benefitted. What is often lacking is up-front funding to make the more affordable provision of water possible. For some desperately poor, the typical grant approach would be the only option for funding, but for a significant portion of the poor, what is needed is a provision of financing so they can afford the capital costs of the water systems that would dramatically affect their lives. Here enters the role of the developing microcredit market. Utilizing this tool would reinforce the community buy-in so important to WaterPartners for sustainability while making access to clean water and adequate sanitation to even more of the poor.

The lack of access of the poor to reasonably priced credit has long been known to be a problem in the developing world. With no collateral the poor are not able to borrow from traditional financial institutions. Instead they are relegated to the informal credit market and outrageous rates of interest that then follow. Recognizing both the inability of the poor to tap into the traditional credit markets and that the very modest sums by Western standards needed by the poor to make investment that would radically alter their lives for the better, Muhammad Yunus began the Grameen Bank. This bank diverged from others by obviating the need for collateral and giving very modest loans to fund small ventures to lift loan recipients from poverty. Yunus began the bank with $27 in 1976, and it has grown to serve more than 7 million borrowers in 2007.

The basic idea of microcredit is that the poor can repay modest, affordable credit if given the opportunity. The original foundation of Yunus' microcredit approach was that small groups of individuals would seek a loan for one member of the group. As the loan was repaid, the funds were available for lending to another member of the group. This approach provided not only affordable and modest credit, but also community support for the success of the projects in which the loan funds were invested.

WaterPartners' WaterCredit Initiative is similar in motivation and structure to Yunus' microcredit approach. WaterPartners' program targets (1) communities that can contribute fully or partially to the capital costs of constructing water provision projects, yet cannot do so in entirety up front and (2) those who are already paying for water and who can benefit immeasurably from more affordable provision of water in their communities. This is not the sole approach to providing clean water and sanitation that WaterPartners utilizes. They acknowledge that there remain those so poor that the traditional grant-funded approach to water projects will remain the only viable avenue. However, the ability to have positive affects on the lives of so many more through the leveraging of funds through microcredit means that many more of those suffering can be helped. The combination of the two approaches really sets WaterPartners apart. The major contribution of WaterPartners really lies in its expertise in understanding when traditional grant-driven approaches are most likely to succeed and when movement into the newer practice of microlending to engender community support and sustainability is the most efficacious approach to meeting the goal of reducing the world water crisis.

This movement by WaterPartners into what would normally be a more business-oriented approach to meeting their organizational goals has also been accompanied by other movements in the same direction. First, as businesses have played a larger and larger role in funding the work of not-for-profits directly or through foundations they form, there have been greater demands for NFP's to "speak the language" of business. This need to speak the language of business holds true in operations, funding development, and reporting of effectiveness to donors. This way of speaking has become even more the case for an organization like Waterpartners, which has additionally taken on business models and tools such as microcredit to meet its goals. Second, as NFP's hire employees from the business world to speak this language and become part of the interface with the donor community, they also begin to structure organizations more like for-profit organizations to meet needs of the donor community for both fundraising and reporting. This trend has been true of Water-Partners as well. A great benefit of this change in NFP's is that it frees up sector specific expertise to delivery of projects to meet organizational goals. The result is potentially an organization that can benefit from the best of both possible worlds.

FERTIGATOR

When longtime friends Dave Cross and Tom Fouch received the offer from national powerhouse True Green/Chem Lawn, the partners had mixed emotions. After all, building their lawn care company's business had consumed them for nearly 20 years. While they were enthusiastic about the potential financial reward from the sale, they could not help but worry about what to do next. The cycle of working countless hours out-doors in the often stifling heat of the St. Louis summers, then spending the off-season trying to build their business, had become their routine. The terms of the sale included strong noncompete language that banned the pair from working in the industry for 5 full years, effectively forcing them to abandon the only work they had known and had started from scratch.

After the final papers were signed to hand over their business, each partner went his own way, dabbling in projects that seemed more about staying busy than pursuing meaningful new careers. As the 5 year anni-versary of their company's sale approached, Cross and Fouch were sur-prised to hear from the lawyer that brokered their original deal with True Green/Chem Lawn. The attorney presented an opportunity that seemed to good to be true. A local entrepreneur was looking to sell his fertiliza-tion technology company to a buyer with experience in the lawn and landscaping industry. The former partners could hardly contain their excitement. The prospect of returning to an industry where they had spent most of their adult lives was invigorating. The company, Fertigator Technologies, even owned a patent on an innovation with national sales potential.

Lawn Care in the United States

There are over 30 million acres of lawns across the United States that are increasingly being managed by professional lawn and landscaping companies. A recent national survey estimated that homeowners spend nearly $12 billion annually on their lawns. Consumers believe that healthy lawns play an important role in home sales, and realtors report that beautiful lawns and landscapes can increase property values by 15 to 20%. However, there are issues created by irresponsible practices, such as environmental degradation through the overuse of fertilizers and excessive water usage for irrigation.

Chemigation

The application of any chemical through an irrigation system is generically called "chemigation." The most common form of chemigation is fertigation, which involves applying fertilizer through irrigation system watering. Products that are typically used by large agricultural enterprises include insecticides, fumigants, soil amendments, and other compounds. Fertigation has distinct advantages in comparison to other application methods, including a more even distribution of the nutrients and significant reductions in water and energy usage.

Fertigator Technologies, Inc.

At the heart of the company Cross and Fouch were buying was a patented technology the inventors named the FertiPro. The product was originally designed to work within existing irrigation systems, delivering varying levels of fertilizer to each watering zone based on the programmed requirement for each particular zone. For example, a zone with a planting bed of perennials would receive a different amount of fertilizer than a zone mostly made up of grass.

The inventors designed the FertiPro to be relatively simple to install, with only three critical components that worked in concert with the irrigation process. The "brain" of the product was the controller, which was designed to be wired into the existing sprinkler system's controller. The injector would receive instructions from the controller as to which zone was logging in for sprinkling and inject the proper amount of fertilizer into the irrigation system pipes, effectively mixing it with the water for optimal distribution. The injector drew the fertilizer from its container, which could be installed anywhere on the premises

The developers of the FertiPro positioned the product as an added value to any irrigation system. Their original marketing claim was that installing the FertiPro enabled any commercial or residential property to reap substantial benefits, including healthier plants and grass, more efficient water usage, and a reduction in the amount of fertilizer applied. The original business model established by the inventors of the FertiPro created a network of irrigation and landscape companies as the primary distributors for the product. Since the positioning of the device was that it worked as a value added feature within an end user's existing irrigation system, the party responsible for installing or maintaining that system was the logical choice to distribute the product. The ease of installation added only minor labor costs to the irrigation/landscape company's bottom line, yet increased the potential revenue generation capacity substantially by extending its product line. The FertiPro inventors pursued an aggressive marketing campaign directed toward potential end users in an attempt to create demand that their network of distributors would fill.

The New Fertigator

With their purchase of Fertigator Technologies complete, Tom Fouch and Dave Cross were ready to use their patented technology to revolutionize the industry and earn their share of the billions spent on lawn care every year. The new ownership deal was finalized in December of 2003, just in time for the spring selling season. The reunited partners were excited to begin meeting the customers they had inherited from the previous owners, some of which were large multinationals like John Deere and Ewing Irrigation. Their hope was to increase sales within the existing customer base and acquire new customers by applying the knowledge they had gained through their 20-plus years of experience in the lawn care industry.

The first step was to visit their existing customers to gain a better understanding of the opportunities to grow their new business. They scheduled a meeting with their largest customer near their St. Louis, Missouri headquarters. When they arrived, the owner of the company met them at the door and said "that (expletive deleted) John Smith better not be with you," referring to the previous owner. Cross, who had assumed the role of president of the new business, felt a sinking feeling in his gut. He glanced toward Fouch, vice president of operations in the new endeavor, for support. For the next 2 hours the deflated partners were presented with a litany of issues they needed to address immediately.

After that initial meeting, the new partners spent the ensuing months visiting other customers to learn the extent of the problems with their newly acquired business. Of primary concern was that the FertiPro technology had not been tested using a variety of fertilizers. As end users applied mass marketed brands of fertilizers, the unit stopped functioning. Unfortunately, the distributor network had been convinced by the former owners to sell the unit based on the assurance that it was simple to operate and flexible enough to fit with any irrigation system. The problems were exacerbated because the previous owners were not staffed for repairs and maintenance.

The new owners embarked on a research mission to understand what their options were, learning from industry trade shows and interviewing anyone even peripherally familiar with the FertiPro. It became clear to Cross and Fouch that the first priority was fixing the technology problem. That challenge was substantial as neither partner had an engineering background. They also learned that allowing the use of all fertilizers was a variable that could not be controlled for, creating the potential for ongoing service issues.

The solutions came slowly, but eventually the partners stabilized the FertiPro through an investment in standard plastic molds to retrofit on the hardware. They also bought their own fertilizer to be used exclusively with the FertiPro. Finally, they developed a basic version of the FertiPro with similar features except the ability to differentiate fertilization rates by zone. Solving the problems took longer than expected and the company missed most of the selling season. The partners needed help from their distributor network to get their revamped products to market quickly in order to recover some of their costs.

Unfortunately, in spite of the improvements, their distributor network was not convinced. The issues caused by the previous owners were fresh in their customers' minds, and too much credibility had been lost. The irrigation and lawn/landscaping industries were typically slow to embrace change, and they controlled access to the large commercial end users. Additionally, while their customers in the Midwest may have understood the benefits to society of reducing fertilizer usage, the average cost for water was so low it was difficult to sell water usage reduction as a benefit.

The Newer Fertigator

Their frustration with existing customers forced Cross and Fouch to reassess their business model. As they reflected on their dilemma, the partners realized that if the distributors who were their existing customers were not interested in the benefits their products and services offered, they would focus on different end users—consumers. They formulated a new strategy based on meeting the needs of a targeted niche of consumers that would value the "green" benefits their products.

The immediate challenge was identifying high priority markets where the environmental benefits of their products would be valued. Their analysis defined the Southeast as a natural fit, with a particularly urgent opportunity in Florida, where regulations on water usage and pollution concerns had effectively created a huge market for "green" products and services. The partners decided to relocate the company's headquarters to Florida and to begin to distribute their products directly to consumers whose monthly water bills were five to 10 times greater than the Midwest.

Their strategic positioning as an environmentally focused lawn care company immediately began to resonate with consumers in central Florida. In addition to their Pro model fertigation device (formerly FertiPro), the company offered the less expensive Flo model for consumers. Both models were tested and proven to improve water usage significantly, effectively reducing monthly water bills to consumers by nearly 50%. Consumers with a quarter acre lawn would see decreases of $50-$75 per month.

The company increased their environmentally focused product offering as well, adding a soil moisture sensor that would activate the sprinkler system only when the soil in a zone reached a programmed level of dryness. The soil moisture sensor could triple the reduction rate in water usage. Their service offerings also emphasized an environmental advantage. Customers could sign monthly service agreements that provided personalized services such as plant inspections for insects and targeted use of environmentally sensitive bug deterrents (versus chemical pesticides). The partners even developed custom lawn and sprinkler monitoring services for targeted groups such as the so-called "homesteaders" that lived away from their Florida home for long periods of time.

The new business model focused on promoting a healthier environment through water conservation and reduced pollution seemed to work. The company recently opened a second branch in northern Florida, and signed a service agreement with an entire community in Sarasota, an area known for its environmental initiatives.

CONCLUSION

This essay has set out to illustrate the increasing convergence in the worlds of for-profit businesses and not-for-profit organizations. While these groups are often presented as opposite sides of a continuum, the reality is that organizations from both sides are becoming increasingly vocal about the learning they can engage in from the other. The brief case studies highlighted here have shown how NPOs such as WaterPartners have drawn inspiration for some of their new initiatives such as Water-Credit from the for-profit world; at the same time, they have shown that for-profit firms such as Fertigator are increasingly looking to balance profit maximization with broader social and environmental objectives. Their approach to business is very much along the lines of what Charles Handy and Andrew Savitz have written. This level of convenience does not suggest that the line between NPOs and FPOs has been eradicated:

the fundamental missions of both sets of organizations do remain distinct. However, the often trumpeted chasm between the two sides may not be as wide as is commonly portrayed, and in fact may be narrowing. We believe this is fundamentally a good development as both sides have much to learn from the other. If NPOs are able to increase their operational efficiencies and to target more clients and communities by introducing new programs, then they and their target audiences will be the better for it. And, as FPOs seek to effect a more comprehensive balance between social, environmental, and shareholder interests, then it is quite natural that they will look to an array of NPOs for inspiration and ideas.

REFERENCES

Fertigator. (2008). *Fertigator home page*. Retrieved June 14, 2008, from http://www.fertigator.com/

Friedman, M. (1970, September 13). The social responsibility of business is to increase its profits. *The New York Times Magazine*, pp. 32-33.

Handy, C. (2002). What's a business for? *Harvard Business Review, 80*(12), 49-56.

McGuigan, J., & Moyer, R. C. (1989). *Managerial economics* (5th ed.). Minneapolis/St. Paul, MN: West.

Porter, M., & Kramer, M. (2002). The competitive advantage of corporate philanthropy. *Harvard Business Review, 80*(12), 56-69.

Savitz, A. W., & Weber, K. (2006). *The triple bottom line: how today's best-run companies are achieving economic, social, and environmental success-and how you can too*. San Francisco: Jossey-Bass.

WaterPartners. (2008). *WaterPartners homepage*. Retrieved June 14, 2008, from http://www.water.org/

CHAPTER 6

WHAT IS
SUSTAINING PRACTICE?
HOW IS IT LEARNED?

Jenni Goricanec and Roger Hadgraft

This chapter describes the authors' experiences of attempting to embed sustainability into tertiary education, through a variety of initiatives, both inside and outside of the university system: these initiatives are linked with models and approaches. We begin by describing our understanding of the nature of our predicament—an unpredictable, turbulent macroenvironment; this turbulence is being further exacerbated by climate change. We expand further on climate change adaptation and specifically adaptation as a response. We also describe our operating environment (the university system). Given the nature of our predicament and our potential responses, we believe that we need to educate "the total person for survival in an unpredictable, turbulent future." We propose the need for transformation "by generating active, ongoing practices that shift a culture's experience of reality."

This chapter follows the authors' journeys, both individually and collectively, over 6 years, as we have sought to create higher education programs with a clearer focus on sustainability, at both undergraduate and postgraduate levels. These journeys have included research on:

Global Sustainability Initiatives: New Models and New Approaches
pp. 103–136
Copyright © 2008 by Information Age Publishing
103

- the *nature of our predicament*—the environment within which, and to which, we are responding including, of course, the specific of *climate change*;

- notions of sustainability (often seen as responding in environmental, social, and economic areas) and more importantly from our perspective, *sustaining*, "a system of production that fulfils desires for economic and ecological *abundance* and social *equity* in both the short and long terms—becoming *sustaining* (not just sustainable) *for all generations*;

- the *role of professions* in sustaining;

- science and particularly its necessary role of observing and *knowing* about the world;

- the role of engineering as *doing*, and "creating what can be," using (knowing) the science;

- *philosophy*: not only epistemology (ways of knowing) but also ontology (ways of being and doing); as well as an understanding of ontological politics—that we may choose a certain way of being because it is "better" than others.

- working with profoundly different conceptual/cultural constructs (e.g., Western ways of being (the world is constructed) versus other cultures views (the world is); or science versus engineering; or social, environmental, economic, and technical views).

- values are critical as they serve as coordinating mechanisms within a turbulent world. When shared, they add predictability to an otherwise unpredictable set of relationships and enable networks to grow; in a postmodern view of the world, whose values do we honor?

- education and the need to educate the total person for survival in an unpredictable, turbulent future; where facts, concepts, theories, intellectual skills, and well-developed cognitive maps are not enough;

- plus more as everything is interconnected.

We have, over this time, our 6 year journey, undertaken various "experiments" (initiatives) which we will describe and aim to closely link to our theoretical notions (our models and approaches). But first we will focus on the nature of our predicament of sustaining for future generations to provide a context for our experiments; as the process philosopher, Alfred North Whitehead, said "consciousness is the acme of emphasis" (Whitehead, 1933, p. 231)

OUR PREDICAMENT

Living in a world "with the property of 'turbulence'" or in the words of John Law (2004, p. 7) "generative flux" means that not only time but also space can shift, as can the "rules," individually and/or collectively. Who would have thought, in early 2006, that climate change would become such a big issue, given that environmentalists and businesses had been in a tug-of-war for decades. Now, not only is Australia's (new) Federal Opposition trying to "buy-in", but also the president of the United States, our previous Australian prime minister became a climate change "realist" after denying it for many years. New "players" are starting to emerge— the Australian Business Partnership on Climate Change, the Energy Futures Forum, the Asia Pacific Partnership on Clean Development and Climate, and even the Global Nuclear Energy Partnership, which is 38 nations trying to create a "closed circle of nuclear-fuel production" (Murphy, 2007, p. 15) globally. In 2007, the then Australian government, despite signing up to the partnership, declared that Australia would not share stewardship of nuclear waste with the rest of the world!

Local governments are moving on energy efficiency, state governments attempt regulation; The Government of Victoria has renewed the licence to extract coal for our dirtiest brown-coal-fired power station. New solutions are being touted— clean coal; renewable energy systems are proliferating particularly in Europe; Kyoto targets continue to be pursued, including beyond Kyoto; the Intergovernmental Panel on Climate Change (IPCC) have said climate change is happening faster than expected; the Stern Report (Stern, 2007) has said it is more economic to mitigate earlier rather than later. Al Gore is traveling the world "teaching" people about the situation and recently has pointed to large areas of Arctic ice disintegrating with its potential impacts on the thermohaline ocean circulation, weather, and sea levels, but we continue with business as usual.

At the same time, who and what was prepared for the prolonged drought in Australia, the lack of water for agricultural, industrial, public, and residential uses? The lack of water has led to various proposals—new dams; fixing the irrigation system in the Goulbourn to supply Melbourne via a north-south pipeline; recycled water piped from Melbourne's Eastern Treatment Plant for power stations in the La Trobe Valley, releasing potable water for Melbourne; desalination—proposed, decried, agreed, popping up in a number of states; connections to power sources and concomitant increases in greenhouse gases; recycling—not for drinking here, but at the same time already in place for irrigators in Werribee from the Western Treatment Plant and at Melbourne's Eastern Treatment Plant for golf courses and gardens. Increased variability of flow and recognition of crisis has driven the call for a national response in the Murray Darling Basin, which the Victorian government has blocked; environmental flows are on again, off again. All the action on drought could go cold if we get lots of rain over the next few years. Other regions of Australia though have had record flooding; cyclones have become more intense, happen more often and with more damage.

This is the type of environment within which we and our students will need to lead change for our future. How can choices be made within this turbulent environment?

NATURE OF OUR PREDICAMENT—THE ENVIRONMENT *WITHIN WHICH,* AND *TO WHICH,* WE ARE RESPONDING

In order to contextualize sustaining, we need to establish how it fits into the causal texture of our (global) environment. In order to do this, we require a way of talking about systems, and their environments that does justice to the complex web of interactions that characterize system-environment relations (shown topologically in Figure 6.1), and to the emergent phenomena which these interactions coproduce. There are relationships within our environment, the dynamic conditions with which *all* systems/organizations (such as nations, businesses, corporations, governments) which share the environment must adapt. Trends include:

- increasing application of technologies to all aspects of life and work;
- increasing penetration by women into all social economic and political arenas of Western societies. (The fact that this trend penetrates all contexts, but is strongly resisted in some contexts—e.g., senior management of many organizations—and the degree to which people will go to resist, are all indicators of its extreme potency.);
- increasing resistance to, and conflict over, the extreme laissez-faire position taken by many governments, and institutions (e.g., World Trade Organization, International Monetary Fund) globally;
- increasing homogeneity of global culture and increasing conflict over this trend; and
- increasing average global temperatures and concomitant increase in volatility in weather patterns, increasingly driven by our past, current, and planned future approaches to energy production.

It should be noted that we use the word environment throughout this chapter in its broadest sense, within a systemic construct, where a system

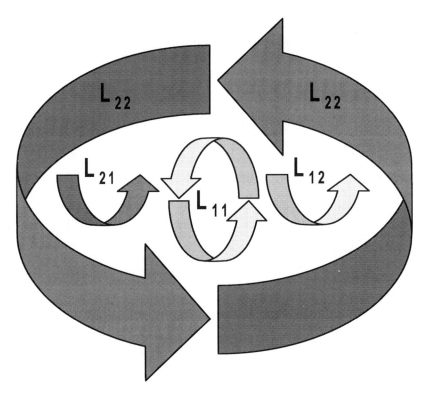

Figure 6.1.   Topological representation of a system in its environment.

is within an environment which thus includes all things—not only the natural environment but also the social, the manmade, and so on.

Focusing on the environment of today, the most important *emergent property* has been the phase change into a "turbulent" environment. In a turbulent environment, the dynamics emerge, not only from the interactions of identifiable component systems—what happens within the system itself (L_{11}), what happens between the system and its environment (L_{12}) (loosely known as outputs), what happens from the environment to the system (L_{21}) (loosely known as inputs)—but also from the environment itself (L_{22}) (Figure 6.1). The ground is set in motion.

Four trends contribute to the emergence of these dynamic field forces:

- The growth of organizations, and linked sets of organizations, to meet disturbed, reactive conditions, that is, where each one of a number of similar, competing organizations improve their chances of hindering others by responding with an operation, a planned series of tactical initiatives, followed by calculated reactions by others, and counteractions. They are so large that their actions are both persistent, and strong enough, to induce out-of-control resonance (autochthonous processes) in the environment—like the wooden bridge which will, itself, resonate as a consequence of soldiers marching over it in step.

- The deepening interdependence between economic and social goals—to the point where economic considerations can come to dominate decision making, and some would claim "there is no such thing as society—only the economy" and, concomitantly, that one should strive for continual economic growth at the expense of all other considerations.

- The increasing reliance on research and development to achieve the capacity to meet competitive challenge. This leads to a situation in which a change gradient is continuously present in the environmental field.

- The increased dependence on fossil fuels to power all of this and the effect that this is having on our natural environment, that is to say, climate change.

The resulting increased complexity, and the unexpected directionality of causal interconnections, produces increased *relevant uncertainty* about the requirements for adaptation. Individual organizations—here we include corporations, governments, and nations—no matter how powerful, cannot expect to adapt successfully, simply through their own direct actions.

What is required in a turbulent environment, over and above tactics, strategy, and operations is *active adaptive planning*, based on an understanding of system-environment interactions in a turbulent field (Figure 6.1).

WITHIN THE CONTEXT OF OUR PREDICAMENT—CLIMATE CHANGE ADAPTATION (AN EXTRACT FROM A RECENT APPLICATION FOR A GRANT FOR CLIMATE CHANGE ADAPTATION SKILLS FOR PROFESSIONALS BY *oases*[1] GRADUATE SCHOOL)

We remind again that emphasis is the acme of consciousness (Alfred North Whitehead). Our emphasis is with our predicament and responses, but for the purpose of this section we will place our attention on climate change adaptation and the skills that professionals will require to respond effectively.

The IPCC (2007, p. 30) in its latest assessment report says that, and we quote as a reminder, "warming of the climate is unequivocal, as is now evident from observations of increases in global average air and ocean temperatures, widespread melting of snow and ice, and rising global average sea level." And that "most of the observed changes in globally averaged temperatures since the mid-20th century is *very likely* due to the observed increase in anthropogenic GHG [greenhouse gas] concentrations" (IPCC 2007, p. 39, emphasis in original). Also, "there is *high agreement* and *much evidence* that with current climate change mitigation policies and related sustainable development practices, global GHG will continue to grow over the next few decades" (IPCC 2007, p. 44, emphasis in original).

The IPCC (2007a, p. 869) defines adaptation as "the adjustment in natural or human systems to actual or expected climatic stimuli or their effects, which moderates harm or exploits beneficial opportunities." Also, "adaptive capacity is defined as the *ability of a system* to adjust to climate change (including climate variability and extremes) to moderate potential damages, to take advantage of opportunities or to cope with the consequences."

But Emery (1997), an Australian social ecologist, identifies a more complex relationship between adaptation and purposive activity (purposive is distinct from purposeful here, as being purposive requires the declaration of intent over and above the internalized intention). In his papers he says that "adaptation refers to the responses available for dealing with emergent environmental circumstances" (p. 887). And that this represents only the passive form of "directive correlation," where the concept of "directive correlation encompasses adaptation in that it allows for that system of causal relations in which the environment is actively influenced to determine the kinds of responses that will subsequently be adaptive" (p. 887) or more succinctly purposive adaptation.

The abstract representation of the directive correlation is reproduced in Figure 6.2 (after Sommerhof, 1950, 1969) and we remind readers that this is a very difficult, turbulent environment within which to plan.

Note that the unit of analysis (or the unit of *intention*) is the system in its environment, or using the nomenclature above, the (L_{22}, L_{11}) relationship (Figure 6.1) and, thereby, adaptation is defined as a dynamic relationship, not a state of affairs. Further, the L_{21} and L_{12} *coproduce* the future.

Introducing Active Adaptive Planning

The active adaptive planning diagram in Figure 6.3 extends the directive correlation via a planning cycle. Where the directive correlation identifies the sought conditions—the *desirable and feasible* system in its

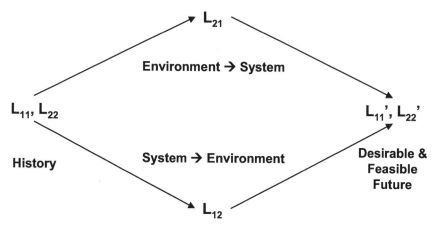

Figure 6.2.   Directive correlation.

environment' (L_{11}', L_{22}') this planning frame also identifies the achieved system in its environment (L_{11}'', L_{22}'') and enables the identification of gaps between what is sought and what is achieved which together with all that was understood previously, can then be the subject of further active adaptive planning. Note that the diagram is indicative of a process which includes the system in its environment at various stages (historical, sought, achieved), via system → environment and environment → system relations.

By focusing on adaptation as described by the IPCC (2007), where the coordination of adaptation needs ought to be aligned with economic and social development suggests some other people that are more expert including organizations such as governments and businesses do the adapting. In this conception, most people are relegated to waiting for mitigation or adaptation to occur—it should be noted here that this is the way that we, at least in Western societies, have been trained to think, that, while many people just continue their lives, others do the work of changing or responding and eventually change will be done to those who have been passively continuing their lives.

We return now to the theme of passivity—the sort of waiting and inherent expectation that someone(s) else will make the changes required, that is, respond, by mitigating the damage or adapting, to the predicament that we find ourselves in (one part of which is climate change). We reflect that much higher education, heavily content oriented, encourages a sort of *feed me* passivity in many of those who interact with it (Hiley & Goricanec, 2006). We believe that a certain personal and professional responsibility is required for the ecological footprint (Global Footprint Network,

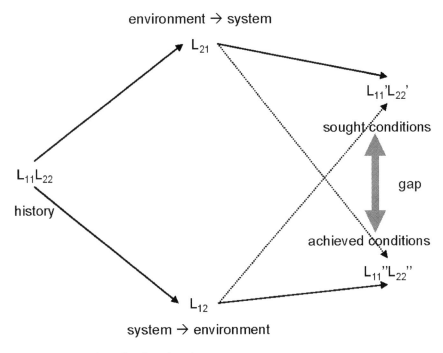

Figure 6.3.   Active adaptive planning.

2006) and fingerprint (Vox Bandicoot, 2006) that we place on the world, both individually (in our own dwellings and lives) as well as collectively (in the cities in which we live, in our organizations, etc.). We need to develop ways of sustaining life on our planet *now* that is congruent with sustaining people in future generations.

Responses May Be Maladaptive

Social ecologists like Emery and Trist (1975) argue that responses to turbulence (Crombie, 1972) may be maladaptive. Tim Flannery argues in *The Future Eaters: An Ecological History of the Australasian Lands and People* (1994) that Australians' "maladapted cultures" are dramatically incompatible with the extremely fragile, difficult, and alien environment where the El Nino Southern Oscillator brings dramatically longer weather cycles than the normal yearly seasons, combined with very different soils and biology. Examples of these cultures are: introducing such things as the traditional Christmas feast that broke the interminably cold barren period to our abundant southern summer; proscribing fires in national parks; refusing to consider eating meat from other sources than sheep, cattle, pigs, and chicken (Flannery, 1994).

Social ecologists like Baburoglu (1987, 1988) also note that initially maladaptive responses may be first order and either passive, such as superficiality, segmentation, dissociation, or active, such as, authoritarianism, synoptic idealism, evangelicism but if these maladaptive responses are not extinguished, they will harden into more intractable second order responses:

- Monothematic Dogmatism—Depth is captured "once and for all" as in "The End of History." Superficial satisfaction of the overriding values to guide behavior in turbulence. Hence dogma becomes the normative base for distinguishing right or wrong, good from bad. There is a single, crystal clear truth (closed system, closed future). Some examples in an Australian university context—neoliberal dogma, wedded to the so-called knowledge economy, applied to universities—"The market is the answer"; "It's the bottom-line"; "The answer is that academics must become more business-like." "You are either with us, sonny boy, or against us" (No, not George W, but the vice chancellor of a prestigious Melbourne university).

- Stalemate—Represents a "crystallization" of progression. The power disparity is lost. Inability to articulate, design and, in particular, pursue, sometimes even the most mechanical ends of the *whole* system. *An obsessive concern with the means at almost complete expense of the ends.* (e.g., as in "on-line education" economies of scale versus "value adding" economies of scope as competing responses to cost pressures, etc.). The system becomes clinched, *qualitative progress ceases.* Academics and managers each see the other as blocking progress and, rather than cooperate, engage in bitter, self-indulgent battles for supremacy.

- Polarization—Crystallization of the breadth dimension produces clear in-group, out-group dynamic, viewing the world as "us" (academics) and "them" (managers). Coupled with the dogmatic style it reduces the complex intertwining of reality to simplistic, black and white, god or evil, terms such as where the "entrepreneurial university" is posited as the evangelical leading edge, positive and negative valence toward this evangelical vision provides groups with a (albeit pathological) sense of identity, leading to "blind giants" and the "angry dispossessed." Produces social enclaves (like gated communities), and social vortices (social "no-go" zones).

In the Australian university system there has been a clear emergence of these second order maladaptive responses (Young & Goricanec, 2003). In order to "unfreeze", a clear policy framework is required, prior to the application of traditional planning (Gloster, 1999). The key difference between the planning conditions which apply in the current decade and those applied in the last quarter of the twentieth century, is that systems now have to be "unfrozen", before traditional planning can occur. This can only be done by "forcing" the external world, in all its dimensions, into the planning space in a way that enable the participants to make judgements about it rather than being overwhelmed by it. Simply surrendering to the external environment leads directly to maladaptive responses. One of the more challenging aspects of the current social and economic debates is the assumption that specific environmental trends (e.g., so called "globalization" as expressed in global cultural homogeneity) have an inevitability about them which means that those who challenge, are naïve. This surrender obviously undermines adaptive behavior and, in fact, it undermines any attempt at long-term thinking.

On the other hand, the process of deliberate and systematic unfreezing, followed by traditional adaptive planning, enables individuals, outside the planning sessions, to act within the contextual knowledge established within the planning sessions (i.e., essentially system capability, in the context of relevant external dynamics and, coordinated by the desirable and feasible scenario), and with the sanction of the other actors to

- mobilize resources (logistics);
- form coalitions with other colleagues;
- develop alliances;
- act on public representation; and
- continue to work on the development of the integrated whole solution development and design (Goricanec & Young, 2001; Latour, 1999).

This is not an easy path to follow and we are reminded that

creating and sustaining such an environment puts tremendous responsibility on all those involved in "pre-figuring the new." It is an integral act—an act of enduring integrity. We need to have resilience and active, engaging tolerance. (Hiley, 2006, p. 23)

Further, we are beginning to meet the hopes of the French sociologist and philosopher Pierre Bourdieu in his book *Acts of Resistance—Against the Myths of Our Time* (Bourdieu, 1998) that:

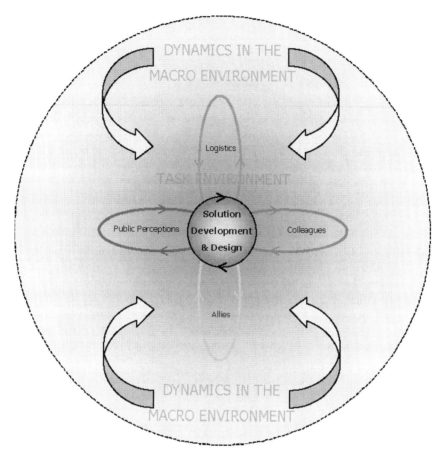

Figure 6.4.   A nonlinear action planning model based on Latour's (1999, p. 100) reality of science practice plus dynamics in the macroenvironment.

> there still exist forces which … work to invent and construct social order which is not governed solely by the pursuit of self-interest and individual profit, and which makes room for collectives oriented towards rational pursuit of collectively defined and approved ends. (p. 42)

WITHIN THE CONTEXT OF OUR PREDICAMENT—UNIVERISITIES

In this section we will refer to two "initiatives" undertaken by David Young and Jenni Goricanec in universities using the models and processes described so far. These descriptions provide a relevant view of the context within which we were working for our initiatives described later. The issues of concern identified here are not specific to these particular initiatives they are endemic in the Australian university system, as well as in our shared turbulent environment.

1. In the year 2000, a leading Australian university invited us to facilitate the development of a new program. The program was intended to position the university at the leading edge of business education, and to serve as the core of an export "product" for the Asian "market" (Goricanec & Young, 2001; Young & Goricanec, 2003).

2. The second initiative was a sequence of conceptualizing, developing, and sustaining an alternative model for higher education outside of the established system—Akademos. Initially we proposed "a complete re-conceptualization of the university, in our dynamic environment, using processes specifically designed to address this level of task (M. Emery, 1993) in a context where all existing institutions have been thoroughly penetrated by the pathology of managerialism" (Goricanec & Young, 2001, p. 1) and further we developed an "Action Research (AR) project that emerged and aimed at developing and sustaining an alternative model for tertiary education—Akademos" (Young & Goricanec, 2003, p. 1).

From these two examples we extract indicators of the university environment within which we were (and continue) working.

When we entered the first project they had been attempting to develop the prospective program for some time, and progress was at a *stalemate*, with a war of attrition taking place between the teaching and learning cadre and the academics on the one hand, and senior management, on the other. Senior management were committed to exclusively electronic means of delivery, to generate economies of scale, and to demonstrate that they were "world's best practice" trendsetters. On the other hand, the academics and learning strategists were seeking a balance between face to face and electronic delivery, especially in a context where the first Asian target market had extremely limited Internet access. The stalemate was reinforced by the complete refusal of senior management to address the ends of the new program in anything but the most authoritarian and rhetorical manner, thereby amplifying the message that the only meaningful debate could be over means. At the same time, there was clear evidence of dogmatism (e.g., satisfying the mass market, lowest common denominator, small (e)business market in Asia is the overwhelming driver (unpacking this criterion for "what to do next," leads inexorably to courses which look more like something a TAFE would offer), for an "entrepreneurial university"), and polarization (e.g., between those academics seeking a full, systemic strategy—that is, the program conceived as a system of subjects, managed by a team of educators, where the relationships between the subjects were as important as the content, and where the relationships were to be coordinated by the purpose of the program. This is distinguished from programs which are composed of an aggregation, or heap of existing subjects, managed as a production line, and coordinated by the need of each school to have its "slice of the action") and the functional managers, who were looking to minimize costs and, at the same time, preserve or enhance their own status through incremental change and "heaping together" existing courses).

In addition there was a significant level of polarization within the academic group over the degree to which leadership status would accrue to the "hard" subjects (like accounting, economics, engineering) and the "soft" ones (like human relations, organization development, strategic thinking). This, in turn, made the development of a truly systemic program, coordinated by the (student) outcomes being sought, extremely problematic.

In our second initiative the intervention was designed as a four-stage, modified *searching* process, which is a general mode that educates "our perceptual systems to better *search* out the invariant characteristics and distinguishing features of our personal, social and physical environments rather than an education in how to someday *research* an accumulated pile of so-called social knowledge" (Emery, 1981, p. 34), with short-cycle reflection to evaluate progress between each step. After 16 months and, partly as a consequence of the ongoing analysis reported in our paper (Young & Goricanec, 2003), the following long-cycle outcomes emerged (in the absence of a formal long-cycle group, the authors took this role):

1. An institutional representation of the outcomes, "Akademos," has been established as a cooperative (see http://www.akademos.org.au) and many "offerings" were being established, but for the purposes of this chapter the more important aspects were that

2. ... there are a number of interrelated trends in the project which pointed toward the persistence of maladaptive responses as well as hypotheses about their nature.

    • Continuing reduction in diversity of the participants (keeping "cosy" in the enclave)

    • A general lack of interest in researching the history of development of universities in general, and Akademos, in particular, despite records being available on the list server.

- A discontinuity in the searching process as originally designed; search data is ignored, focus is placed on means (a cooperative) without articulation of ends, and there is a failure to take formal responsibility for the action and reflection cycle (which includes stubborn resistance to the *public* recording of discussions, and a constant slide into committee structures).

- Contextualizing has been reduced. There has been a return to inside-out thinking (instead of outside-inside-outside) and very little effort is focused on engaging people outside of Akademos in the thinking and activities.

- Hope has disappeared from the agenda it is being replaced by comfort/habit—this is exhibited in choice of venue (a comfortable, traditional library), the focus on socializing and a lack of interest in bringing in new members, or new ideas/perspectives. (events which have occurred during the writing of this paper indicate that this block may be shifting)

- *Monothematic dogmatism—the normative base for distinguishing right from wrong, good from bad*—on the one hand, this comes in easily recognizable packaging; "it's all about community development," or "the answer is a cooperative university," but on the other, it comes in the guise of the contextualist framework itself. Translating contextualism from a theory which has substantial support, into practice, has led to a stubborn and possibly intractable performative contradiction. As the cycle between contextualist theory and AR practice proceeds, it is becoming obvious that the practice of contextualism, especially in so far as it is used to map the external world (the L_{22}), and highlight which trends (L_{21}) to respond to, is being experienced by many in the group as an example of the monothematic dogmatism we are all seeking to unlock.

- *Leading to polarisation—reducing the complex intertwining of reality to simplistic, black and white, terms*—Again, there are the relatively common examples: "They are evil," "We need to be different from them," "Some people ...." However, the contextualist framework of AR is also polarizing, since it is not being applied "off the billiard table." The sometimes dogmatic assertion of this framework by people "on the billiard table" acts, in and of itself, as a driver of polarization. The contradiction is, as we stated above both stubborn and possibly intractable.

- *Stalemate—qualitative progress ceases*—The most common symptom of this second-order response is the obsession with means— a cooperative plus a Web site is all we need; a policy, governance and procedure subcommittee are looking at orthodox policy before courses have been designed (i.e., how, comes before, what, and why); together with lots of fight/flight and "keep your head down." However, again, the application of the contextualist framework and AR is part of the problem. *AR practice is, in itself, a "means"*—we would argue it is simply good science, applied to *complex-organized systems,* with high degrees of freedom (that is, social systems—rather than the simple-organized systems of billiards, and solar systems, or the complex-random systems of subatomic physics and thermodynamics). However, in an interdisciplinary group which is nevertheless homogeneous (all the active participants, with the exception of the authors are employed in universities) the framework-in-practice is often interpreted as just another decision making process, like committee meetings.

In addition, in a context where a significant number of participants seem to identify the alternative to authoritarianism ("the rules") as laissez faire ("my rules"), rather than democracy ("our rules") (democracy is, in fact, the alternative to the opposition between authoritarianism and laissez faire), the situation has become further exacerbated. While a hierarchy, formal committee structures and ex-cathedra evaluations are somehow seen as ideology free, participative AR processes are, sometimes, interpreted as pure ideology. (Young & Goricanec, 2003, p. 3)

From the long-cycle reflection the trend toward *localized vortical* (Gloster, 1999) conditions becomes clearer. *In so far as the group is attempting to implement the concept of an enclave, with a formal cooperative structure, we can hypothesize that we are:*

- attempting to create a placid, clustered institution (e.g., like a monastery, homogeneous values, identity based on language, rites of passage, distinctive competence and referent power, and a hierarchy of structure, headed by the old men of the tribe);
- within an operating environment being manipulated by government as disturbed, reactive (i.e., neoliberal dogma—centers of excellence, competitive free market, user pays, product focused, and subordination to the main plan of, increasingly, online, export-oriented, courses); and
- within a turbulent global environment. (Young & Goricanec, 2003, p. 4)

In a situation where there is a deeply imbued sense of authority (if not authoritarianism), a highly individualist model of scholarship, and a deep seated fear of "the mob" (i.e., uninitiated outsiders, those who neither recognize, nor respect, the academic hierarchy—for a detailed discussion of this phenomena, under the heading of "The Modernist Settlement" (Latour, 1999), polarization and stalemate have become strong "attractors."

OUR FIRST UNDERGRADUATE STORY

This is a story of working within the university system, it should be noted that working inside a system brings with it all sorts of potential constraints not least of all leaders unwillingness within the context described above to take action which would seem to naturally flow from their espoused beliefs but which for reasons of political expediency and or habit they appear unwilling to take.

This story begins in 2002 when the Royal Melbourne Institute of Technology was beginning the renewal of its undergraduate engineering programs. Forums were held with industry partners, such as in chemical engineering, using some key *searching* questions (Hadgraft & Muir, 2003):

1. What are the *emerging trends* in the environment that will have an increasing impact on your organization?
2. What *attributes* will organizations, yours included, require if they are to survive and thrive in this environment?
3. How are you, and your organization, *dealing/coping* with the pressures to survive and thrive in this environment at the moment?
4. Given 1-3, what *capabilities* will employees, specifically, graduate engineers, require if they are to effectively contribute to their work organizations and communities in the twenty-first century?
5. What can or should be done to ensure that (chemical, natural resources or civil) engineers from Royal Melbourne Institute of Technology are *better prepared* to meet the demands in their lives as professionals and citizens?

The results of the scan were summarized as a mindmap, in Figure 6.5, in which the need for sustainability emerged strongly in terms of competitive advantage, attracting investors, production efficiency and dealing with waste products.

Consequently, the role of sustainability was made more explicit in the school's three undergraduate programs: chemical, civil, and environmental engineering. Students each take a course in first semester that requires them to work on a project in which they must make choices on the basis of economic, environmental, social, and technical criteria. They learn upfront about decision-making methodologies (e.g. using constraints and a weighted ranking approach).

Students then encounter projects in subsequent years in which they must again choose alternative solutions on the basis of these four basic criteria. Previously, engineering students tended to be taught to use only two criteria: technical sufficiency and economics.

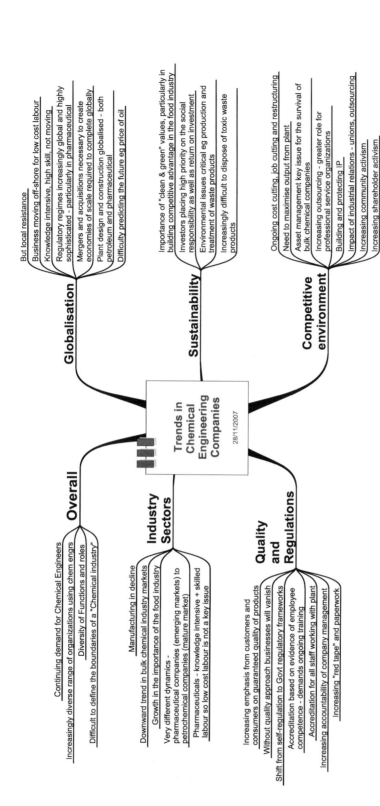

Globalisation
- But local resistance
- Business moving off-shore for low cost labour
- Knowledge intensive, high skill, not moving
- Regulatory regimes increasingly global and highly sophisticated - particularly in pharmaceutical
- Mergers and acquisitions necessary to create economies of scale required to complete globally
- Plant design and construction globalised - both petroleum and pharmaceutical
- Difficulty predicting the future eg price of oil

Sustainability
- Importance of "clean & green" values, particularly in building competitive advantage in the food industry
- Investors placing high priority on the social responsibility as well as return on investment
- Environmental issues critical eg production and treatment of waste products
- Increasingly difficult to dispose of toxic waste products

Competitive environment
- Ongoing cost cutting, job cutting and restructuring
- Need to maximise output from plant
- Asset management key issue for the survival of bulk chemical companies
- Increasing outsourcing - greater role for professional service organizations
- Building and protecting IP
- Impact of industrial relations - unions, outsourcing
- Increasing community activism
- Increasing shareholder activism

Trends in Chemical Engineering Companies

28/11/2007

Overall
- Continuing demand for Chemical Engineers
- Increasingly diverse range of organizations using chem engrs
- Diversity of Functions and roles
- Difficult to define the boundaries of a "Chemical industry"

Industry Sectors
- Manufacturing in decline
- Downward trend in bulk chemical industry markets
- Growth in the importance of the food industry
- Very different dynamics - pharmaceutical companies (emerging markets) to petrochemical companies (mature market)
- Pharmaceuticals - knowledge intensive + skilled labour so low cost labour is not a key issue

Quality and Regulations
- Increasing emphasis from customers and consumers on guaranteed quality of products
- Without quality approach businesses will vanish
- Shift from self-regulation to Govt regulatory frameworks
- Accreditation based on evidence of employee competence - demands ongoing training
- Accreditation for all staff working with plant
- Increasing accountability of company management
- Increasing "red tape" and paperwork

Source: Hadgraft and Muir (2003).

Figure 6.5.   Mindmap—trends in chemical engineering companies.

The shift of emphasis that occurred through this renewal was from a curriculum heavily focused on "knowing" to a *more* active program of "doing" (projects) in each of the years with a practical use of knowledge gained (e.g., chemistry, processes, health and safety, environmental impacts, project planning, risk assessment). Sometimes in attempting complex projects students shifted to searching for new (for them) knowledge to answer the questions that arose. Also students come to understand that in making decisions on the basis of economic, environmental, social and technical criteria that they are making value judgements.

In these programs the project courses previously described are delivered alongside other more traditional courses (i.e., math, physics, chemistry, structural design, chemical processes, etc.) and no clear integration or synthesis is provided for the students, nor is there academic support provided to students for the epistemological and ontological dilemmas that arise from having to consider the social, environmental, and economic aspects of what for many is seen as a basically technical project/discipline. Further, more needs to be done on values in this curriculum—people value different things, there is no clear access to these differing views and also consideration needs to be given to obtaining collective agreements on values. Also the program provides in its design no access to students to the macroenvironment within which the design of their projects and products occur.

OUR FIRST POSTGRADUATE STORY

It also became obvious to us in 2002-03 that there were (and we note that there still are) many existing practitioners (of all types—not only engineers) who are coming up against sustainability issues in their practice and need to get their heads around this new way of working, where the social and environmental is as important as the technical and economic and that it is also important to move toward making "good" things happen, as our panel of sustainability practitioners put it "move from rhetoric to reality."

We return now to our predicament and note that energy, water, and waste are intensely connected and that there are issues of values, including how much we are willing to pay for possible solutions, how much are we willing to accept declining water yields, and reining in our usage? How much are we willing to pay for transport costs and for the flow on effect of increased fuel prices? Further, where will the energy come from for baseload, for existing demands and any increased demands? What will this do to our capacity to meet our state's, country's, world's GHG emissions over the coming years, when the extra energy produced will probably be produced by coal-fired power stations? What will be the environmental impact (on land, sea, and air), particularly if extrasalty brine is pumped back into the ocean from desalination plants? What happens to the solid waste from these processes? Do the locals want this plant in their backyard? What will it do for their land values?

How do governments come to their solutions? What problem are governments trying to solve? If one of the problems is defined as replacing the water in Melbourne's catchments (note that the desalination plant is not to be built in Melbourne) then were alternatives considered, such as, waste water recycling, stormwater harvesting? And what are these alternatives impact on energy and concomitant GHG emissions?

If on the other hand we posed the problem differently we might consider other alternatives—reducing household water usage from the current average in Australia of around 320 liters per person per day (figure comes from session 2 in Watermark Australia, 2005), capping or even reducing the population of Melbourne/Victoria, demanding industry change its water practices (including the coal-fired power industry—a profligate user of water!) and changing our agricultural practices, including irrigation. We might also look at the embodied energy and virtual water in the products that we use, as well as the connections between logging in old-growth forests, replanting of young trees and greenhouse gas emissions and water flowing into our catchments. Is this the best we can do in responding to climate change?

How do we prepare people for roles in these complex, interconnected value-laden discussions? In trying to answer this question we developed the idea of a postgraduate program in sustainable practice. In the design of the program we provided a space within which people could prepare for these types of discussions. This was done in part by continually developing, through theory and practice, the following capabilities over the 3-year program:

- communicating with a range of people and groups; particularly an affected community and particularly where a change of direction is required;
- being aware of self and the process being used;
- identifying the problem;
- developing research skills;
- developing understanding of sustainability principles;
- developing alternatives;
- planning implementation;
- understanding tools and techniques of sustainability;

- detailing proposals, attempting implementation, getting into action, planning evaluation; and
- refining implementation, comprehensive evaluation, reflecting on the journey.

Gestation

In trying to develop university support for what was to become the master of sustainable practice (MSP), we developed the concept loosely and walked it around the university in meetings across many schools and institutes. From this networking and through discussions at our sustainability forum we started to understand that there was a wide and deep range of expertise in sustainability across the university but that it tended to be associated with the discipline or area in which it was based. This is reflected most aptly in a book from the Global Sustainability Institute produced at that time titled *Protecting the Future: Stories of Sustainability from RMIT University* (Caswell & Holdsworth, 2004) which provides a collection of stories from mainly individuals within traditional disciplines struggling with sustainability.

We also noted during this time that the university's emphasis was very much on the reorganization from faculties and departments to portfolios and schools and despite the strategic rhetoric being about "dissolving the boundaries" new boundaries were very firmly being put in place. In this operating environment we kept a low profile and almost despite the university "system" we kept the process moving.

Designing the Curriculum

On the basis of our understanding—of the turbulent macroenvironment (including the universities environment), the reorganized operating environment of this university and that there was a lot of sustainability expertise spread across the university but that much of it was "trapped" in the disciplines,

- and a growing understanding that students needed to understand about different aspects of our predicament depending on their needs (e.g., scientists needed to know about the social and the economics, the marketers needed to know about the economics and the science; everybody needs to develop an understanding of our environment);
- also that there was a need for students to integrate knowledge from across disciplines;

- and understand the different ways of knowing in the intersecting areas;
- as well as be able to "do" something about what they perceived as problems; and
- preferably do something good.

we chose to design a postgraduate program that had a core series of contextualist, integrative, project-based learning courses, so that we continued to see and support the students regularly throughout their program. Selection of electives consistent with their needs from across the university (from any discipline area) was embedded. The participants could share an understanding of the environment within which they were trying to make change occur and that they may begin to understand that they may have to change the environment within which their organization resides as well as the organization itself, to get their innovations to be sustaining, within the ongoing core series of courses.

The core series of courses provided the space and extended time (slow learning as distinct from the often fast learning in many other programs) in which the students could begin to research (with guidance) and integrate their learning experiences—those that they had at work, in their private lives, through their projects and supervision, through their electives, through writing or reflection. This core series of courses began with a scan (searching) of our environment, developing a shared understanding of the dynamic context within which they were undertaking the MSP, their projects, and so on. This was done with a view to developing a personal understanding of capabilities required and a learning contract for each participant.

In designing it this way, with a core series of courses, we were attempting to overcome the issue described earlier of programs that are simply composed of an aggregation, or heap of existing subjects, managed as a production line, and coordinated by the need of each school to have its "slice of the action," where the students do all the integrating in an ad-hoc fashion. This had implications for program leadership. See comments further on.

The other important aspect of the program's design was assessment and here we use a quote from our interview with Royal Melbourne Institute of Technology's online learning and teaching journal as representative of our thinking—

> We've had to get creative. There's the project and there's a personal learning mentor who looks after the personal learning contract. So we want the students to think about, "what capabilities do I personally want to develop?" as distinct from these general ones that we say we're developing. We want them to actually articulate their learning and develop that as a contract with

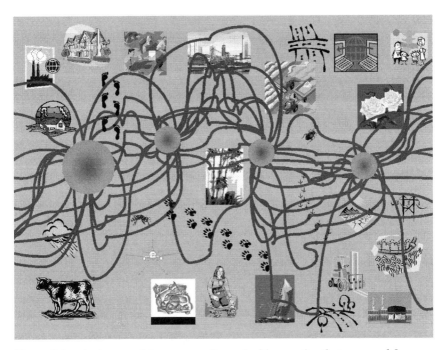

Figure 6.6.   An image of the master of sustainable practice that emerged from "living" it.

themselves. Plus they do regular presentations of their work. They also do a personal journal and the portfolio and the program exegesis. Semester by semester, we use the portfolio to actually assess how they're going. So it's a physical review of their portfolios and they review other people's portfolios. (Goricanec & Hadgraft, 2007, p. 5).

The image in Figure 6.6 emerged from "living" the MSP as at the same time that we were facilitating the inaugural first year core courses and leading the program, Jenni was researching water and she came across a rather vivid image of the Australian landscape called "Children's Water Dreaming with Possum Story" (Bardon & Bardon, 2004). This painting became an inspiration for the living MSP—individual participants and facilitation staff (13) going out and journeying in our environment, coming up against "stuff" in the environment bringing back their experiences into the four workshops. The core courses are designed in more detail by the facilitation staff as we went along—as the participants "came up" against issues in their journeying, in the environment, in their work, in their personal lives. The journeys start and end beyond the MSP.

Designing

In an interview for the new online journal for learning and teaching we reflected that "we started off hoping that the masters of sustainable practice would be a university-wide program with lots of different schools contributing to it and so on, but in the end we put it up for approval within our school because it just seemed too hard to get lots of different schools all to own and share" (Goricanec & Hadgraft, 2007, p. 2).

But having established the program in a school we found that we were "building alliances with other masters programs, like environment and planning and the MBA. So, someone can go there and do perhaps some eight courses out of their program and for electives come and do four of our courses, or vice versa" (Goricanec & Hadgraft, 2007, p. 2). So once the program was established the universitywide model gradually started to emerge.

Program Leadership as "Holding the Whole"

> To our minds much higher education, heavily content oriented, encourages a sort of "feed me" passivity in many of those who interact with it. In this, the master of sustainable practice offers a real difference. It expects, and depends on, a commitment and vibrancy and vitality within participants that may well be new to their adult educational experience. We expect them to participate with energy, with passion and with congruence between what they are learning and how they are behaving in their professional (and personal) practice. We expect them to recognize and work with the complexity and ambiguity and linkages within their workplaces and interests, holding "the whole" in mind as they develop their sustainable practice. We figure it is critical for us to also do this within the MSP.
>
> We believe it is critical for program leadership in sustainable practice to be congruent with the implicit and explicit intent of the program itself and, in order to be so, needs intentional, ongoing attention to holding the whole. Indeed, we believe that the primary task of MSP program leadership is holding the whole on behalf of its students, its staff, the university and the program itself. (Hiley & Goricanec, 2007)

Difficulties

The progress that we were making in our wider university model was not reflected in the school in which it was based. A difficulty for a program using a universitywide model is that the system within which it sits has very distinct "silos." This can be seen in the financial system. Students pay fees to the university. The university takes around 50% from these fees for "centralized" functions. The remaining fees are then distributed to the schools that deliver the courses. This means that even though students see themselves as enrolled in a university, they are actually enrolled in a series of courses in different schools. The university sees itself as separate delivery units (schools) and a centralized unit. Any school setting up a program bears all the costs of setting up the program (initiation, design, development of the program, and the core courses, including working across the university to keep the actor-network in play—what we have called "holding the whole") even though it is only delivering part of the program (the core courses) directly—in this case they ended up with about 25% of the money from the students. It is not in the financial interests of a school to set up a new program and certainly not one that also operates by offering students access to elective courses across the university.

In this system the parts are very much autonomous and look after their own interests above those of the whole, this is seen in the "trapping" of the knowledge of sustainability in the disciplines as described above. Another aspect of autonomy is the attitudes of the academic staff within each part—their allegiance is very strongly with the school within which they are based, particularly for teaching—there was a very strong reaction (accusations of poaching) to the idea of having academic staff from any of these other schools teach in our core courses. On the other hand an academic's research interest is focused on their own small, carefully defined area—if there is strong alignment between the student and the academic's interest it can be very fruitful, but if not there is little to no possibility of supervision (mentoring) of a potential project. At the same time the schools' administrators are very happy to have MSP students in their existing courses as they get extra fees and their established courses are more profitable.

In keeping with this, the schools are generally set up to deliver ongoing established programs and therefore operate in a business-as-usual and tactical mode, particularly where the work relates to students. They expect the students to manage their own enrolment (even though they are enrolling across organizational boundaries), their engagement with this novel program, while also having full-time work commitments and evolving personal and family lives, without any targeted support from the school.

On the other hand the master of sustainable practice as a strategic initiative was designed to network together expertise and knowledge in sustainability across and beyond the university as well as to provide a safe place for students to undertake integration, synthesis, and practice these new ways of working. In the early stages of the program, students' relationship to the university is fragile (part-time, other responsibilities, wider experience, higher levels of expectation) and care needs to be taken to support them; this is at odds with the normal approach of sink or swim for the mass of undergraduates.

The support for this program became a real challenge for the school and the university when the program leader left for a role at another university. The gap in resources—financial, as well as, personal and institutional commitment to strategic program leadership—what we called holding the whole needed to support this fledgling program were then clearly visible.

OUR SECOND UNDERGRADUATE STORY

In 2008, another university in Melbourne offered, for the first time, a bachelor of environments, which is an entry point to graduate study for architects, civil engineers, environmental engineers, geomatic engineers, construction managers, planners, landscape architects, agriculturalists, and foresters. The aim is to develop in these students the abilities to grapple with complex problems of the kind described in our desalination example.

Some of the characteristics of the bachelor of environments include:

- explore the contemporary *theory and practice* of natural, constructed, and virtual environments;
- solve challenges like climate change, urban growth, and sustainability, and the management of scarce resources, such as water, using *innovative and integrated thinking*;
- use a *variety of learning experiences,* including lectures and classes, studios, field trips, laboratory sessions, site visits, and workshops;
- turn theory into action by engaging with *real-world problems* and community projects; and
- select a *major field of study* complemented with subjects taken both from other majors in the bachelor of environments and with subjects from outside the degree program.

All of this seems quite reasonable. A problem is that this program has clearly highlighted the difficulty that most academics have in delivering these learning outcomes. A serious impediment is that most academics are specialists. They are hired for their ability to conduct research, usually in a small, carefully defined area. Consequently, curricula reflect this specialization, with technical disciplines separated in different courses (subjects). This has already happened in the design of the first year of the bachelor of environments, with eight subjects created, of which students will do six:

- natural environments (natural sciences);
- reshaping environments (sciences, engineering, architecture);
- urban environments (planning);
- governing environments (regulation);
- mapping environments (geomatics);
- designing environments (architecture);
- constructing environments (engineering); and
- virtual environments (visualization).

These subjects reflect the discipline areas that have defined them and despite good intentions of multidisciplinary teaching teams, most subjects are being presented from a strong knowledge perspective in one discipline, as shown above.

Even where multidisciplinary teams meet to teach the subject, the focus is on the *knowledge* that students will need, some examples are:

- Discuss how *sustainable management* and design stems from a respect for our planet's natural systems;
- Describe the processes that led to the *formation of the Earth* and the continents;
- Describe and begin to quantify the principles and nature of the *global atmospheric circulation system* and implications for patterns of global climate and weather;
- Describe the nature of *climate change* and variability and begin to quantify the planet's energy balances, especially as they relate to current global warming;
- Describe the attributes of the major *biogeographical* realms; and
- Discuss different approaches to the *principles of ecology* and the interactions between the physical and biological that lead to ecological systems of differing character and scale.

It is hard to imagine that students will see that they need to do anything more than learn what will be on the exam. These sorts of learning objectives encourage surface learning at the bottom levels of Bloom's Taxonomy (Bloom, 1956). Where will they learn to grapple with climate change and complex, dynamic environmental problems? Where is the integrated and innovative thinking, the multiple perspectives, the real-world problems?

Science as Knowing and Engineering as Doing

The development of this program has highlighted the difference between the scientific view of the world and the engineering one. Science seeks to understand and to know. It endeavors to use objective means to remove the effect of the observer. It seeks to stand aside from the world, to see it as it really is.

But in *The Art of Possibility: Transforming Professional and Personal Life* (Zander & Zander, 2000, p. 11) the authors remind that "the 'real world' is a construct"—science constructs the world in a particular way. Also they remind us that Einstein said "it was nonsense to found a theory on observable facts alone: In reality the very opposite happens. It is theory which decides what we observe" (p. 11). It is the theories of science that have us see the world in a particular way; this is also true of other disciplines, for example, engineering, which sees itself, as immersed in the world.

Engineering's declared raison d'être is to provide humanity with the infrastructure for survival—clean water, food production, clothing, shelter, energy, transport, communications. In more recent times, at least in the developed world, we have moved far beyond survival (Maslow, 1943) and now engineering has expanded into entertainment and other diversions. Where once, not so long ago, engineering was seen as an unarguable good, it became obvious in the nineteenth and twentieth centuries that the waste products of engineering were spoiling the environment. Where engineering was well suited to the modernist view, it is not so well adapted to a postmodernist view.

At the same time we have had an extended, continuing process of

> fragmentation and the growth of a large number of disciplines, each devoted to the study of some specialised segment of knowledge.... In order to accommodate the need for ever-increasing depth of knowledge, there is generally a narrowing of the scope of knowledge possessed by any individual. (Sage, 2000, p. 158)

We now quote from a recent application for accreditation from *oases* Graduate School, of which the first author was a participant, about the broader process—

> the breaking down, narrowing, reductionist program of the last three centuries, attempting to break complex systems into increasingly smaller and simpler parts, has been "spectacularly successful" (Kauffman, 1995), leading to fragmentation, competition, and reactiveness (Kofman & Senge, 1993), and thus to our present crisis (Sheldrake, 1994). This reductionism is now triumphant on a global scale; built into the official orthodoxy of economic progress and educational achievement, becoming a kind of religion. (Hiley, 2006, p. 12)

And from the same source some of the consequences of this are that

> we have "privileged" certain data and knowledge without acknowledging that they had interpretation and meaning systems overlaid. Perhaps we shouldn't be surprised that a society based upon structure and logic should determine the answer to most questions by laying out the manner in which

they are posed (Saul, 1993). It really comes down to what we *value*. What are so-called "distractions" in one worldview are the heart of another. Indeed they may be the most important things we need to "know", especially in times of crisis. (Hiley, 2006, p. 32)

Somehow we as leaders in education need to reprivilege this other data and knowledge, we need to put back together—defragment or think holistically, we need to collaborate and become mindful, responding carefully and subtly—how do we do this?

TRANSFORMATION THROUGH PRACTICES

We propose moving beyond knowing to transforming our practices.

The history of transformational phenomena—the World Wide Web, for example, or paradigm shifts in science, or the spread of new religion—suggests that transformation happens less by arguing cogently for something new than by generating active, ongoing practices that shift a culture's experience of reality. (Zander & Zander, 2000, p. 4)

The sorts of practice change that we need are "not about making incremental changes that lead to new ways of doing things based on old beliefs.... They are geared instead toward causing a shift of posture, beliefs, and thought processes. They are about transforming your entire world" (Zander & Zander, 2000, p. 4)

How do you *purposively* generate active, ongoing practices (collective desirable and feasible futures)?

Who do you generate these with? Who has these types of practices already?

OUR SECOND POSTGRADUATE STORY
AND NEW HIGHER EDUCATION PROVIDER

oases Graduate School, which has recently been accredited as a higher education provider by the Victorian Qualification and Registration Authority, sees itself as responding to our predicament by establishing an integrative and transformative studies program. This is an example of a program that has the potential to educate "the total person for survival in an unpredictable, turbulent future; where facts, concepts, theories, intellectual skills, and well developed cognitive maps are not enough" (Davies, 1993, p. 258).

oases Graduate School's information booklet provides a brief description of the program and philosophy:

Integrative and Transformative Studies encourage us to participate with others in conversation and dialogue in a way which makes us aware of the restrictions of our own way of seeing and so opens a space for us to view things from the *integrative perspective* of "the whole," as the most effective way to realize the *transformative action* that needs to emerge for our interrelated, sustainable well-being. There is a continuous spiral of renewed, regenerating participation-integration-transformation across the dimensions of the aesthetic, social, ecological and spiritual.

Participation—The **oases** program focuses on collaborative learning, dialogue and self-reflection. It encourages participants to bring their experiences into the educational process to grapple with contemporary dilemmas through communicative learning. Participants are encouraged to draw from the arts and from spiritual traditions in their learning.

Integration—**oases** creates and integrates knowledge beyond the confines of traditional disciplines to provide education for a changing world. **oases** values cultural diversity, multiple ways of knowing, spirituality, a sense of social and ecological sustainability, in the joyful presence of a reflective and innovative learning community.

Transformation—The **oases** program aims to support participants to facilitate personal and social transformation. By focusing on the development of capacities to envision, initiate, and engage in transformative change processes, reflection and theory are united with practice. (**oases** Graduate School Community Learning and Research Centre, 2008)

Figure 6.7 shows an image of the integrative and transformative program (Hiley, 2006). There has been some further reimagining, but this particular image and accompanying words are indicative of **oases'** thinking of how the program works—you will notice that we use an embedded water metaphor, as water has inherent properties which provide good metaphoric references.

The integrative conversations, are described as "a space, the primary 'holding' environment for the 'whole'; the learning clusters; and, whilst not the only place, major project discussions; theoretical integration discussions; and experiencing and reflecting on embodied integral praxis" (Hiley, 2007). These conversations continue throughout the program. In the first phase they are partnered with four entries—here we enter into the social, the ecological, the spiritual, and the aesthetic. In the second phase the participants are beginning to think about their project, which can be in any mode, and can be about anything—by the end of this phase they are asked to articulate a project proposal. During this phase they are called to consider their "poem" (Hiley, 2003, p. 39)—the congruence of their philosophical, epistemological, ontological, and methodological settlements. They also undertake four units. In the last phase they are wholly immersed in their projects—the integrative conversations provide a peer supervisory role and the whole academic collegium is available to interact with their work. We allow this latter phase to continue to allow participants project work to emerge as a whole—a bit like birth really.

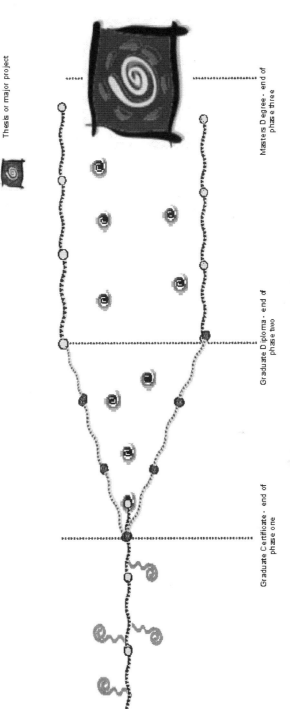

Figure 6.7. Pictorial view of integrative and transformative studies program.

CONCLUDING REMARKS

In this chapter we have taken you on our long journey, the aim of which has been to shift practice to transform our world in response to our predicament, which includes climate change. We describe those models and approaches that we have found helpful in implementing various initiatives within (and without, at least initially) the higher education sector, both undergraduate and postgraduate. We have also declared the difficulties and concerns that we have had along the way.

We have described two new master's programs in our environment, which seek to use adult learning principles; we guide students' explorations rather than requiring memorization; they engage with the macroenvironment rather than "surrendering" to it, with an integrative perspective to realize transformative practice, all within an inquiring mode rather than one where we believe that we know the answers. We have also shown processes that aim to transform and how these have been successful or otherwise in these endeavors.

Our practices include searching or scanning to develop awareness of context which provides the "material" backdrop for, designing, going out and trying things, being aware of what is around, bringing back reflections, and reflecting together with others. We aim to align assessment and activities with outcomes being sought, particularly the capabilities, which we believe are essential if we are to educate leaders of change for the future.

NOTE

1.   *"oases"* appears in a lowercase, bold italic font, intended to stand out but without the formality of an initial capital. It orginally arose from the letters of an acronym "organic integration of aesthetic, spiritual, ecological, and social." It is the sense of the word that is now more important as we are creating oases from the dynamic, complex world within which we live and developing spaces within which we can learn, learn to learn, and learn to learn with others.

REFERENCES

Baburoglu, O. N. (1987). *A theory of stalemated social systems and vortical organizational environments: The Turkish experience and beyond.* Unpublished doctoral dissertation, University of Pennsylvania, Philadelphia.

Baburoglu, O. N. (1988). The vortical environment: The fifth in the Emery-Trist levels of organisational environments. *Human Relations, 41*(3), 181-210.

Bardon, G., & Bardon, J. (2004). *Papunya: A place made after the story.* Melbourne: Miegunyah.

Bloom, B. S. (Ed.). (1964). *Taxonomy of educational objectives: The classification of educational goals.* London: Longman.

Bourdieu, P. (1998). *Acts of resistance—Against the myths of our time* (R. Nice, Trans.) Oxford, England: Polity Press.

Caswell, T., & Holdsworth, S. (Eds.). (2004). *Protecting the future: Stories of sustainability from RMIT university*. Melbourne: CSIRO.

Crombie, A. D. (1972). *Planning for turbulent social fields*. Unpublished doctoral thesis, Australian National University, Canberra.

Davies, A. (1993). An alternative general studies curriculum. In M. Emery (Ed.), *Participative design for participative democracy* (Rev. ed., pp. 258-270). Canberra: Centre for Continuing Education, Australian National University.

Emery, F. (1981, Spring). Educational paradigms. *Human Futures*, 1-17. Retrieved July 19, 2008, from http://www.moderntimesworkplace.com/archives/ericsess/sessvol3/QEMEDPARp230.pdf

Emery, F. E. (1997). The next thirty years: Concepts, methods, and anticipations. *Human Relations, 50*(8), 885-931.

Emery, F., & Trist, E. L. (1975). *Toward a social ecology: Contextual appreciations of the future in the present*. New York: Plenum.

Emery, M. (1993). *Participative design for participative democracy*. Canberra: Australian National University, Centre for Continuing Education

Flannery, T. F. (1994). *The future eaters: An ecological history of the Australasian lands and people*. Chatswood, Australia: Reed Books.

Global Footprint Network. (2006). *Ecological footprint: Overview*. Retrieved June 25, 2008, from http://www.footprintnetwork.org/gfn_sub.php?content =footprint_overview

Gloster, M. (1999). *A grounded socio-ecological theory of managing active adaptation of stalemated social systems in localised vortical environments*. Unpublished doctoral thesis, Southern Cross University.

Goricanec, J., & Hadgraft, R. (2007). Design: Designing a new program. *The RMIT Learning and Teaching Journal, 2*(1). Retrieved July 18, 2008, from http://emedia.rmit.edu.au/ed/Issue/2007A/Design/0_cover_Design.html

Goricanec, J., & Young, D. L. (2001). *From resignation to active adaptation—Confronting the managerialist pathology in universities*. Paper presented at the Transforming the University, Association of the Public University, Melbourne, Australia.

Hadgraft, R., & Muir, P. (2003). *Defining graduate capabilities for chemical engineers at RMIT*. Paper presented at the proceedings of the 14th annual Australasian Association for Engineering Education, Melbourne.

Hiley, T. (2003). *Living and working in the first person—Emancipating the 'silent' voice and the 'deaf' ear*. Unpublished doctoral thesis, RMIT University, Melbourne.

Hiley, T. (2006). *Application to Victorian Registration and Qualification Authority for accreditation of oases' Integrative and Transformative Studies Program*. Melbourne: *oases* Graduate School.

Hiley, T. (2007). *oases Academic Board Working Party Report—Reconceiving the integrative and transformative studies program after accreditation*. Hawthorn, Australia: *oases* Graduate School.

Hiley, T., & Goricanec, J. (2006) *Proposal* [to the Head of School] *for the program leadership for the master of sustainable practice—"Holding the whole."* Melbourne, Australia: RMIT University.

Hiley, T., & Goricanec, J. (2007). *Proposal for program leadership for the master of sustainable Practice—"Holding the whole."* In Head of SECE—RMIT University (Ed.). Melbourne, Australia.

Intergovernmental Panel on Climate Change. (2007). *Climate change 2007: Synthesis report. Contribution of Working Groups I, II and III to the fourth assessment* Geneva: Author.

Intergovernmental Panel on Climate Change. (2007a). *Glossary. Appendix 1.* Retrieved July 18, 2008, from http://www.ipcc.ch/pdf/glossary/ar4-wg2.pdf

Kauffman, S. (1995). *At home in the universe: The search for laws of self-organization and complexity.* London: Oxford University Press.

Kofman, F., & Senge, P. (1993). Communities of commitment: The heart of learning organizations. *Organizational Dynamics, 22*(2), 5-23.

Latour, B. (1999). *Pandora's hope—Essays on the reality of science studies.* Cambridge, MA: Harvard University Press.

Law, J. (2004). *After method: Mess in social science research.* London: Routledge.

Maslow, A. H. (1943). A theory of human motivation. *Psychological Review, 50*, 370-396.

Murphy, K. (2007, September 27). Don't mention the 'N' word. *The Age*, p. 15.

oases Graduate School Community Learning and Research Centre (2008). *2008 masters degree program in integrative and transformative studies.* Hawthorn, Australia: Author.

Sage, A. (2000). Transdisciplinarity perspectives in systems engineering and management. In M. A. Somerville & D. J. Rapport (Eds.), *Transdisciplinarity: reCreating integrated knowledge* (pp. 158-170). Oxford, England: EOLSS.

Saul, J. R. (1993). *Voltaire's bastards: The dictatorship of reason in the West.* Ringwood, Victoria, Australia: Penguin Books.

Sheldrake, R. (1994). *The rebirth of nature: The greening of science and God—Notes.* Sydney, Australia: Rider.

Sommerhof, G. (1950). *Analytical biology.* London: Oxford University Press.

Sommerhof, G. (1969). The abstract characteristics of living things. In F. E. Emery (Ed.), *Systems thinking: Selected readings* (pp. 147-202). Harmondsworth, United Kingdom: Penguin Books.

Stern, N. (2007). *The economics of climate change: The Stern review.* Cambridge, United Kingdom: Cambridge University Press.

Vox Bandicoot. (2006). *The ecological fingerprint—Hands on for our future.* Retrieved June 25, 2008, from http://vox.3legs.com.au/ecofingerprint/

Watermark Australia. (2005). Retrieved June 14, 2008, from http://www.watermarkaustralia.org.au/

Whitehead, A. N. (1933). *Adventure of ideas.* New York: Macmillan.

Young, D., & Goricanec, J. (2003). *Akademos—Developing and sustaining an alternative model for tertiary education.* Paper presented at the Action Learning, Action Research and Process Management Conference, Tweed Campus, Southern Cross University, Australia.

Zander, R. S., & Zander, B. (2000). *The art of possibility: Transforming professional and personal life.* Boston: Harvard Business School Press.

PART III

CHANGING PRACTICES, PROCESSES, AND SYSTEMS: CONCEPTS, INITIATIVES, SUCCESSES, AND DISAPPOINTMENTS

CHAPTER 7

TRANSPORT SUSTAINABILITY AND THE AIRPORT CITY

Michael B. Charles and Paul H. Barnes

The ability to make critical infrastructure systems more sustainable is particularly problematic in the transport sector, which is becoming increasingly scrutinized on account of its enormous reliance on fossil fuels and substantial impact on the global environment. Airports are increasingly becoming more "citylike" and thus exposed to the kinds of long-term planning and sustainability issues presently confronting urban municipalities throughout the world. An increasing demand for air travel and the airborne transportation of goods also brings with it the threat of underexamined social, environmental, and ecological impacts on the region supporting the airport metropolis, especially regarding the need to expand existing airport facilities. This chapter reports on the concepts and issues underpinning the development of innovative sustainability indicators that will inform enhanced understanding of the operational needs of airport metropolises throughout the world. The incorporation of sustainability indicators as core functional elements is expected to inform management decision making with regard to the potential impacts of an airport's operations from a social, environmental, and ecological perspective.

Global Sustainability Initiatives: New Models and New Approaches
pp. 139–158
Copyright © 2008 by Information Age Publishing
All rights of reproduction in any form reserved.

139

INTRODUCTION

The notion of air travel is a ubiquitous fact of life in the modern world and is more or less taken for granted, at least in the developed and newly industrialized nations of the world. Concomitant to this ubiquity is the movement of air cargo as an element of globalized supply chains and just-in-time (JIT) logistics systems, all of which is designed to give a competitive advantage to those firms participating in these time-based strategies. In a world beset with problems surrounding our apparent inability to curb greenhouse gas (GHG) emissions, which are thought to be a major contributing factor to anthropogenic global warming (Intergovernmental Panel on Climate Change [IPCC], 2007), growth in air transport continues to advance, seemingly inexorably. For example, the Intergovernmental Panel on Climate Change, prognosticates a rough figure of 5% annual growth until 2015 (Vedantham, 1999). More air transport obviously necessitates greater investment in the infrastructures that support it. Indeed, many airports around the world are finding it difficult to cope with current volumes of traffic, let alone the volumes that they will be expected to handle if current growth trends continue. As a result, space set aside for air transport operations also looks set to increase dramatically. Furthermore, with the introduction of even larger commercial airplanes such as the Airbus A380, new runways, or at least significant upgrading of existing ones, are clearly needed. In addition, terminals need to be expanded, while maintenance facilities require expansion in order to cope with the larger numbers of aircraft using the airport.

The growth in aviation industry activity, however, brings with it a variety of challenging sustainability concerns, not least of which is the idea of fusing the airport as a provider of aviation infrastructure with conventional notions of a satellite city, or at least bringing about a merging of the host city and airport landscape. The blending of the two concepts into an airport city, referred to in a range of commercial and academic literature as an "aerotropolis," warrants critical assessment. While the concept of the airport city, with its eclectic conurbation of living space, supportive industries, and wealth generators symbiotic to the airport and the industry it supports, is inherently interesting from an economic geography perspective, realization of the aerotropolis concept requires careful consideration of a range of factors central to the notion of sustainable growth.

In view of the considerations outlined above, this chapter will analyze selected sustainability issues pertinent to the "airport city," which we will henceforth refer to (if only for the sake of convenience) as the aerotropolis, and will canvass the types of information relevant to adaptive management of airport growth into the future. In particular, the chapter will look at the various kinds of indicators that can be used to assess the suitability of infrastructure projects on airport sites. It is envisaged that these indicators will aid in the decision-making process, thereby allowing airport administrators, in addition to other relevant stakeholders, to make effective decisions regarding the sustainability or otherwise of the airport and adjacent facilities.

REALIZING THE AIRPORT CITY

At this point, it is necessary to give a brief overview of the rationale behind the phenomenon known as the aerotropolis. Although the aerotropolis might sound like a future goal or an endpoint of sorts, it is, in fact, a reality in some regions of the world. In other cases, we are slowly seeing a transmutation from the traditional transport-oriented airport to something that is far more multifunctional in its nature. In essence, the aerotropolis arises from the notion, mentioned in the introduction to this chapter, that air transport has become an intrinsic part of modern world commerce and trade and is thus no longer merely a transport hub, but has the potential to become a city in its own right, with various industries, leisure and recreation centers, urban developments, and many of the other attributes of a conventional city (Charles, Barnes, Ryan, & Clayton, 2007a). Since air transport, at least according to proponents of the aerotropolis, has become so paramount in international trade and passenger transport, the airport has thereby become the gateway to the surrounding region, and thus a major driver of the regional and even national economy.

The most significant driver of the aerotropolis, of course, is the need for speed, and the observation that speed has a significant economic value attached to it (Kasarda, 2005). Indeed, proponents of the aerotropolis view speed as *the* most important attribute of modern transport. Since the airplane is easily the fastest of all current transport modes, in as much as it takes the least amount of time to travel between two points, there will be a significant shift from other transport modes, such as road, rail, and sea, to air. While air transport, because of its fuel inefficiency, has been mainly regarded as a carrier of passengers and low-weight high-value items, the aerotropolis concept relies on more medium-weight items being carried by air, thereby necessitating larger air freighter fleets and the appropriate augmentation of supporting infrastructure (Charles et al., 2007a). When placed in the context of international business, the aerotropolis emerges as an import infrastructure in realizing JIT supply chain strategies, on which many industries, especially those producing high-value outputs, are now based (al Chalabi & Kasarda, 2004). As will be highlighted further below in this chapter, the airline manufacturing industry itself relies to a great degree on a JIT strategy.

The promise of the aerotropolis therefore implies a high degree of co-location of transport infrastructure and the industries that benefit from the receipt of factor inputs and components transported by air (Charles et al., 2007a). Thus factories relying on these inputs are built within the vicinity of the aerotropolis in order to avoid additional transportation costs (Kasarda, 2000/2001). The finished products, ideally, will then be transported by air to markets around the world. In other cases, they will be shipped by means of the other transport modes connected to the aerotropolis system. In particular, connectivity between air and sea transport emerges as an important component of the model (Charles et al., 2007a). In many cases, the marginal nature of port lands has meant that the logical place to position airports has been close to maritime infrastructure.

Given that factories require skilled and semiskilled workers (even in today's highly automated world), while the other services that function within the aerotropolis, such as cleaning agencies, food and beverage outlets, recreational facilities, and even security, also require personnel, the aerotropolis planning model envisages that workers reside (and would want to reside) close to their place of work (Kasarda, 2000). Thus they live, work, and participate in recreational activities either within or else very close to the aerotropolis, and take their children to educational facilities located in the immediate vicinity, thereby ensuring that transit costs are reduced to a bare minimum, in addition to the time taken to travel to their place of employment. The aerotropolis therefore operates more or less independently of the conventional (or "host") city that necessitated the construction of airport facilities in the first place, even though it is likely that it is connected to water, electricity and sewage provided by the "host city."

By extension, globetrotting professionals, or so it is hoped, will live in prestige urban developments located close to the airport (Kasarda, 2000). Since these busy and career-driven professionals spend much of their time traveling to other airports in order to conduct business, it makes sense, or so the model goes, for them to live close to the airport. A further implication is that face-to-face meetings, which will continue despite information-communication-technology developments such as videoconferencing on account of the context-rich nature of face-to-face communication or "co-presence" (Boden & Molotch, 2004), will no longer occur in conventional cities. Rather, business will be conducted in specifically built conference facilities at the destination airport. Instead of traveling from Bangkok to Singapore, therefore, the professional will travel from Suvarnabhumi Airport to Changi Airport. Real estate located near the aerotropolis will also rise in value, as has already been seen around the world, such as at Amsterdam's Schiphol Airport (Kasarda, 2004).

In short, the aerotropolis model implies that the region or major city of that region is no longer necessarily the destination. It is the airport itself and the adjacent facilities and infrastructure, known collectively as the aerotropolis that will increasingly become the destination, not only for passengers, but also for industrial inputs, and even, in some cases, finished products ready to be transported to market.

ARE AIRPORTS SUSTAINABLE?

Before this chapter turns its attention to sustainability issues in a more general sense, it is worthwhile to ponder on some of the specific sustainability issues that modern air transport faces.

The notion that airports, and aerotropolises by extension, are sustainable is most certainly subject to debate. In its present incarnation, the airport, and indeed air transport in general, represents an especially unsustainable transport mode. Of that there can be little doubt. Let us start at the beginning. The manufacture of a modern aircraft necessitates the transport of numerous inputs to an assembly location. To take the European airline manufacturer Airbus Industrie as an example, components of the finished product are manufactured at various points around Europe, and indeed in other parts of the world. These components are air-freighted to Toulouse, in southern France, where they are assembled into an Airbus airliner such as the small short-range A319, or the enormous long-range A380. Aside from the operation of these completed airliners, the manufacturing and carriage of these components has a substantial emissions penalty.

To put things more succinctly, the basic material from which the airframes of a modern airliner are manufactured is aluminum. Consider the energy required to mine bauxite in the first instance, the energy required to transport this ore to a refining facility, the energy required to turn this raw material into aluminum, and then the energy required to transport the aluminum to a site where it is transformed into ailerons, rudders, winglets, and other aeronautical components. To make matters worse, the airliner is powered by an ultrarefined petroleum product requiring the greatest amount of energy of all petroleum-based fuels to refine, and which is burnt up at astonishing rates to power what is still, after all, an appreciably heavy vehicle through the rigors of wind resistance and oftentimes a nagging headwind.

With respect to fuel, there are concerns regarding the exhaustion of fossil fuels in the not too distant future (Charles et al., 2007a; Vedantham,

1999). The date of peak oil, after which oil production will dwindle, causing prices to skyrocket, is subject to much debate. What is clear is that economically viable alternative to fossil-fuel-derived jet fuel has not yet emerged. Studies have been undertaken with regard to using liquid nitrogen, but this necessitates a major rethink of aeronautical design given the space constraints of housing a fuel that, while it has three times the energy content as modern jet fuel, requires four times the space to store it (Faa, 2001). Moreover, this supposedly environmentally friendly fuel must be stored pressurized, in a liquid state, at very cold temperatures (-253°C). This naturally requires large amounts of electricity, as it does to produce the liquid nitrogen in the first place (Birkenstock, 1998). Fuel derived from biomass, that is, plant matter, is another possible alternative. Yet the synthesis of kerosene from biomass again requires very large amounts of energy (Lopp & Stanley, 1995). If this energy is not clean in the first place, substantial environmental costs will ensue. Progress with second-generation biofuel production techniques that use the whole of the plant material should give some cause for optimism (Charles, Ryan, Ryan, & Oloruntoba, 2007b), yet systems capacity may still militate against adequate harnessing of natural resources for fuel production. Moreover, if, as seems likely, the world's economies become closely tied to national, regional and even international emissions trading schemes (ETS), the cost of purchasing unclean energy may also become unfeasible.

The scenarios articulated above obviously do not mean the end of air transport in the short or even medium term. The point, here, is that air transport may become much more expensive than it currently is. The aerotropolis model, of course, requires fuel prices to remain relatively stable if growth is to continue. Any appreciable hike in fuel prices, or indeed general operating costs resulting from economic penalties arising as a result of an ETS, may mean that goods and passengers are transferred to more economically and environmentally efficient transport modes such as road or sea. A question of underutilized capacity at the aerotropolis arises if fuel prices continue to rise, and then increase exponentially as resources run out, while new technology remains inaccessible because of cost and underdevelopment (Ryan & Charles, 2007).

As has been seen, modern air transport carries a significant environmental burden. When this is combined with activities on the ground, there is reason to be concerned about the industry's greenhouse gas emissions. In an aerotropolislike environment, the environmental penalties go beyond merely GHG emissions from aircraft. Without clean energy, ground vehicles contribute to the environmental woes, as do the operation of the adjacent facilities. In the absence of nuclear power or renewable power sources such as wind, solar, hydroelectric, or geothermal, coal-fired power stations are required to provide energy for the operational of terminals and adjacent facilities.

But that is not where the environmental pressures end. As airports grow, which seems to constitute a necessary feature of the aerotropolis model (at least in the vast majority of cases, which vary from being "space rich" to "space poor"), pressure is placed on the physical environment of the airport, in addition to that of the surrounding region. Expansion means the clearing of vegetation, the disruption of ecosystems and an accompanying rise in noise levels, which may affect the lifecycles of fauna accustomed to dwell in the vicinity of the airport. The point to consider, here, is that airports are often located in what might well be termed "marginal" areas. Further below, we will see this in the case of Suvarnabhumi Airport in Thailand, a facility constructed on reclaimed marshland generally regarded as unsuitable for other purposes. Areas that are more desirable are required for other purposes, such as residential housing in particular (at least traditionally).

Yet the landscapes on which airports are built or located next to, although not likely to elicit approval or particular interest from the general public, are important ecosystems in their own right. Mangrove swamps, wetlands, and littoral landscapes house a variety of life that is worth protecting in the same way as the denizens of tropical rainforests. This brings into play public value conflicts between, on the one hand, economic growth, job creation, and societal progress, and, on the other, environmental sustainability and the protection and continued preservation of life. In such situations, public value trade-offs are necessitated as part of the negotiation process conducted between project stakeholders (de Bruijn & Dicke, 2006). Public values that have the potential to lead to more quantifiable and substantive outcomes, such as those introduced above, are often given undue salience at the expense of less well articulated and oftentimes abstract ones (Koppenjan, Charles, & Ryan, 2008). During project implementation, actors will be involved in a process of "pulling and pushing" with respect to value prioritization (Kirlin, 1996). In these circumstances, economic values are often those most likely to prevail.

Assumptions inherent in the aerotropolis model, over and above the more traditional form of airport, are potentially problematic. The model posits that the airport and its immediate vicinity will attract urban developments, the residents of which will have moved there either to (a) work at the aerotropolis, or (b) to be close to the domestic and international connectivity that the aerotropolis provides. Regardless of whether these movements actually take place, a growth in residential development within the aerotropolis (or at least on its immediate periphery), necessarily signals a radical change in land-use that will conceivably impact on existing ecosystems. Aside from the development of land, housing development place considerable pressure on infrastructure, especially with respect to electricity provision, water reticulation and sewage.

There is a final environmental point to consider. Construction work on project sites often necessitates the release of carbon dioxide (CO_2) trapped in soil, buried vegetation, or in living plants, thereby increasing the environmental footprint of the airport space even before flights have commenced. This is particularly the case on space-rich sites.

To conclude this area of analysis, the sustainability or otherwise of the aerotropolis must inevitably focus on two important areas. These are energy and space. A shift to alternate forms of energy will entail specific challenges for airport planners and aircraft operators. Expansion of the physical dimensions and capacity of the aerotropolis will perhaps entail even greater challenges to maintaining the continuity of operations, abating noise increases, and ensuring a minimum of impact on the physical environment.

THE AEROTROPOLIS: A ONE SIZE FITS ALL APPROACH?

It is clear that the aerotropolis, be it called thus or some cognate term such as "airport city" or "airport-centered development," is a popular issue in the air transport industry. We have previously seen what, in its broadest sense, the aerotropolis signifies. The question to consider here, especially with regard to the sustainability or otherwise of the model as it stands (which will obviously be subject to change over time), is whether one size does truly fit all; that is, can a successful aerotropolis model used in, for example, Schiphol Airport in the Netherlands, be successfully transplanted to what might seem a rather different sociocultural, economic, jurisdictional, and perhaps even ideological context, such as, a site in Latin America, or in Africa? In short, the following analysis looks at the problems inherent in transplanting a model that works reasonably well in one socioeconomic, jurisdictional, and environmental context to another, which may be quite different. Proponents of the aerotropolis, necessarily prophets of globalization and the benefits that it (arguably) brings, would naturally contend that global similarities outweigh the differences, that is, that the world's political, economic, and social systems are converging, at least to some degree. Yet, in the following case, we see that this might not always be the case.

First of all, acknowledgment of the fact that governments around the world, and at various levels, are pouring significant resources into the establishment of aerotropolises necessitates the view that not all these centers can succeed, or even match minimal expectations advanced by supporting stakeholders. The aerotropolis is espoused by proponents as an economic panacea, with potentially negative repercussions glossed over, or ignored altogether. Proponents espouse a "build it and they will come" mantra that may not necessarily bear fruit in all circumstances. The implicit notion is that the aerotropolis works, is greatly desirable, and that it will continue to be a dynamic economic model into the short to medium term.

A point worth noting is that many cases that might be referred to as exemplars of the concept in action, such as the aforementioned Schiphol Airport in the Netherlands or Haneda Airport in Japan, function in concert with complex networks of trade-specific commercial operators and related infrastructure (Charles et al., 2007a) and, well-established maritime ports (in the case of Haneda). While this might outwardly appear as if this relative colocation was achieved by design, it is nevertheless important to understand the historical underpinnings to the collocation of airport and maritime shipping infrastructures. These will be explored in a section of this chapter further below.

Other examples are worthy of note. We will now look specifically at the controversy surrounding building an aerotropolis around Thailand's Suvarnabhumi Airport, a plan which has since been put on hold, as will be explained below. This brief case serves as a focal point for the ongoing challenge to balance traditional economic values, usually the most salient with respect to the provision of critical infrastructure, with those pertaining to society and the environment.

In 2006, Suvarnabhumi Airport, located close to Thailand's capital city Bangkok, replaced Don Meung as the city's international airport. The new airport is currently operating with two runways and is capable of handling 45 million passengers and 3 million tons of airfreight per annum. Long-term plans include a total of four runways, two terminals, and the ability to handle 100 million passengers and 6.4 million tons of cargo on an annual basis. The Thai government views the expansion of the airport as an essential component of its plan to ensure that Suvarnabhumi Airport is recognized as the gateway to South-East Asia, and not just merely Bangkok.

Considerable thought seemed to have gone, at least ostensibly, into the planning of the new facility. The airport is connected to the city center of Bangkok via a high-speed railway, while a modern motorway connects it to the eastern Thailand seaboard, where the majority of Thailand's exported goods are manufactured. This was meant to enable Thai industries to benefit from just-in-time logistics strategies. Tourists were also intended to benefit from the new aerotropolis, which would offer a wide array of facilities. Of interest is that the Thai government intended to establish a no-housing zone that would encompass a 10-km buffer zone around the airport. While this might appear to mitigate concerns relating to noise, it calls into question elements of the aerotropolis model, especially the desirability of aerotropolis workers to live very close to their place of employment. It also calls into question the suitability of transport arrangements for dealing with massive influxes of people at peak hours.

Despite these grandiose plans, efforts to turn Suvarnabhumi Airport into an aerotropolis were put on hold by Thailand's interim government in the wake of a military junta removing the elected Thaksin government, accused of corrupt activities, from office in September 2006 (Katharangsiporn, 2006). Although general elections were held in late December 2007, it remains to be seen what will occur with Suvarnabhumi Airport.

It was acknowledged that, while the development of the aerotropolis would have undoubted benefit for Thailand's economy, and especially its burgeoning tourism and industrial sectors, the development would prove detrimental to the regional environment. In particular, the vast complex of planned infrastructure was viewed as having the potential to result in severe drainage problems. This is because the area on which Suvarnabhumi Airport was built was a large water basin. In effect, the airport was built on reclaimed marshland, with an inevitable cost to the natural environment, in addition to quality of the infrastructure, and the tarmacs and taxiways in particular (which have been subject to major cracking and other evidence of structural weakness). There were also major concerns about the impact of the proposed aerotropolis on living conditions in the region as a result of increased air traffic. This represents an interesting case of environmental values being given priority over economic ones, although it must also be acknowledged that the lack of proximity between the airport and the closest maritime facility was also called into question. Moreover, care for the environment did not prevent the marshland from being reclaimed in the first place.

Retrofitting the Airport, or "Aerotropolization"

The proposed aerotropolis based on Suvarnabhumi Airport represents the exception rather than the norm. The possibility of using a green-field site allows airport planners a greater degree of freedom than is the case for sites currently being used for air transport operations, which can be characterized for convenience as space-rich or space-poor. Indeed, in most cases, the aerotropolis will be based on *existing* and indeed *functioning* air transport sites, especially since, despite the rhetoric to the contrary, the airport is still seen as an extension of the host city in the majority of cases, rather than as a conglomeration of infrastructure and economic driver in itself. Thus the legacy of previous planning decisions will undoubtedly affect the operation, and certainly the sustainability, of the aerotropolis. For example, residential neighborhoods located nearby will be affected by any increase in air traffic, augmentation of the facilities will encroach on whatever natural spaces remain near the airport, while conduits to and from the aerotropolis will, in most cases, be suboptimum and difficult to retrofit to the required standard. In particular, the notion of access to and from the aerotropolis emerges as particularly important. The question, here, is to what extent the aerotropolization of an existing airport will be sustainable.

It has been argued that many existing airport sites, such as Schiphol in the Netherlands, exist as part of an urban space in which a number of cities have evolved as critical nodes in an economic meta-system (Batten, 1995). Batten (1995) further refers to such a configuration as a "network city." It may be that the airport city could be examined more readily as part of such an existing system rather than as a unique and emergent economic phenomenon in its own right. Space rich on the other hand, provides a useful label to contrast to these forms. A more viable discriminator may be the degree of space available for expansion and thus for incorporation of facets of the aerotropolis put forward by its proponents.

As a case in point, we look here at Brisbane, Australia. The southeast corner of the Australian state of Queensland has witnessed considerable growth in recent times. The current location of the domestic and international terminals, which are located next to each other, is approximately 13 kilometers from Brisbane's central business district. The site has the largest buffer zone (separating residential from airport land) of any major city airport in Australia. The average distance to residential areas located laterally to the proposed parallel runway is 1.7 km and, along the runways, 6.6 km. As a result, there is a large amount of land available to airport operators for expansion.

At present, plans are progressing that aim to utilize 970 hectares of available land sectioned off into seven integrated precincts. Of this allocation, approximately 80 hectares are planned for business development and include retail, leisure, tourism, general business, and commercial office facilities in addition to three separate export and cargo parks; in short, a typical aerotropolis. Also included in the development plan are hotels, conference facilities, a residential element with shopping village, and medical and childcare facilities. There are currently a number of aviation technology and maintenance businesses operating within the airport, in addition to a large "name brand" factory outlet for clothing and other consumer retail goods. In addition, planning is well advanced for an additional "main" runway that would effectively double the take off and landing capacity of the airport, like Haneda airport and the ports of Tokyo Bay, is in close physical proximity to the port of Brisbane: albeit on the opposite side of a river. The site does benefit from the nearby presence of a major freeway system that is destined for expansion, though it does not yet have a well-established rail cargo network other than a passenger link for transiting people to the airport from the city center.

Thus, once again, it can be seen that previous decisions regarding airport location, in addition to other serendipitous outcomes, weigh heavily on the prospects of aerotropolization. In short, a space-rich environment, in addition to its ability to be connected with other forms of infrastructure, provide the most optimum environment for currently in use airport sites to undergo the process of becoming airport cities, at least in the short to medium term.

INDICATORS OF SUSTAINABILITY

As seems to be evident, the notion of the aerotropolis as a one-size-fits-all concept is problematic. The sustainability of the aerotropolis (or otherwise) is thus contingent on a variety of factors. As seems clear, most aerotropolises will *not* be built on space-rich sites, even though it is the most optimum scenario from a planning perspective, although perhaps less so from an environmental perspective given the likelihood of substantial impact on existing ecosystems and their constituent fauna and flora. In many cases, the aerotropolis will merely constitute an amplification of existing infrastructure. Although the site may once have been located away from large-scale human habitation, urban sprawl in many space-poor locations means that the modern airport is now very much adjacent to built-up areas, or, at the very least, aircraft accessing the airport will need to fly over such areas. Pollution and noise concerns thus ensue.

Sustainable development (or redevelopment) has been an essential question of international environmental policy, at least since the 1992 United Nations summit in Rio de Janeiro. As set down in the 1987 Brundtland Report, a development can only be considered sustainable when it "meets the needs of the present without compromising the ability of future generations to meet their own needs" (World Commission on Environment and Development, 1987). In narrow terms, sustainability also relates to the maintenance of critical environmental processes that remain functional, and regular, for present and future generations (Upham, 2001). At a more detailed level, however, Upham (1999) identifies a range of sustainability principles that can be defined from a variety of disciplinary and political perspectives. Despite being successfully promoted by the Brundtland Commission, sustainable development has no precise or single meaning. Rather, it is a general and benign aspiration seeking the integration of environmental, social, and economic concerns.

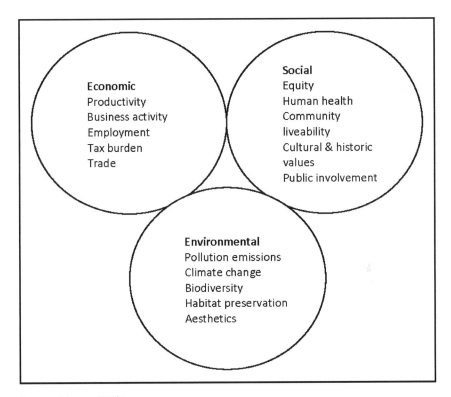

Source: Litman (2007).

Figure 7.1.   Transport sustainability indicator themes.

Recent thought on the integration of these thematic aspects of sustainability within the transport sectors are detailed in Figure 7.1.

The themes detailed in Figure 7.1 are not specifically unique to the transport sector or the aviation industry in a broader sense. They mirror factors common to many "modern" commercial and organizational settings and sustainability criteria used in social and environmental impact assessments historically. At worst, the aspirational aspect of Brundtland might be regarded as an empty "motherhood" statement. In practice, defining and indicating sustainability, especially for performance management, will always be a value-laden process irrespective of the availability of data, or how accumulated scientific and specialist knowledge is used. Moreover, it is evident that each individual element within the three themes shown in Figure 7.1 is inherently specialized in nature. The combination of the knowledge bases of each theme as part of a comprehensive approach to managing and enhancing sustainability in any of the two contexts (i.e., space rich and space poor) of the aerotropolis requires detailed and long-term planning. Effective decisions and planning thus rely on choices about which natural and social features are to be sustained (and conversely which are to be neglected) in the face of development, and in what form (Upham, 2001). This has important implications with regard to arriving at the indicators that might be used to assess the potential sustainability status of decisions involving aerotropolis infrastructure.

In admittedly generic terms, an indicator is a measure of function that points to an issue or condition purposefully selected in order to show how well a "system" is working (Hart, 2007). From a governance and managerial perspective, an indicator should assist decision makers to determine the direction to take when a system is identified as subfunctional. While indicators themselves vary according to their purpose, certain common characteristics might be regarded as indicative of effectiveness and usefulness. In a broad sense, effective transportation performance indicators include the following:

- **Relevant** (indicators show you something about the system that you need to know);
- **Comprehensive** (indicators should reflect various economic, social, and environmental impacts, and various transport activities—such as personal *and* freight transport);
- **Comparable** (data collection should be standardized so that the results are suitable for comparison between various jurisdictions, times, and groups, which means that indicators should be clearly defined);
- **Accessible and transparent** (indicators and the data on which they are based should be available to all stakeholders);
- Based on **accessible data** (information for each of the indicators is available or can be gathered with ease);
- **Reliable** (information that the indicator is providing can be trusted);
- **Easy to understand** (indicator is meaningful, even to people who are not regarded as experts);
- **Cost effective** (information for the indicator(s) should be cost effective to collect, i.e., the decision-making worth of the indicators should outweigh the cost of collecting them);
- **Performance targets** (indicators are selected that are suitable for establishing usable performance targets) (Hart, 1997; Marsden, Charlotte Kelly, & Snell, 2006; Sustainable Measures, 2007).

Some commentators, such as Thomas (2006), have referred to the presence of carbon-neutral airport strategies incorporating renewable energy (e.g., wind, photovoltaic) in addition to noncarbon energy sources (e.g., hydrogen), heat stores, low-energy terminal designs, energy management, and carbon offset programs—all within the context of indicating sustainable activity. Other commentators have examined sustainability in the aviation industry by other means. For example, Hughes and Johnston (2005) have suggested continued economic growth and human development, protection, and extension of social capital with a special emphasis on social equity, and protection of the natural environment. The problem, here, of course is ensuring that these goals are internally reconcilable, for example, can economic growth be achieved at the same time as protecting the natural environment? Or are trade-offs expected in these sort of circumstances?

Likewise, industry groups, such as the United Kingdom's Sustainable Aviation Council, have documented specific *goals,* with set indicators, designed to assist sustainable planning for airports. Specific instances include:

- **Limit and, where possible, reduce the number of people affected by noise:**
  o The area enclosed by and the number of people living within the 57 decibels 16-hour equivalent continuous noise level contour at individual airports;
  o Percentage achievement of continuous descent approaches at individual airports;
  o Progress toward the Advisory Council for Aeronautics Research in Europe target for new aircraft; and
  o Performance of the U.K. fleet relative to International Civil Aviation Organization Chapter 4 standard.
- **Industry commitment and involvement in improving air quality and meeting regulations:**
  o Modal split for transport access by passengers at individual airports; and
  o Modal split of transport used by staff at individual airports.
- **A competitive and commercially viable industry contributing to the economy:**
  o Market share and industry gross value added percentage of gross domestic product resulting from the aviation industry; and
  o Turnover and gross margin of individual companies.
- **Governance and communication:**

  o Full industry commitment to sustainable development and a
    wider understanding of the role of aviation in sustainable soci-
    ety;
  o A competitive and commercially viable aviation industry contrib-
    uting to local, regional, and national economies; and
  o An industry that engenders productive relationships with
    employees, local communities, customers, and industry partners
    in a manner that meets societal needs (Sustainable Aviation
    Council, 2005, 2006).

Such themes and measures, of course, would fit modern airports anywhere and are not unique to the aerotropolis. It is arguable that the
notion of an aerotropolis in its purist form may not actually be achievable
in the space-poor setting of airport activity, thus leaving space-rich as the
only fully relevant setting for the full expression of the concept. This follows the idea posited by Batten (1995), that is to say that the form of the
"network city" has more "goodness-of-fit" in instances where considerable
enmeshing of aviation infrastructure and services exist with trade and
commerce, such as would be seen in well-established and often space-
poor situations.

A key differentiating factor in pursuing the full form of the airport city
may be the availability of land, and by association, distances between
existing built airport infrastructure and differentially zoned (often residential) land—a factor often more likely to be present in a space-rich setting. Concomitant with availability of land is the capacity to plan and
implement the infrastructure and essential services expected of a fully
conceived aerotropolis.

ISSUES AND OPTIONS

A question of relevance to any discussion of the airport city concept is the
way in which it is construed by supporters and doubters alike. Both positions may view it as:

• A stand-alone center of trade incorporating aviation cargo, supportive industry, and people movement;
• A transport node within a networked urban-city conglomeration;
• A new urban form driven by wealth creation (associated with the
  airport and aviation industry activities).

All three descriptors are arguably valid representations of the concept. The means by which sustainability would be monitored, that is, by means of indicators, may also be common across these views. Analytical differences may be discernible in the baseline land-use context, out of which a developmental process toward the airport city emerges: that is, a "renewal" or retrofitting focus for space-poor settings against a room-to-grow developmental flavor for space-rich locations. An important differentiating factor in the space-rich context is the general availability of land and the expectation that distinct pocket(s) of residential land use will be included in the mix. This constitutes a key element of the Brisbane Airport example mentioned earlier.

If the full aerotropolis concept were to be realized, for instance, in Brisbane, it is likely that, in order to be successful, indicators would have to go beyond the industry-specific examples detailed earlier and would include greater emphasis on community sustainability. Why would this be important? While the socioeconomic profile of residential pockets within an aerotropolis is likely to be, as in many specialist urban settings, skilled and professional groupings related specifically to the aviation industry itself, service provision and maintenance would arguably be the responsibility of the airport operator, or would be undertaken conjointly with owners of the residential locations. Notwithstanding the élan of jet-setting business persons, a need is thus likely to emerge that will center on ensuring the presence of community-making via suitable engagement and participative activities. Sustainable communities, largely as a result of the Brundtlandian approach, have been characterized as exhibiting a range of viability factors such as:

- **Governance** (well-run communities with effective and inclusive participation, representation, and leadership);
- **Transport and connectivity** (well-connected communities with good transport services and communications linking people to jobs, health, and other services);
- **Services** (public, private, and community and voluntary services that are accessible to all);
- **Environmental** (providing places for people to live in an environmentally friendly way);
- **Equity** (for everyone, i.e., for both today's and tomorrow's communities);
- **Economy** (a thriving and vibrant local economy);
- **Housing and the built environment** (high-quality buildings);

- **Social and culture** (active, inclusive and safe with a strong local culture and other shared community activities) (Academy of Sustainable Communities (2008).

Longhurst, Gibbs, Raper, and Conlan (1996), in support of this notion suggested that a sustainable airport must, in addition to a number of industry-specific tasks, entertain a dialogue with its customers, offer partnership to the community, be able to meet the needs of its customers, and be involved in debate about the quality of life at local, national, and international levels. In the case of a fully realized aerotropolis, which is the goal in the case of Brisbane, industry and community sustainability indicators may have to merge.

While the development cycle in Brisbane is yet to reach maturity it is arguable that, based on a space-poor and space-rich dichotomy established in this chapter, sustainability indicators for airport cities would vary from those listed by aviation industry groups, which are predominantly designed or chosen (however artfully) to limit negative responses to airport activities. A more complete expression of the aerotropolis concept would, based on the brief analysis presented here, require a multifaceted implementation and inclusion of community-based needs analysis as part of sustainability indicator development, in addition to those defined by industry specific imperatives. The full realization of the concept, however, can be constrained by a range of market, commercial, and socioenvironmental variables or, in the case of Suvarnabhumi Airport in Thailand, what may be construed as a combination of all these factors.

REFERENCES

Academy of Sustainable Communities. (2008). *What is a sustainable community?* Retrieved June 9, 2008, from http://www.ascskills.org.uk/pages/sustainable-communities

al Chalabi, M., & Kasarda, J. D. (2004). Airports: Short- and long-term trends. In A. Frej (Ed.), *Just-in-time real estate* (pp. 81-85). Washington, DC: Urban Land Institute.

Batten, D. (1995). Network cities: Creative urban agglomerations for the 21st Century. *Urban Studies, 32*(2), 313-327.

Birkenstock, W. (1998, September). Hydrogen aircraft fuel research plans. *Flug Revue, 66.* Retrieved June 9, 2008, from http://www.flug-revue.rotor.com/FRheft/FRH9809/FR9809k.htm

Boden, D., & Molotch, H. (2004). Cyberspace meets the compulsion of proximity. In S. Graham (Ed.), *The cybercities reader* (pp. 101-105). New York: Routledge.

Bruijn, H. de, & Dicke, W. (2006). Strategies for safeguarding public values in liberalized utility sectors. *Public Administration, 84*(3), 717-735.

Charles, M. B., Barnes, P., Ryan, N., & Clayton, J. (2007a). Airport futures: Towards a critique of the aerotropolis model. *Futures*, *39*(9), 1009-1028.

Charles, M. B., Ryan, R., Ryan, N., & Oloruntoba, R. (2007b). Public policy and biofuels: The way forward? *Energy Policy*, 35(11), 5737-5746.

Faa, R. (2001). *Cryoplane: Flugzeuge mit Wasserstoffantrieb* [Cryoplane: Airplanes with hydrogen drives]. Retrieved April 13, 2006, from http://www.haw-hamburg.de/pers/Scholz/dglr/hh/text_2001_12_06_Cryoplane.pdf

Hart, M. (2007). *Characteristics of effective indicators*. Retrieved December 12, 2007, from www.sustainablemeasures.com/Indicators/Characteristics.html

Hart, M. (1997). *Johnson Foundation. Evaluating indicators: A checklist for Communities*. Retrieved December 12, 2007, from http://www.johnsonfdn.org/spring97/indicators.html

Hughes, B. B., & Johnston, P. D. (2005). Sustainable futures: Policies for global development. *Futures*, *37*(6), 813-831.

Intergovernmental Panel on Climate Change. (2007). *Climate change 2007: The physical science basis (summary for policy makers)*. Geneva, Switzerland: Author.

Kasarda, J. D. (2000). Aerotropolis: Airport-driven urban development. In R. Fishman (Ed.), *The future of cities* (pp. 32-41). Washington, DC: Urban Land Institute.

Kasarda, J. D. (2000/2001). Logistics and the rise of the aerotropolis. *Real Estate Issues*, *25*(4), 43-48.

Kasarda, J. D. (2004). Amsterdam airport Schiphol: The airport city. In A. Frej (Ed.), *Just-in-time real estate* (pp. 96-104). Washington DC: Urban Land Institute.

Kasarda, J. D. (2005). Gateway airports, speed and the rise of the aerotropolis. In D. V. Gibson, M. V. Heitor, & A. Ibarra-Yunez (Eds.), *Learning and knowledge for the network society* (pp. 99-108). West Lafayette IN: Perdue University Press.

Katharangsiporn, K. (2006, November 3). Aerotropolis plan would have 'pros and cons.' *Bangkok Post*. Retrieved June 9, 2008 from http://archives.mybangkokpost.com/bkkarchives/frontstore

Kirlin, J. (1996). What government must do well: Creating value for society. *Journal of Public Administration Research and Theory*, *6*(1), 161-185.

Koppenjan, J., Charles, M. B., & Ryan, N. (2008). Managing competing public values in public infrastructure projects. *Public Money & Management, 29*(3), 131-134.

Litman, T. (2007). *Well measured: Developing indicators for comprehensive and sustainable transport planning*. Victoria, British Columbia, Canada: Victoria Transport Policy Institute. Retrieved June 9, 2008 from http://www.vtpi.org/wellmeas.pdf

Longhurst, J., Gibbs, D. C., Raper, D. W., & Conlan, D. E. 1996. Towards sustainable airport development. *The Environmentalist, 16*, 197-202.

Lopp, D., & Stanley, D. 1(995). *Soy–diesel blends in aviation turbine engines*. West Lafayette, IN: Aviation Technology Department, Purdue University.

Marsden, G., Charlotte Kelly, C., & Snell, C. (2006). *Selecting indicators for strategic performance management*. Presented at the Transportation Research Board annual meeting. Retrieved June 9, 2008, from http://www.mdt.mt.gov/research/docs/trb_cd/Files/06-0378.pdf

Ryan, N., & Charles, M. B. (2008). Science and technology: Policy futures. In G. Hearn & D. Rooney (Eds.), *Knowledge policy: Challenges for the 21st century* (pp. 106-119). Cheltenham, United Kingdom: Edward Elgar.

Sustainable Aviation Council. (2006). *Sustainable aviation progress report, UK.* Retrieved June 9, 2008, from www.bata.uk.com/Web/Documents/media/pubs/ SustainableAviationReport02006.pdf

Sustainable Measures. (2007). *Indicators of sustainability.* Retrieved May 5, 2008, from http://www.sustainablemeasures.com/Indicators/index.html

Thomas, C. (2006, October). *Sustainable airport development.* Paper presented at the Towards Sustainable Airport Development Conference, Dublin, Ireland.

Upham, P. (2001). A comparison of sustainability theory with UK and European airports policy and practice. *Journal of Environmental Management, 63,* 237-248.

Upham, P. J. (1999). *An assessment of the natural step as a framework for technology choice.* Unpublished doctoral dissertation, University of Manchester, Manchester, England.

Vedantham, A. (1999). *Aviation and the global atmosphere. A special report of IPCC working groups I and III in collaboration with the scientific assessment panel to the Montreal Protocol on substances that deplete the ozone layer.* Philadelphia: University of Pennsylvania. Retrieved June 9, 2008 from http://repository.upenn .edu/cgi/viewcontent.cgi?article=1066&context=library_papers

World Commission on Environment and Development. (1987). *Our common future.* Oxford, England: Oxford University Press.

CHAPTER 8

SUSTAINABLE AVIATION

Challenges and Solutions in a Carbon Constrained World

Dawna L. Rhoades

As consensus over climate change and carbon dioxide emissions grows, the aviation industry is coming under increasing scrutiny. Three questions are raising debate within and outside of the industry. First, what is the extent of the problem? Second, what are the solutions? Third, at what level should they be implemented? This chapter reviews the extent of carbon emissions in aviation, actions to address emissions, and future prospects for aviation in a carbon constrained world.

On December 19, 2006, the cover story of *USA Today* proclaimed that "Concern grows over pollution from jets: Aviation emissions will take off along with worldwide air travel." The article reported that each passenger on a commercial jet from New York City to Denver would generate between 840 and 1,600 pounds of carbon dioxide, roughly the same amount of carbon as a sports utility vehicle driven over the period of a month. Given projected increases in air travel, aircraft emissions could become one of the largest contributors to global warming by 2050 (Stoller,

Global Sustainability Initiatives: New Models and New Approaches
pp. 159–172

2006). While the European Commission has proposed including emissions from civil aviation into the European Union (EU) Emissions Trading Scheme by 2011 for all internal EU flight and 2012 for all flights to and from EU airports, the issue is not currently on the agenda of the U.S. government and is strongly opposed by U.S. airlines (Pilling & Thompson, 2007). The issue has become so contentious in the EU that Britain's Prince Charles was forced to defend his decision to fly to New York in January 2007 to accept the Global Environmental Citizen Prize (Reuters News Agency, 2007). The British Parliament is even considering measures to limit the growth rate of aviation to the rate at which the industry improves its fuel efficiency. Locally, governments and citizens are rejecting planned increases in aviation activity such as new airport runways or additional flights due to concerns over the environment and global warming (Stoller, 2006). Meanwhile, groups such as Sustainable Aviation are working to insure that aviation becomes part of the solution to the problem of greenhouse gases (GHG) through (1) full industry commitment to GHG reduction, (2) incorporation of aviation into a global policy framework, and (3) reduction in the environmental footprint of aviation (Sustainable Aviation, 2006).

The United States now appears poised to "Go Green" (Adler, 2006; Kaihla, 2007; Stone, 2006). In a world that consumes 85 million barrels of oil every single day (Tertzakian, 2006), the United States accounts for roughly 25% of total daily consumption, consuming approximately 22 million barrels a day for the week of August 18, 2006 (Energy Information Administration, 2006). Oil is the largest source of primary energy for the United States, making up almost 40% of the energy needs. Transportation accounts for roughly two thirds of total oil consumption (National Energy Policy Development Group, 2001). Aviation has only recently received any attention in the debate over global warming. In fact, the Kyoto Protocol did not mention aviation emissions as they were believed to be a minor contributor to global warming when the agreement was being negotiated (Stoller, 2006).

As the industry struggles to recover after September 11th, it is reluctant to address carbon emissions and even less thrilled with the predictions of some geologists and environmentalists such as Colin Campbell, author of *Oil Crisis* and a chief proponent of an early peak for oil production. Campbell has predicted that the "airline business will go into near extinction as fuel costs soar. Very few people actually need to travel by air. Modern communications makes most business travel unnecessary" (2005, p. 298). Lester R. Brown, president of the Earth Policy Institute, has offered a less dire prediction for the aviation industry, but he still suggests that cheap airfares, fresh fruit transported by aircraft to out-of-season consumers, and citizens willing to "subsidize this high-cost mode of transportation for their more affluent compatriots" will soon be a thing of the past (Brown, 2006).

The purpose of this chapter is to explore the current state of understanding about the role of aviation in global warming with a special emphasis on efforts by various sectors of the industry to address this impact. The costs, benefits, and challenges of possible voluntary and mandated actions are also discussed.

GLOBAL WARMING AND TRANSPORTATION

While the debate about the reality of global warming and its causes has largely been settled in much of the world, it still remains a topic of dispute in the United States as a recent visit by former U.S. Vice-President Al Gore to the U.S. Congress illustrated (Kluger, 2007). As the EU moves to cut energy use 20% by 2020 and increase the share of renewable energy to 12% by 2010, the United States currently does not have a comprehensive plan to address the issue of energy use, carbon emissions, or renewable energy. Instead, the United States is relying heavily on markets to drive change (Brown, 2006; McKinnon & Meckler, 2006). To the extent that carbon emissions have received attention in the United States, they have been confined to discussions of power generation or automobile use. There are calls for greater use of nuclear power or "clean coal" and renewed interest in ethanol production, but until recently the aviation industry was largely untouched by this debate. Their primary concern has been the cost of petroleum-based jet fuel not carbon and other emissions, and their primary focus has been on technological improvements and air traffic modernization (Pilling & Thompson, 2007).

Impact of Aviation

The Federal Aviation Administration (FAA) is predicting that the number of U.S. passenger aircraft will increase 47.3% between 2005 and 2020. The projected increase in fuel consumption is expected to be even greater at 68.7% for airlines in passenger and cargo service. Fuel consumption by general aviation aircraft is predicted to triple over the same period due to the development and projected popularity of very light jets (Bond, 2007). At present, all transport modes are responsible for 23% of the total carbon emissions with air transport accounting for 12% of this total (Ott, 2007). The chief source of carbon emissions for the industry overall is the jet engine. A jet engine will emit more carbon dioxide than the actual weight of the fuel that creates combustion (Bond, 2007). According to

Environmental Defense, burning a gallon of jet fuel will produce 21.1 pounds of carbon dioxide or about half a pound per passenger per domestic mile or one pound per passenger per international mile. It is not clear at this time whether emissions at high altitude represent a greater problem for global warming than those that occur at sea level (Environmental Defense, 2007; Stoller, 2006). Further, some sources suggest that noncarbon dioxide GHG emissions may be even more significant. These include nitrogen oxide, sulfur oxide, soot, and water vapor (Stoller, 2006).

The aviation industry can be roughly divided into six segments-airlines, manufacturers, airports, general aviation, airspace, and air cargo. While these segments exist throughout the world, there are important structural differences. In the United States, airlines and air cargo operators are privately owned. Most are publicly traded stock companies and are subject to financial as well as operational reporting. Airports, on the other hand, are largely owned by the city or county in which they are located. All but a small number of airports are open to general aviation traffic. Airspace is tightly regulated. The air traffic system is managed by the U.S. Federal Aviation Administration and controllers are public employees.

In much of the rest of the world, full or partial government ownership of airlines is common, while airports are increasingly being privatized or the management of the airport outsourced. General aviation is much less common and many airports are closed to this type of traffic. Airspace is less restricted and in some cases such as in Africa, radar coverage is limited (Rhoades, 2003). Although these differences are probably not a significant factor in the current approach of the aviation sectors in different regions, it could affect future support of carbon constraint. Currently, each segment contributes to carbon emissions in a multitude of ways and each is approaching (or not approaching) the issue of emissions at its own pace and in its own way.

Airlines

U.S. airlines use approximately 53.4 million gallons of jet fuel per day for a total of U.S.$19.5 billion per year. Fuel constitutes 20-30% of the total operating costs of an airline, surpassing labor as the single largest expense (Air Transport Association, 2007b). The U.S. Environmental Protection Agency sets aircraft emissions standards while it is the responsibility of the Federal Aviation Administration to enforce established standards. U.S. guidelines roughly mirror international standards set by the International Civil Aviation Organization (ICAO). ICAO's Committee on Aviation Environmental Protection recently approved new guidelines that include recommendations on emissions trading, however, the guidelines are not binding on any nation (Ott, 2007).

Aircraft emit carbon dioxide and nitrogen oxide both on the ground and while in flight. On the ground, fuel can be burned when aircraft back from the gate under power, taxi to the runway, or reposition on the airport, either to a new gate or a maintenance hangar on airport property. This on ground fuel burn has tended to raise more concerns about local air and noise pollution rather than carbon emission. However, it is the in-flight, upper atmosphere emissions and the creation of contrails (condensed water vapor formed in the wake of an aircraft and believed to contribute to cloud cover) that has raised the most concern (McKinnon & Meckler, 2006).

Manufacturers

Aircraft engines have continued to increase the efficiency of their fuel burn. It is estimated that new technologies have doubled fuel efficiency over the past 40 years and several manufacturers are committed to a further improvement of almost 50% (Sustainable Aviation, 2006). These technologies have also helped reduce carbon dioxide emissions, however, it is estimated that nitrogen oxide emissions in new engines have increased by about 40% over the same period (McKinnon & Meckler, 2006). Unfortunately, the replacement of existing fleets with newer, more fuel efficient aircraft is a slow process given the cost to aircraft operators and the potential modifications to existing aircraft would yield only modest improvements in efficiency (Bond, 2007).

In addition to improved design for engines, there are possibilities for the use of alternative fuels. The turbine engine of a large commercial jet uses a high octane form of diesel fuel, commonly called Jet A. Jet A must perform under extreme temperature conditions, particularly the cold of high altitude. Smaller general aviation aircraft use what is called *avgas*. As the name implies, avgas is more closely related to gasoline than diesel (U.S. Department of Energy, 2005).

Airports

Airports have been a focal point for resident and environmental groups concerned about environmental impacts arising from noise and air pollution. In addition to the activity of the aircraft themselves, airports utilize powered vehicles for baggage transfer, aircraft maintenance, emergency response, terminal-to-terminal transportation, terminal-to-parking transportation, and so on. In the United States, most airports are accessed through private automobile and parking fees represent a substantial source of revenue. Although airport master planning in the United States requires intermodal transportation issues be addressed through the design of parking facilities, rental cars, and public transportation access, the reality is that only 14 airports in the United States are linked to rail systems, one of the least polluting forms of transportation, leaving the other airports to rely on other forms of surface transportation. (Airport Council International & Air Transport Action Group, 1998).

General Aviation

General aviation includes all noncommercial, nonmilitary aviation. While the general aviation segment includes business jets that would use biodiesel similar to large commercial jets, most of the industry is dominated by nonjet aircraft that range from small single engine aircraft to multiengine propeller craft. These craft use avgas rather than Jet-A fuel. Avgas is more closely related to ethanol. There are over 320,000 general aviation aircraft including helicopter, single, piston engine craft, and turbo-props. In the United States, general aviation aircraft fly over 27 million hours annually (General Aviation Manufacturers Association, 2006).

Airspace

Airspace is restricted to a certain extent in all countries due to noise, security, safety, and radar coverage. In the United Space, airspace is more tightly controlled than in many other regions and is the responsibility of a single entity, the FAA. In regions such as the European Union, multiple air traffic control systems reduce the efficiency with which airspace is used. Another source of global inefficiency are country limitations on the entry of foreign aircraft either by closing entrance or charging fees for entry or overflight, thus encouraging fly around and additional flight times. The current system of air traffic management utilizes step-down approaches that require progressive altitude changes and thrust applications in descent to landing, adding to fuel burn (Hughes, 2007).

Air Cargo

World air freight growth, which is closely linked to the overall growth in world GDP, has recovered slowly since 2001. Recent forecasts predict annual growth to be 6.8% through 2015 with Asia, particularly China, leading the regions of the world (Graham, 2006). Air freight is carried either as belly cargo on commercial airlines or on dedicated freighter aircraft some of which are operated by the airlines themselves. As airlines have struggled to return to profitability, many have turned to a greater reliance on air cargo. Cargo revenue for the world's airlines has increased from a post-2001 low of U.S.$38 billion in 2002 to roughly U.S.$56 billion for 2006 (Putzger, 2006). Other all-cargo operators act as air freight forwarders, handling the air segment of a shipping operation. This includes operators handling oversized cargo such as Volga-Dnepr. Oversized carriers use some of the largest aircraft in the world—C-17 and AN 124—to ship large industrial equipment. Firms such as those in the oil and gas industry often consider the time saved by shipping equipment by air rather than slower modes of transportation to be an ideal tradeoff to get operations up and running quickly (Nelms, 2007).

The best known shippers are the so-called integrated carriers such as UPS, FedEx, and DHL. While air forwarders such as airlines and all cargo operators are responsible for only the air portion of travel and require shippers to make their own arrangements to get freight to and from the airport, the "integrated" carriers combine all modes of transportation to provide seamless, door-to-door shipping. FedEx started life as an overnight air freight delivery company while UPS began as a ground delivery company that expanded into air freight later in life. Their differing histories have not stopped either company from amassing an air fleet that would rank them among the largest airlines in the world (Niemann, 2007).

CURRENT ACTIONS

The aviation industry is pursuing a number of actions to reduce GHG emissions. The primary hope of significant reduction lies in new technologies, but certain sectors are currently engaged in actions to change existing processes and/or pursue a holistic approach to the GHG issue.

New Technology

Aircraft and engine manufacturers are currently working on technologies to redesign aircraft wings to reduce drag and fuel burn, utilize advanced light-weight composite materials, and replace existing technology with fuel cells (Sustainable Aviation, 2006). The Advisory Council for Aeronautics Research in Europe (ACARE) has established a goal of reducing nitrogen oxide emissions by 80% and carbon dioxide by 50% by 2020 (Norris, 2007). The two major U.S. engine manufacturers—General Electric (GE) and Pratt and Whitney, part of United Technologies (UTC)—are founding members of the Pew Center Business Environmental Leadership Council which is dedicated to addressing global climate change (Hoffman, 2006). UTC is part of the Dow Jones Sustainability index and was named one of the top 100 sustainable companies at the 2005 World Economic Forum in Davos, Switzerland. UTC and Pratt and Whitney are committed to reducing GHG by 12% over the next 4 years and include key performance indicators for air and carbon dioxide emissions in their public reporting (United Technologies, 2007), GE is committed to reduce GHG 1% by 2012 and the intensity of GHG emissions 30% by 2008 (Hoffman, 2006).

The only "drop in" alternative fuel for Jet-A is synthetic jet fuel, manufactured through a conversion process from natural gas or coal. Unfortunately, the conversion process produces 1.8 times the carbon dioxide of conventional jet fuel production. All other alternative fuel technologies require engine modification. The use of 100% biofuels is not currently viable as they freeze at the normal cruising temperatures of large commercial aircraft (Daggett, Henricks, Walther, & Corporan, 2007). The Renewable Aviation Fuels Development Center (RAFDC) at Baylor University has run a series of experiments using alternative fuels for aviation. RAFDC tests examined biodiesel blends of 5, 10, 15, 20, and 25%. The best results were obtained for the 20% blend. Beyond this level of blend, major changes in engine configuration would be required. Boeing is currently exploring the use of cryogenic hydrogen and liquid methane (Daggett et al., 2007). For general aviation, nonjet fuels, RAFDC has tested ethanol and eythyl tertiary butyl ether (ETBE) against avgas in the piston engines commonly used in general aviation propeller aircraft. Although some engine modification is required, tests showed that efficiencies were higher for ethanol than avgas and even greater gains were seen with increased compression. Fuel consumption comparisons indicated that at 80% power, ethanol consumed 11% more fuel than avgas. Ethanol and ETBE were shown to produce lower emission of carbon monoxide and unburned hydrocarbons, but increase the emission of carbon dioxide and nitrogen oxide because of lower energy conversion rates, a fact reflected in the level of fuel consumed (Shauck & Zanin, 2000). In a real world test, a modified piston aircraft was flown without significant problems across the Atlantic using ethanol (Shauck & Zanin, 1990). During the transatlantic flight no fuel-related problems were encountered. The overall cost of the ethanol for the crossing was U.S.$160 compared to U.S.$230 for avgas, even including the reduced mileage (Shauck & Zanin, 2000). Results indicate that ethanol burns more completely and cleanly than gasoline. There is, however, a reduction in range (mileage) between 10-15% (Johnson, Shauck, & Zanin, 1998).

There are a number of technologies that would improve airport arrival and departure procedures. The Next Generation Air Transportation System of the FAA is looking at technologies such as 4D trajectory management which would involve runway-to-runway planning with autonegotiation equipment in the aircraft that could adjust the flight plan as necessary to accommodate weather, aircraft separation, airport delays, and so forth. Air traffic management (ATM) changes to step-down approaches, mentioned above, are also in testing. This technology relies on global positioning satellites and Automatic Dependent Surveillance-Broadcast to implement proper spacing. It is estimated that continuous descent arrivals could save between 100-300 pounds of fuel (Hughes, 2007). The U.S. Air Transport Association, a trade organization representing U.S. airlines, and the FAA support the airspace management initiative called Secure America's Future Energy (SAFE). SAFE would link a satellite-based air traffic system to ground-based technologies in order to reduce delays and shorten travel. SAFE estimates that implementation of these action could save 400,000 barrels of oil daily by 2030 and reduce carbon emissions by 57.5 million metric tons per year (Air Transport Association, 2007a). The European equivalent of these programs are the Single European Sky ATM Research Programme and the Advisory Council for Aerospace research in Europe.

Changing Processes

Airlines are taking a number of actions that reduce fuel burn and emissions on the ground, primarily because of fuel cost concerns. These actions include the elimination of power backing (backing the airplane from the gate using its engines) in favor of small tugs that push the aircraft back from the gate and "supertugs" that can be used to tow aircraft around the airport itself.

EU airlines are addressing governments and customer concerns by developing explicit plans to manage and report on a range of environmental issues. For example, British Airways has a section on their Web site that reports on their environmental actions in the area of noise, air quality, waste, and biodiversity. It also includes a way to calculate and offset carbon dioxide emissions. British Airways is one of several EU airlines to affirm their support for the Emissions Trading Scheme and call for action on an international scheme for emissions trading (British Airways, 2007). Air France reports on their actions toward sustainable development, including their tracking reports for emissions and efforts to reduce emissions through fleet renewal, alternative fuel ground vehicles, and air-rail link options (Air France, 2007).

U.S. airlines do not include any information of this nature in their investor reports or on their Web sites. In fact, only a few mention environmental issues at all, usually only to affirm their "commitment" to the environment, although some U.S. airlines will direct concerned customers to GoGreen to explore means of offsetting carbon emissions.

U.S. airports have been more aggressive in their approach to environmental issues. Several examples highlight some of the many actions that airports are employing. Dallas-Fort Worth Airport (DFW) is the world's third busiest airport with 1,900 flights per day. DFW is also an example of an airport that has taken a very proactive approach to environmental issues. This fact was recently recognized when the U.S. Environmental Protection Agency named it to the National Environmental Performance Track program. Over the prior 5 years DFW has reduced its air emissions by 95% and converted 100% of its light-to-medium on field fleet as well as bus and shuttle operations to alternative fuels (DFW News Release, 2007). Another example of proactive environmental response is the Port of Seattle which includes not only the Sea-Tac Airport but the seaport in Seattle. The port has a staff of 22 individuals responsible for environmental issues and compliance. Like DFW, they have converted much of their on-airport vehicles to natural gas and redesigned field operations to reduce the number of tanker trucks needed on the airfield (Port of Seattle, 2006).

In the United Kingdom, the Airport Carbon Management Group was created to explore ways to reduce carbon emissions, primarily through improved energy use. To date, the efforts of this group have reduced carbon emissions by 13,000 tons per year (Sustainable Aviation, 2006). As of 1998, there were 40 airports in Europe with air-rail links and an additional 49 links planned. It is estimated that the Heathrow Express will remove 3,000 cars a day from London roads (Airport Council International & Air Transport Action Group, 1998).

The integrated carriers are making the greatest efforts to address environmental concerns, including carbon emissions. DHL has launched its GoGreen program that allows shippers to select low carbon emission modes of shipping. This option was provided to delegates attending the World Economic Forum in Davos as part of the forum's carbon neutral goal for the last conference. DHL is exploring the use of biogas, hybrid, and fuel cell vehicles for ground shipping and packaging options that reduce GHG emissions (Charlesworth, 2008). FedEx is also exploring alternative fuels for its ground vehicles and has recently launched 18 Optifleet E700 hybrid vehicles to its fleet. On the aviation side, FedEx has retired its remaining B727 aircraft and hush-kitted older aircraft, both of which reduce the overall fleet emissions and noise levels (FedEx, 2007). UPS has taken a number of actions to reduce fuel consumption and emissions from its ground fleet including trailering trucks onto railcars and optimizing driving routes as well as adding 50 hybrid vehicles to its fleet in 2006. These hybrids join a fleet of 12,000 low emission vehicles already in operation (Niemann, 2007). UPS has also established key performance indicators (KPI) for environmental performance, which include ground and aviation emissions. These are reported on their Web site (UPS, 2007).

DISCUSSION

With the exception of U.S. airlines, other U.S. sectors of the aviation industry are taking steps to address GHG and climate change. While it would be incorrect to say that the airline industry has taken no actions to reduce energy use, switch to renewable fuels, or reduce emissions, these actions have been driven by higher fuel prices rather than other concerns. This may not be surprising given that U.S. airlines as a group are only now beginning to recover from the effects of September 11th. This segment of the industry has also struggled over time to post consistent profits (Loomis & Buffet, 1999). Unfortunately, airlines have tended to react to their external environment rather than take a proactive stance. This reactive posture is not the case with much of the rest of the industry in the U.S. where pro-environmental action has occurred. Still, U.S. industry is behind its European counterparts in a number of respects in part because there has been no political or consumer pressure to act. Environmental groups have found themselves refighting the same issues on the broader issue of climate change and have not been able to focus on the specifics of carbon emissions in the aviation industry.

MANAGERIAL IMPLICATIONS

A number of recent publications offer guidance to firms in preparing strategies to meet environmental challenges such as GHG emissions. The Pew Center on Global Climate Change recently published the results of a survey of the 31 members of their Business Environmental Leadership Council (Hoffman, 2006). The report provides guidance on assessing emissions profiles, gauging risk and opportunities, evaluating options, setting goals, developing financial mechanisms, engaging the organization, formulating policies, and managing external relations. It also indicates that companies that are proactive in the area of GHG emissions have been able to identify a number of ways to reduce their "footprint" while at the same time lowering costs and increasing their reputation, both inside and outside the company.

In a newly released book titled *Green to Gold: How Smart Companies Use Environmental Strategy to Innovate, Create Value, and Build Competitive Advantage,* Esty and Winston (2006) offer advice and examples of strategies and tools for addressing environmental issues. Their research focusing on so-called "waveriders" confirms the Pew findings that proactive firms are outperforming others in their respective industries. The research suggests that environmental initiatives fail for one or more of the following reasons: seeing the trees but not the forest, misunderstanding the market, expecting a price premium, misunderstanding the customer, middle-management squeeze, silo thinking, eco-isolation, claims outpacing actions, surprises, wasp stings, unintended consequences, perfect is the enemy of good, inertia, ignoring stakeholders, and failing to tell the story. One example of seeing the trees but not the forest that they cite is the Ford Motor Company's investment in creating a green roof on its River Rouge plant and supporting Conservation International with a U.S.$25 million grant while Toyota was investing in hybrid technology. Another example of failure occurred when Monsanto misunderstood the differences in markets between the United States and Europe and were surprised to find that Europe did not welcome genetically modified food as a sustainability effort.

In short, the advice to firms in any industry would be to become proactive in managing the risks and opportunities presented by carbon constraint and other environmental issues. Such companies gain advantage by being slightly ahead of rivals when regulations do arise. They identify which courses of action present better overall results. They address and manage the concerns of key stakeholders, earning goodwill and reputation. Even in the United States, where the climate debate continues, "a growing number of companies believe that inaction is no longer a viable option. All companies will be affected to varying degrees, and all have a managerial and fiduciary obligation to at least assess their business exposure to decide whether action is prudent" (Hoffman, 2006, p. vii). U.S. airlines risk much by their inaction, particularly given the recent U.S.-EU multilateral air service agreement and the European decision on emissions trading.

REFERENCES

Adler, J. (2006, July 16). Going green. *Newsweek,* pp. 43-52.
Air France. (2007). *Sustainable development.* Retrieved June 13, 2008, from http://developpement-durable.airfrance.com/FR/en/local/demarche/N4_responsabilite_enjeux.htm

Air Transport Association. (2007a). *ATA and 'SAFE' agree that modernized ATC will significantly reduce fuel consumption and U.S. oil dependence* (News release). Retrieved June 13, 2008, from http://www.airlines.org/news/releases/2006/news_12-13-06.htm

Air Transport Association. (2007b). *US airlines support development of alternative fuels*, [ATA Issue Brief. Retrieved June 13, 2008, from http://www.airlines.org/government/issuebriefs/Alt+Fuels.htm

Airport Council International & Air Transport Action Group. (1998). *Air rail links: Guide to best practice*. Geneva, Switzerland: ACI-ATAG Press.

Bond, D. (2007, August 19). Green is for go. *Aviation Week and Space Technology*, pp. 52-55.

British Airways. (2007). *Respecting our world*. Retrieved June 13, 2008, from http://www.britishairways.com/travel/csr-corporate-responsibility/public/

Brown, L. R. (2006). *Plan B 2.0*. London: W.W. Norton.

Campbell, C. J. (2005). *Oil crisis*. Essex, United Kingdom: Multi-Science.

Charlesworth, A. (2008). DHL to cut emissions by 30 percent by 2020. *ClimateBiz*. Retrieved June 13, 2008, from http://www.climatebiz.com/news/2008/04/16/dhl-cut-emissions-30-percent-2020

Daggett, D. L., Henricks, R. C., Walther, R., & Corporan, E. (2007). *Alternative fuels for use in commercial aircraft*. Retrieved July 16, 2008 from http://www.boeing.com/commercial/environment/pdf/alt_fuels.pdf

DFW News Release. (2007). *DFW international airport's environmental success lands EPA recognition—Earns participation in National Environmental Performance Track Program*. Retrieved June 13, 2008, from https://www.dfwairport.com/mediasite/pdf/07/03/070301-epa.pdf.

Energy Information Administration. (2006). *Prime supplier sales volumes*. Retrieved June 13, 2008, from http://tonto.eia.doe.gov/dnav/pet/pet_cons_prim_dcu_nus_a.htm

Environmental Defense. (2007). *How your pollution is calculated*. Retrieved June 13, 2008, from http://www.fightglobalwarming.com/content.cfm?contentid=5043

Esty, D. C., & Winston, A. S. (2006). *Green to gold: How smart companies use environmental strategy to innovate, create value, and build competitive advantage*. New Haven, CT: Yale University Press.

FedEx. (2007). *The environment*. Retrieved June 13, 2008, from http://about.fedex.designcdt.com/corporate_responsibility/the_environment

General Aviation Manufacturers Association. (2006). *Industry facts*. Retrieved June 13, 2008, from http://www.gama.aero/aboutGAMA/industryFacts.php

Graham, M. (2006. May). Emerging markets drive growth. *Air Cargo World*, pp. 21-34.

Hoffman, A. J. (2006). *Getting ahead of the curve: Corporate strategies that address climate change*. Arlington, VA: Pew Center on Global Climate Change.

Hughes, D. (2007, August 19). ATM is no silver bullet. *Aviation Week and Space Technology*, pp. 66-68.

Johnson, G., Shauck, M. E., & Zanin, M. G. (1998, September). *Performance and emissions comparison between avgas, ethanol, and ETBE in an aircraft engine*. Paper presented at the the XII International Symposium on Alcohol Fuels Technology (ISAF XII), Beijing, China.

Kaihla, P. (2007, January/February). Go green. Get rich: Problem #1-Global warming. *Business 2.0*, 68-69.

Kluger, J. (2007, April). Why now? *Time*, 50-60.

Loomis, C., & Buffet, W. (1999). Mr. Buffet on the stock market. *Fortune, 140*(10), 212-220.

McKinnon, J. D., & Meckler, L. (2006, August 9). Bush eschews harsh medicine in treating US oil 'addiction.' *Wall Street Journal*, pp. A1, A9.

National Energy Policy Development Group. (2001). *Reliable, affordable, and environmentally sound energy for America's future*. Washington, DC: US Government Printing Office.

Nelms, D. (2007, April). Oversized ambitions: The outsized air cargo market is growing rapidly. *Air Cargo World*, 16-20.

Niemann, G. (2007). *Big brown: The untold story of UPS*. San Francisco: John Wiley and Sons.

Norris, G. (2007, August 19). Green machines. *Aviation Week and Space Technology*, pp. 62-64.

Ott, J. (2007, August 19). Clearing the air. *Aviation Week and Space Technology*, pp. 54-55.

Pilling, M., & Thompson, J. (2007, February). Carbon storm. *Airline Business*, 54-56.

Port of Seattle. (2006). *Environmental programs*. Retrieved June 13, 2008, from http://www.portseattle.org/community/environment/index.shtml#SEPA

Putzger, I. (2006, June). Can cargo yield profits. *Air Cargo World*, 21-25.

Reuters News Agency. (2007). *Prince Charles cancels ski trip to help save planet*. Retrieved June 13, 2008, from http://uk.reuters.com/article/topNews/idUKL2013566020070120

Rhoades, D. L. (2003). *Evolution of international aviation: Phoenix rising*. Aldershot, United Kingdom: Ashgate.

Shauck, M. E., & Zanin, M. G. (1990). *The first transatlantic flight on ethanol fuel*. Retrieved June 13, 2008, from http://www.wrrc.p2pays.org/ref/35/34813.pdf.

Shauck, M. E., & Zanin, M. G. (2000, June). *The present and future potential of biomass fuels in aviation*. Paper presented at the the First World Biomass Conference, Seville, Spain. Retrieved June 13, 2008, from http://www3.baylor.edu/bias/publications/bomassfuels.pdf.

Stoller, G. (2006, December 19). Concern grows over pollution from jets: Aviation emissions will take off along with worldwide air travel. *USA Today*, pp. 1A-2A.

Stone, B. (2006, November 13). The color of money. *Newsweek*, E10-E15.

Sustainable Aviation. (2006). *Sustainable aviation progress report 2006*. Retrieved June 13, 2008, from http://www.sustainableaviation.co.uk/images/stories/key%20documents/report06final.pdf.

Tertzakian, P. (2006). *A thousand barrels a second: The coming oil break point and the challenges facing an energy dependent world*. New York: McGraw-Hill.

U.S. Department of Energy. (2005). *Biofuels encyclopedia*. Washington, DC: Author.

United Technologies. (2007). *Environment*. Retrieved June 13, 2008, from http://www.utc.com/responsibility/environment.htm

UPS. (2007). *Key performance indicators*. Retrieved June 13, 2008, from http://www.sustainability.ups.com/popup/performance/main.html

CHAPTER 9

CLOSED-LOOP SUPPLY CHAIN MANAGEMENT FOR GLOBAL SUSTAINABILITY

Matthew J. Drake and Mark E. Ferguson

While the focus of traditional supply chain management has been on the forward chain of bringing raw materials and components together to assemble products and distribute them to the end-customers, there is increasing interest on the original equipment manufacturer's part about what happens to the product after the customer receives it. This broader view of supply chain management, termed *closed-loop supply chain management*, includes the customer returns process, the end-of-use options available to the customer, and the options available at the product's final end-of-useful-life. While much of this increase in interest has been driven by firms who are beginning to look seriously at the global environmental footprint of their products (either due to environmental legislation or societal pressure), there are also many proactive companies that view this area as a potential source of long-term competitive advantage. These progressive organizations are adopting a holistic approach in designing their supply chains by incorporating reverse logistics and end-of-life product issues into the initial planning of product design, production, and forward distribution operations. In this chapter, we review the closed-loop practices of several of these firms along with the findings from the academic research in this field.

Global Sustainability Initiatives: New Models and New Approaches
pp. 173–191

With the introduction of advanced connective technologies into business applications in the late 1980s and early 1990s, many firms began to examine their logistics processes with the hope of realizing substantial cost savings while simultaneously improving customer service. In traditional logistics theory, cost reduction and improved service are inversely-related measures. Companies must incur extra costs, often in the form of maintaining excess inventory or capacity, to provide higher levels of customer service. Similarly, a common consequence of reducing inventory levels is customer service degradation. The new connective technology, however, enables firms to collaborate with their suppliers and customers more efficiently and effectively, which allows them to substitute available real-time information for large inventory stocks or safety capacity to improve customer service. The practice of working with external suppliers and customers to meet end-customer requirements is a hallmark of the extension of logistics known as *supply chain management* (SCM).

SCM is primarily concerned with the management and coordination of flows of materials, products, services, information, and financial payments from the initial supplier who mines the raw materials or produces the basic chemical compounds all the way to the final consumer who will use the product or experience the service. Depending on the complexity of the product, there could be hundreds, thousands, or hundreds of thousands of different companies that affect the ability of the supply chain to meet the customers' requirements. In addition, a single firm may play a significant role in hundreds of different supply chains, especially if the firm is a raw material supplier, distributor, or retailer. The dispersion of these firms around the world adds another layer of complexity to the system. There is significant potential for the effects of decisions made in the supply chain for one product to ripple through to other seemingly unrelated supply chains because of the cross-pollination of suppliers and customers in the supply chains for different products. This interconnectedness between supply chains has led several experts to suggest that a more accurate metaphor for the system would be "supply web" rather than the linear-focused "supply chain" (e.g., Gattorna, 2006).

To date, the primary focus of product and materials flow management in SCM is on the "forward" flows from suppliers through the production and physical distribution processes to the end-users. In many, if not all, supply chains, however, there is some degree of reverse flow from buyers back to the suppliers for any of a variety of reasons. These flows could vary from the simple return of new items that were shipped incorrectly in the forward distribution system to products that are collected from users at the end of their useful lives. Every type of flow impacts the profitability of firms in a goods' supply chain, and the decisions that the companies make about the handling, processing, and disposal of these goods can have significant implications for long-term global sustainability. As a result, many firms are starting to incorporate the "reverse" flows of products and materials that exist in their supply chains into the managerial purview of their SCM initiatives.

In this chapter, we discuss the sources of the reverse flows and highlight tactics that can be employed to control these flows effectively. We also detail the practices of some innovative firms that have been able to create value from these reverse flows and have turned this into a competitive advantage in their industries. We conclude the chapter with some strategies that are likely to experience widespread adoption in the next decade and will substantially improve the interaction between the supply chains for manufactured goods and the sustainability of the global environment.

THE GENESIS OF REVERSE FLOWS IN THE SUPPLY CHAIN

The reverse flows in the supply chain originate from a number of sources, and the condition and utility of the materials and products largely depends on the sources of the flow. These sources can be broadly classified into two categories: product returns near the point of sale and end-of-use product returns.

Regardless of their environmental sensibilities, every company that sells products must have an effective strategy for handling product returns. These returns could be the result of the incorrect product being shipped to a customer, the product being of poor quality or being damaged in transit, or a generous returns policy that enables customers to return products within a certain time frame for any reason, including buyer remorse. These flows can represent significant costs for many companies. In the United States, consumer returns of general merchandise are estimated to represent 6% of firms' revenue (Rogers & Tibben-Lembke, 2006), and the average return rate across all industries is an estimated 10-15% and can exceed 40% for catalog and Internet retailers (Horvath, Autry, & Wilcox, 2005). All of the transportation, inspection, and administrative activities associated with processing returns can represent significant costs. Wyld (2004) estimates that logistics costs of managing returns are approximately 4% of total logistics costs, and the total cost of all of these activities can approach $150 per unit. Companies that are able to improve their returns processes can experience a significant contribution to their bottom lines. Because these products are returned soon after their original sale date, they are likely to come back in close-to-original condition (unless they have quality problems or were damaged in transit) and can be resold as "new" or "like new" after very little repair or refurbishing.

There is an additional reverse flow when customers want to dispose of products after the products no longer meet their needs (end-of-use). Because these flows are generated by customers who want to replace or upgrade the products, the condition of the items has a wide degree of variability which can often hinder their usefulness after subsequent processing. In the past, most of these flows terminated at landfills or third-party recycling facilities that had no affiliation to the manufacturers who originally produced the goods. In recent years, however, many manufacturers have taken responsibility for collecting these end-of-use items (or have arranged for private third-party firms to manage the process on their behalf).

The impetus for the active participation of original equipment manufacturers (OEMs) in the management of end-of-use product flows is predominantly a factor of the geographic location of the customer base. The European Union (EU) has adopted legislation in the form of the European Waste Electrical and Electronic Equipment (WEEE) Directive which holds electronic-product OEMs responsible for managing the end-of-life flows of their manufactured goods to prevent these products from populating landfills (Mollenkopf, 2006). The EU focused on electric and electronic equipment due to the proliferation of WEEE products in recent years and the limited existing options for responsible disposal of these goods. The stated objectives of the WEEE Directive are "to improve waste management processes, eliminate hazardous substances, increase recycling capacity, and introduce harmonizing legislation" (McIntyre, 2007, p. 239).

The United States does not have comprehensive producer responsibility legislation comparable to the WEEE Directive in Europe. The U.S. government has gradually increased the stringency of environmental legislation on producers' manufacturing operations and material specifications over the past 3 decades, but (with the exception of a few states imposing regulation) producers' environmental responsibility for the goods currently ends the instant the products are sold (Clift, 2003; Guide, Harrison, & Van Wassenhove, 2003). Because they are not guided by national legislation, U.S. companies must be able to realize some form of value from engaging in end-of-use product management.

This value could be an intangible benefit that comes from enhancing the firm's brand equity. A strong movement among the general public in the United States advocating corporate environmental responsibility has gained significant momentum over the past 5 years. Terms such as "sustainability," "eco-friendly," "carbon-neutral," and "environmental footprint" have crept into the public's vernacular. As a result, many companies have marketed their environmental responsibility initiatives to meet their customers' increasing social requirements. Indeed, it is not outrageous to hypothesize that all companies will have to demonstrate a significant level of environmental responsibility to remain viable in the U.S. market within the next decade. This growing social conscience about corporate environmental responsibility is not limited to the United States. Mollenkopf, Russo, and Frankel (2007) conclude from their analysis of several Italian manufacturers and distributors that the effective management of reverse product flows will necessarily be a part of European firms' corporate social responsibility (CSR) initiatives in the near future.

THE REVERSE SUPPLY CHAIN DECISION ENVIRONMENT

Regardless of the source of the reverse flow, the supplier must have a strategy for handling and possibly processing the returned item. The customer's reason for returning the item largely determines the set of feasible alternatives that is available to the supplier. For example, a product that is returned due to incorrect order fulfillment can likely be returned to the forward chain immediately after a brief inspection. Defective items, on the other hand, may no longer be sold as new items but may be available to enter a secondary market at a reduced price after replacement or repair. Rogers and Tibben-Lembke (1999) identify the following options that suppliers have for returned product disposal, depending on the quality of the returned items received:

- return the product to an upstream supplier;
- resell the product as new;
- sell the product through an outlet store or distributor;
- salvage the product;
- recondition, refurbish, or remanufacture the product and sell it through a secondary market;
- donate the product to charitable organizations;
- reclaim materials from the product;
- recycle the product; or
- send the product to a landfill.

Almost all of the options above yield less unit revenue than selling the product in the primary forward distribution channel. The supplier must also finance an inspection process to assess the condition of the returned products and to determine which of the options above are feasible. If the item is a consumer return of a new product, the supplier will likely need to provide the customer with a replacement item, often shipping the good via expensive expedited transportation to minimize the customer's loss of goodwill due to the return. As Mollenkopf et al. (2007) note, these costs can increase significantly for returns associated with international customers. Product returns also generate a variety of hidden costs including poor space utilization in warehouses and higher taxes because the returned items increase a firm's taxable asset base (Mannella, 2003). When these costs are added to the administrative costs of processing returns, it is easy to see how the total cost of handling returns can approach $150 per unit.

Compared with the flow of products in the forward supply chain, the reverse flows create several unique managerial challenges for suppliers. Table 9.1 provides a comparison between some general characteristics of forward and reverse flows in supply chains. One of the main challenges of the reverse flows is that they are very difficult to forecast accurately and are difficult to track internally once they have been received. This causes problems for inventory planners as returned items are sometimes reabsorbed into inventory counts unexpectedly. The lack of effective forecasting methods can create bottlenecks at the processing centers if unanticipated returns arrive at the same time. Consumer returns also create problems for accounts receivable and cash budgeting because it is likely that customers will be credited for returns that should not have been authorized to maintain lofty customer service requirements. These

Table 9.1.   Comparison of the Characteristics of Forward and Reverse Flows in Supply Chains

Forward Flows in Supply Chains	Reverse Flows in Supply Chains
• Forecasting is relatively straightforward	• Forecasting is more difficult
• Product quality is uniform	• Product quality is varied
• Product packaging is uniform	• Product packaging is varied
• Standardized channel	• Exception-driven channel
• Distribution costs are closely monitored by accounting systems	• Costs are less directly visible
• Marketing methods are well known	• Marketing methods are complicated by several factors
• Importance of speed is recognized	• Speed is often not considered a priority
• Product destination/routing is clear	• Product destination/routing is unclear
• Real-time information is readily available to track product	• Visibility of the flows is less transparent

Source: Tibben-Lembke and Rogers (2002).

unauthorized units also contribute to the firm's inventory control problems (Norek, 2002).

In addition to processing and handling individual returns, suppliers must make a host of strategic and tactical decisions related to the reverse flows in the supply chain. Some additional questions that organizations must answer are as follows:

- Where will returns be processed? At the store? At one centralized distribution center? At every distribution center?
- Should we use a third-party logistics provider to manage our returns processes?
- Under which circumstances will we authorize returns? How will we give credit to our customers for these returned items?
- Will the sale of refurbished and remanufactured items affect our primary market for new goods? Can we take measures to minimize this cannibalization effect?
- What criteria should we use in our inspection process to assess the condition of returned items?
- What is the process for deciding between refurbishing, remanufacturing, dismantling, recycling, or land-filling of the returned items after inspection?

In the next section we discuss several tactics that companies can employ to address these questions and manage the reverse flows in their supply chains more effectively. We also include many practical examples of firms that have achieved success with these methods.

STRATEGIES FOR MANAGING
REVERSE FLOWS IN THE SUPPLY CHAIN

Companies typically view the reverse flows in their supply chains according to a spectrum that defines their goals in managing the process. On the one end of the continuum, the firm views the reverse flows solely as a cost center; thus, firms with this perspective seek only to minimize the cost of processing and handling the returned products. On the other end of the spectrum, the firm views the reverse flows as a value-creating opportunity. This value is often manifested in the company's ability to use the returned product to satisfy demand by either remanufacturing the goods and selling them in a secondary market or using the returned product as a low-cost source of components for the production of new items. These organizations are willing to commit significant financial and human resources to coordinating the reverse flows with the goal of capturing value from the process, ultimately creating a sustainable competitive advantage in the marketplace. In practice, most firms fall somewhere in the interior of the spectrum, reducing costs as much as possible while taking advantage of some of the value-creating opportunities inherent in the reverse product flows.

Our discussion of strategies for managing the closed-loop supply chain to reduce processing and handling costs or to add value (or both!) follows the decision model developed by Guide, Pentico, and Jayaraman (2001) and Guide and Pentico (2003). The major advantage of this model is that its explicit focus is on developing the most profitable closed-loop supply chain plan while requiring very few assumptions about the external factors and parameters that affect the flows.

Product Acquisition

The first stage of the model concerns the characteristics of the reverse flows including the volume, timing, and quality of the returned product and the firm's visibility to the acquisition process. Because the reverse flows are almost always initialized by the customer, firms experience a great degree of variability in the amount of returned product they receive, the time at which they receive the product, and the quality of the product when it is received. As we discussed earlier, suppliers receive products from their customers for a number of reasons. Goods returned in response to an incorrect initial shipment are likely to be of very high quality, whereas products returned because they were of poor quality or were damaged in transit are obviously in worse condition. End-of-life product returns run the gamut of quality. The unit may be fully operational, but the customer may wish to dispose of it to upgrade to a newer model with enhanced features. On the other hand, the good could truly be at the end of its useful life, prompting consumer disposal.

The condition of the returned product largely dictates its value to the supplier. Higher-quality goods can be directed toward the more lucrative disposal streams such as remanufacturing or refurbishing. Lower-quality goods, on the other hand, present limited opportunities for the supplier to capture value through their re-use. These goods are likely to be relegated to the materials reclamation, recycling, or landfill disposal streams.

Companies have two main options in managing their product acquisition process: a waste-stream system and a market-driven system (Guide et al., 2001). A waste-stream system is a passive strategy that uses the fewest number of resources possible. The firm simply accepts the products that the customers decide to return without doing anything to influence the customers' behavior. Companies solely trying to minimize the costs of managing the reverse flows would likely employ this strategy. In contrast, firms seeking to capture some value from their reverse flows have begun to use market-driven mechanisms that attempt to influence the customers' decisions to return products to the supplier.

These market incentives can take a variety of forms including cash deposits, leases, and trade-in allowances that are applicable toward the purchase of new products. Cash deposits are often applied to short-term-use products such as beer kegs and soft drink bottles and cans. Leases are primarily used for capital equipment such as machinery and computers. Trade-in allowances have been used by automobile dealers for many years. Ferguson and Souza (2007) analyze the impact of trade-in rebates on a firm's ability to practice perfect price discrimination for semidurable goods in the presence of a secondary market for remanufactured goods.

Regardless of the firm's focus on capturing value from their reverse flows, the company can improve the efficiency of its returns-management process by introducing automation. This technology adds much-needed visibility to the incoming products as well as the ability to track their status while they are being processed. These capabilities enable the inventory planners to regain the balance that is normally disrupted by the returned units. Automation can also limit the amount of expensive labor resources traditionally devoted to the returns process. Labor can be saved in scheduling the pickup of returned items and the delivery of their replacements, staffing call centers dedicated to handling customer inquiries about returns, reducing the amount of duplicate data entry, and inspecting the condition of the returned items. An automated returns process can also help to maximize adherence to the organization's standard procedures and regulations for accepting and processing returns (Norek, 2002).

Many firms have realized significant efficiencies by adding automation to their returns management processes. Ashford.com, an online gift retailer, used technology to reduce the amount of labor required to process each return by approximately 70%. Ashford was also able to simplify their returns process, thereby reducing the number of errors that they incurred while handling returns. PeoplePC, a company that bundles complete computer systems with Internet service, implemented a third-party returns management system which has reduced the cost of processing and handling returns by 75%. An interesting beneficial byproduct of implementing this system is that the data collected and the added visibility of the in-process returns have increased the accuracy of PeoplePC's financial reporting (Norek, 2002).

Of course, there is a limit to the efficiencies that an organization can capture by utilizing technology in managing the reverse flows in the supply chain. To reduce the cost of processing and handling returns further, the firm must focus on reducing the *number* of items returned soon after their original sale (not necessarily the end-of-life products that they receive). The first way to curb the number of returns received is to apply the firm's established returns authorization policy consistently. If this policy is developed appropriately, a larger proportion of the goods received will exhibit the characteristics that qualify them for the more-desirable disposal streams (such as using the goods to satisfy new demand or selling the goods in "like-new" condition after minimal repackaging and retouching).

The firm could also consider the impact of its current supply chain contracting mechanisms on the volume of returns that are generated. (See Tsay, Nahmias, & Agrawal [1999] for a comprehensive review of the literature about supply chain contracting.) If the firm currently uses a buy-back contract in which the buyer is able to return all or part of an order if unsold items remain at the end of the selling season, there will often be a significant number of returns due to the buyer's tendency to overorder. The seller could instead utilize a revenue-sharing contract which achieves an equivalent level of supply chain coordination and does not incorporate buyer returns. The majority of supply chain contracting mechanisms do not consider the impact of product returns. One exception is the target rebate contract developed by Ferguson, Guide, and Souza (2006), which seeks to minimize the number of units that are returned due to lack of effort on the retailer's part on better matching the customer's needs with the right product and not because the products have any functional or cosmetic defects.

Another effective way to reduce the number of product returns is to eliminate the causes of consumer returns and to satisfy the customers' expectations completely with the initial delivery of the item. A firm can approach this lofty operational goal by improving the quality of all processes—from product design to manufacturing and distribution to customer service. Philips Consumer Electronics was able to reduce its annual consumer returns by more than $100 million by making their products easier to use, revamping its after-purchase service, and consistently enforcing company return policies (Sciarotta, 2003). Initial customer satisfaction can be increased by implementing established quality programs such as Total Quality Management (TQM) or Six Sigma, but quality can also be improved by realigning the firm's internal performance metrics. Focusing on the "perfect order fulfillment" metric to assess the performance of the distribution process, for example, rather than the traditional fill rate measure can potentially reduce the number of product returns. Perfect order fulfillment ensures that all facets of the customer's order are delivered according to the desired specifications to signify acceptable performance. Presutti and Mawhinney (2007) develop a hierarchy for adopting additional performance metrics for supply chain processes that support perfect order fulfillment.

Operational Planning and Costing

After the products populating the reverse flows have been acquired, the organization must have a strategy for processing the item and for identifying the best option (e.g., remanufacturing, material reclamation, recycling, landfill, etc.) for each individual unit. As previously mentioned, the feasible set of options available for each returned item is largely dependent on the condition of the item when it is received. Thus, quality inspection is an essential initial phase of the closed-loop supply chain process upon product receipt.

The first operational question that suppliers must answer concerns the location of the collection and inspection processes for the returned items. These processes could take place at a central store or distribution center, which allows the firm to take advantage of scale economies; or it could be done at each individual retail store or local distribution center, which provides the supplier with information about a product's condition faster than the centralized system does. The time-value of returned items is often ignored in practice, but it can have a significant effect on the value that a supplier can extract from its reverse product flows.

The flow times of the return and remanufacturing processes are especially crucial for products with short life cycles. Firms should pay special attention to the amount of time that elapses from when these products arrive at a collection facility to when they are ready to be either resold in the primary market or sold in the secondary market after remanufacturing. Blackburn, Guide, Souza, and Van Wassenhove (2004) estimate that short-life-cycle consumer electronics items such as PCs can lose more than 1% of their value weekly, and this rate accelerates as the item approaches the end of its useful life. An item such as refurbished Hewlett-Packard notebooks experience an average processing delay of 4.3 months (or 18 weeks) before they are available for sale in the secondary market. It follows that they have lost approximately 20% of the initial value they possessed at the point of collection by the time they reach the market (Guide, Muyldermans, & Van Wassenhove, 2005). Thus, delays in the logistics network can severely erode suppliers' ability to capture value from their reverse supply chain flows, especially in distribution channels for products with short life cycles.

Firms facing time-sensitive returns can likely benefit significantly from utilizing the principles of "preponement," proposed by Blackburn et al.

(2004), to design a responsive reverse logistics network. The major goal of preponement is to inspect and verify returned item's condition as soon as possible after collection to quickly identify the best option for each particular unit. This minimizes the amount of time that the high-value returns—units designated to be restocked or refurbished—spend in the reverse logistics network and makes these items available for sale as soon as possible. Conducting the inspection directly at the collection point creates the most responsive reverse logistics network. Krikke (2001) provides a general reverse logistics network design model appropriate for products whose value has little time sensitivity. A variety of technological applications such as data loggers that are built directly into the products themselves can often facilitate an inexpensive preponement strategy. Employees at Bosch Tools' facilities, for example, use data loggers to quickly assess the maximum speed at which each unit has been operated, a factor that affects the unit's ability to be refurbished or remanufactured profitably.

It is likely that products that are returned soon after their initial shipment to the customer can be reintroduced into the forward distribution channel as new products after a minimal amount of refurbishing. This type of return usually occurs as the result of an order-picking error at the distribution center or as a common byproduct of Internet commerce in which customers order multiple sizes or styles of an item with the intention of keeping only one of the units and returning the rest that either do not fit or do not meet their style preferences.

L.L. Bean, a major outdoor clothing and accessory retailer that was founded in 1911 and is known for its excellent customer service, handles its consumer returns at a dedicated 135,000-square-foot reverse logistics facility. The company's generous returns policy of allowing a customer to return any product for any reason contributes to its annual return volume of 6 million units (out of a total 48 million units shipped in the forward channel). Reverse logistics managers are more than willing to have workers spend 5 minutes refurbishing a returned shirt if that means that it can be sold as a new item, yielding the maximum possible revenue. Recently L.L. Bean updated its information systems in the reverse logistics center to link the return processing operation with the forward order processing system. This linkage allows the firm to fulfill new customer orders directly from recently-processed returns (if they are available) without having to readmit the returns into the forward inventory. Because L.L. Bean receives new orders for over 50% of their returned items within 48 hours of their arrival, the company stands to realize tremendous inventory turnover benefits from the ability to satisfy new demand directly from its pool of customer returns (Johnson, 2006).

Of course, products that are returned due to initial quality defects or damage in transit cannot usually satisfy the strict governmental requirements of products that are sold as new items, even after substantial refurbishing. These items, along with end-of-use returns, are often routed to the following streams, listed in decreasing order of value to the supplier: remanufacturing or refurbishing for secondary-market sale, materials reclamation or dismantling, recycling, and depositing in landfills. The supplier often transfers the product to a third-party processing firm in the latter two disposal streams, which concludes its role in the product's reverse supply chain.

A growing number of suppliers, who have identified their reverse logistics competencies as a potential source of competitive advantage, have developed in-house remanufacturing and disassembly operations to capture value from their reverse flows. Most of these companies operate in industries from which consumers are willing to purchase remanufactured units at significant prices. Hewlett-Packard, for example, recognized that 50-70% of their used notebooks could be remanufactured in-house instead of via a third-party company. This internal remanufacturing operation resulted in an estimated monthly savings of $147,000 (Guide et al., 2005). IBM designed its return network to be a source of spare parts for its after-sales service and repair operations and has been able to save several million U.S. dollars annually by decreasing the average cost of spare parts (Fleischmann, van Nunen, & Grave, 2003). Schultmann, Engels, and Rentz (2003) describe a company that went one step further by designing a reverse logistics network in which approximately 100% of the collected used batteries could be recycled for use in newly-manufactured items such as steel construction products.

Several factors complicate manufacturing planning strategies for disassembly and remanufacturing operations. Unlike traditional production planning environments, the supply of returned products delegated to these streams and, thus, made available for use in these operations is highly variable. Adding to the complexity is that even within a given set of items marked for disassembly or remanufacturing, the quality and value potential is not necessarily homogeneous from product to product. Gupta and Veerakamolmal (2001) develop an aggregate planning model that determines the number of end-of-life products to disassemble to supply enough components to a remanufacturing process while minimizing the acquisition and disposal costs for excess products and components. Ferguson, Guide, Koca, and Souza (2007) consider the production planning problem for a remanufacturing firm whose returns can be classified according to several quality grading levels. Because remanufacturing costs decrease as the quality of the returned products increase, they find that firms can capture substantial value by dividing the returns into no more than five quality grade levels instead of treating the returns as homogeneous for production planning purposes.

If a company plans to include disassembly and remanufacturing operations, the firm's design engineers should consider these end-of-life processes when generating the initial product design and specifications. Significant operational cost savings are possible if the engineers design the product so that workers can easily assess the condition of the product and to facilitate disassembly of the unit when it is returned at the end of its useful life. Krikke, Bloemhof-Ruwaard, and Van Wassenhove (2003) examine the interaction between the initial product design and the closed-loop supply chain network design for refrigerators. Their model suggests that system performance is maximized when the product is designed such that its components can be reused again and again rather than relying on new raw material and component production.

Pricing and Demand Management

As the examples above suggest, a supplier can capture significant value from its disassembly operations by using the components reclaimed from these processes as a source of raw materials or spare parts. Regardless of the efficiency of a supplier's remanufacturing operations, however, the ultimate value a firm can realize from these operations is predicated on the existence of a viable secondary market for the remanufactured goods. Not-for-profit organizations that receive donated goods are also dependent on the existence of a viable secondary market to convert these goods into funds that can be used to help their beneficiaries; see Reyes and Meade (2006) for a transshipment model that maximizes the revenue a not-for-profit organization realizes from its donations.

An interesting example of this principle is found in the market for retreaded tires. Many companies provide retreading services for truck tires, but very few perform the same operations on passenger-car tires. The main reason is that commercial trucking companies have relied on retreads for low-cost replacement tires for decades, and typically pay for tires through a service arrangement based on a per-mile fee. Passenger-car drivers, however, are less educated about the quality of retreaded tires and would rather pay extra for new tires instead of buying retreads. As a result of the lack of a viable secondary market, retreading operations for passenger-car tires are practically nonexistent.

In industries that do enjoy a viable secondary market for remanufactured products, firms are cognizant of the potential for cannibalization to occur between their new products and remanufactured items. The magnitude of the cannibalization effect is largely dependent on the attitudes of the consumers in the market. Firms should be most concerned about cannibalization when the perceived difference between new and remanufactured items is small; in the consumers' eyes, the goods are almost perfect substitutes. The coupling of used cars with extended warranties along with the reduction in the average age of used cars on the market has leveled the new- and used-car markets for some consumers.

A growing body of literature is considering the market characteristics for remanufactured products as well as the interaction between the markets for new and remanufactured goods. Bayindir, Erkip, and Gullu (2007) develop a decision-support model that is helpful in estimating the profitability of a remanufacturing operation in a market that includes consumer substitution between new and remanufactured products. Oraiopoulos, Ferguson, and Toktay (2007) model an OEM's incentives to foster or to eliminate a secondary market for its remanufactured goods as a function of the OEM's competitive position in the market, the main product characteristics, and consumer preferences. They determine the optimal relicensing fee (fees required in the IT market before a product can be transferred between customers) the OEM should offer in the secondary market to maximize overall profitability. Savaskan and Van Wassenhove (2006) examine the impact of a supplier's collection network structure (either direct or indirect through retailers) and pricing decisions in the forward distribution channel on total supply chain performance. They highlight the importance of coordinating forward- and reverse-channel decisions to maximize the overall performance of the closed-loop supply chain.

THE NEXT FRONTIER OF
CLOSED-LOOP SUPPLY CHAIN MANAGEMENT

The strategies discussed thus far are useful to reduce the costs of managing the reverse supply chain flows, and in some instances they can create value for suppliers and can even become a source of competitive advantage. From the long-term, systems point of view of society as a whole, all of these practices may still be suboptimal. The remanufacturing of used products and the reuse of their components in the production of new items does not necessarily guarantee a sustainable society because these practices ignore the consumption part of the global economy. Regardless of the methods employed by manufacturers to guide products to renewable waste streams, scholars such as Dobers and Strannegard (2005) and Schaefer and Crane (2005) posit that a sustainable society is only possible if global per-capita consumption decreases. Many companies' traditional business models, however, are based on increasing consumption levels to attain higher levels of profitability. Clearly, firms will only participate in consumption-reduction efforts if they can find other ways to provide value to their customers.

Several progressive organizations have identified opportunities to reduce consumption of their products while maintaining and even enhancing their profitability by offering services in addition to their products. McGriff Treading Company implemented a gain-sharing-based service contract with its third-party fleet operators to reduce overall tire consumption by providing the operators with access to the expertise of McGriff's personnel about their products (Yadav, Miller, Schmidt, & Drake, 2003). Chrysler worked closely with two of its suppliers to maintain the suppliers' profitability while decreasing Chrysler's consumption of their products. Gage Products, a producer of chemical blends for automobile painting processes, offered a new, environmentally friendly product that cleans the paint circulation process in automobile assembly plants and enables Chrysler to purchase lower quantities of Gage's chemical blends. Gage also acted as a consultant in teaching Chrysler employees how to use less cleaning solution in the paint processes. PPG placed its employees on-site at the Chrysler plants to manage inventory of PPG paint and to assist Chrysler in monitoring regulatory compliance. To provide PPG with adequate compensation for the use of their employees and to ensure incentive alignment between the two companies, PPG and Chrysler implemented a gain-sharing contract similar to the one used by McGriff. Xerox, a company best known for its copiers, introduced a new Office Document Assessment (ODA) consulting tool to its customers such as United Health Services Hospitals (UHSH) of Binghamton, NY. This tool assesses the total cost of various documentation processes, and it often suggests that significant cost savings could be captured by consolidating the number of document devices (e.g., printers and copiers) that an organization employs. The recommendations from the ODA tool generated $60,000 in annual savings for UHSH. Obviously, consolidation would reduce the amount of paper and toner that the company consumes, reducing the firm's eco-footprint. Xerox's service division generated 22% of the company's overall sales revenue in 2005, and Xerox estimates that the size of the market for its services will approach $20 billion in the future (Rothenburg, 2007).

Firms seeking to shift a significant portion of their sales efforts from products to services face several major challenges. The biggest issue is often the attitude of their internal sales personnel. Salespeople may feel that their compensation basis or even their jobs are threatened by this relative de-emphasis on product sales. There may also be significant resistance from the customers' workforce to suggestions from the supplier's service personnel for altering their traditional daily routine. They may not understand how the supplier's suggestions will add value to their organizations' processes; at worst, they may mistrust the supplier's motivation and undertake measures to undermine the successful implementation of the supplier's recommendations. As several of the examples above suggest, the suppliers that have depended largely on product sales in the past may need to redesign the contracts that they use with their customers to maintain their profit levels while selling fewer products.

CONCLUSIONS AND FUTURE OPPORTUNITIES

Whether they are motivated by governmental regulatory pressure, the potential for new sources of competitive advantage, or principles of corporate social responsibility, an increasing number of companies are likely to consider the environmental impact of their products and their supply chain processes in the future. Progressive organizations should adopt a holistic approach in designing their supply chains by incorporating reverse logistics and end-of-life product issues into the initial planning of product design, production, and forward distribution operations. Firms may also be able to alter their product portfolio to include more services to generate revenue while concurrently reducing consumption levels. These networks, which adopt a closed-loop perspective by considering both forward and reverse flows in their initial design, have the most potential for creating value and long-term competitive advantages for the organization, thereby creating a win-win scenario with the environment and society as a whole. It is no coincidence that this is the true definition of business sustainability; closed-loop supply chain planning helps organizations do their part toward building a sustainable global society while simultaneously ensuring the firm's long-term presence in the global market.

REFERENCES

Bayindir, Z. P., Erkip, N., & Gullu, R. (2007). Assessing the benefits of remanufacturing option under one-way substitution and capacity constraint. *Computers and Operations Research, 34*(2), 487-514.

Blackburn, J. D., Guide, V. D. R., Jr., Souza, G. C., & Van Wassenhove, L. N. (2004). Reverse supply chain for commercial returns. *California Management Review, 46*(2), 6-22.

Clift, R. (2003). Metrics for supply chain sustainability. *Clean Technology and Environmental Policy, 5*, 240-247.

Dobers, P., & Strannegard, L. (2005). Design, lifestyles, and sustainability: Aesthetic consumption in a world of abundance. *Business Strategy and the Environment, 14*, 324-336.

Ferguson, M. E., Guide, V. D. R., Jr., Koca, E., & Souza, G. C. (2007). *The value of quality grading in remanufacturing* (Working paper). Atlanta, GA: Georgia Institute of Technology College of Management.

Ferguson, M. E., Guide, V. D. R., Jr., & Souza, G. C. (2006). Supply chain coordination for false failure returns. *Manufacturing & Service Operations Management, 8*(4), 376-393.

Ferguson, M. E., & Souza, G. C. (2007). *Trade-in rebates for price discrimination or product recovery* (Working paper). Atlanta, GA: Georgia Institute of Technology College of Management.

Fleischmann, M., van Nunen, J. A. E. E., & Grave, B. (2003). Integrating closed-loop supply chains and spare-parts management at IBM. *Interfaces, 33*(6), 44-56.

Gattorna, J. (2006). Supply chains are the business. *Supply Chain Management Review, 10*(7), 42-49.

Guide, V. D. R., Jr., Harrison, T. P., & Van Wassenhove, L. N. (2003). The challenge of closed-loop supply chains. *Interfaces, 33*(6), 3-6.

Guide, V. D. R., Jr., Muyldermans, L., & Van Wassenhove, L. N. (2005). Hewlett-Packard company unlocks the value potential for time-sensitive returns. *Interfaces, 35*(4), 281-293.

Guide, V. D. R., Jr., & Pentico, D. W. (2003). A hierarchical decision model for re-manufacturing and re-use. *International Journal of Logistics: Research and Applications, 6*(1-2), 29-35.

Guide, V. D. R., Jr., Pentico, D. W., & Jayaraman, V. (2001). A framework for hierarchical planning and control for remanufacturing. In J. Sarkis (Ed.), *Greener manufacturing and operations* (pp. 273-287). Sheffield, United Kingdom: Greenleaf.

Gupta, S. M., & Veerakamolmal, P. (2001). Aggregate planning for end-of-life products. In J. Sarkis (Ed.), *Greener manufacturing and operations* (pp. 205-222). Sheffield, United Kingdom: Greenleaf.

Horvath, P. A., Autry, C. W., & Wilcox, W. E. (2005). Liquidity implications of reverse logistics for retailers: A Markov chain approach. *Journal of Retailing, 81*(3), 191-203.

Johnson, J. R. (2006). The returns of an American icon. *DC Velocity, 4*(12), 47-50.

Krikke, H. (2001). Recovery strategies and reverse logistics network design. In J. Sarkis (Ed.), *Greener manufacturing and operations* (pp. 256-272). Sheffield, United Kingdom: Greenleaf.

Krikke, H., Bloemhof-Ruwaard, J., & Van Wassenhove, L. N. (2003). Concurrent product and closed-loop supply chain design with an application to refrigerators. *International Journal of Production Research, 41*(16), 3689-3719.

Mannella, M. (2003). What your returns are telling you. *APICS—The Performance Advantage, 13*, 38-44.

McIntyre, K. (2007). Delivering sustainability through supply chain management. In D. Waters (Ed.), *Global logistics* (5 ed., pp. 238-252). London: Kogan Page.

Mollenkopf, D. (2006). Environmental sustainability: Examining the case for environmentally-sustainable supply chains. *CSCMP Explores..., 3*(3), 1-15.

Mollenkopf, D., Russo, I., & Frankel, R. (2007). The returns management process in supply chain strategy. *International Journal of Physical Distribution and Logistics Management, 37*(7), 568-592.

Norek, C. D. (2002). Returns management: Making order out of chaos. *Supply Chain Management Review, 6*(3), 34-42.

Oriaopoulos, N., Ferguson, M. E., & Toktay, L. B. (2007). *Relicensing as a secondary market strategy* (Working paper). Atlanta, GA: Georgia Institute of Technology College of Management.

Presutti, W. D., Jr., & Mawhinney, J. R. (2007). The supply chain-finance link. *Supply Chain Management Review 11*(6), 32-38.

Reyes, P. M., & Meade, L. M. (2006). Improving reverse supply chain operational performance: A transshipment application study for not-for-profit organizations. *Journal of Supply Chain Management, 42*(1), 38-48.

Rogers, D. S., & Tibben-Lembke, R. S. (1999). *Going backwards: Reverse logistics trends and practices*. Pittsburgh, PA: Reverse Logistics Executive Council Press.

Rogers, D. S., & Tibben-Lembke, R. S. (2006). Returns management and reverse logistics for competitive advantage. *CSCMP Explores..., 3*(1), 1-16.

Rothenburg, S. (2007). Sustainability through servicing. *Sloan Management Review, 48*(2), 83-91.

Savaskan, R. C., & Van Wassenhove, L. N. (2006). Reverse channel design: The case of competing retailers. *Management Science, 52*(1), 1-14.

Schaefer, A., & Crane, A. (2005). Addressing sustainability and consumption. *Journal of Macromarketing, 25*(1), 76-92.

Schultmann, F., Engels, B., & Rentz, O. (2003). Closed-loop supply chains for spent batteries. *Interfaces, 33*(6), 57-71.

Sciarotta, T. (2003). How Philips reduced returns. *Supply Chain Management Review, 8*(6), 32-38.

Tibben-Lembke, R. S., & Rogers, D. S. (2002). Differences between forward and reverse logistics in a retail environment. *Supply Chain Management: An International Journal, 7*(5), 271-282.

Tsay, A. A., Nahmias, S., & Agrawal, N. (1999). Modeling supply chain contracts: A review. In S. Tayur, R. Ganeshan, & M. Magazine (Eds.), *Quantitative methods for supply chain management* (pp. 300-336). Norwell, MA: Kluwer Academic.

Wyld, D. C. (2004). Reverse potential. *APICS—The Performance Advantage, 14*(2), 26-32.

Yadav, P., Miller, D. M., Schmidt, C. P., & Drake, R. (2003). McGriff Treading Company implements service contracts with shared savings. *Interfaces, 33*(6), 18-29.

CHAPTER 10

CONSTRUCTION AND DEMOLITION DEBRIS RECYCLING FOR SUSTAINABLE LOCAL ECONOMIC DEVELOPMENT

Lynn M. Patterson

Local economic development practice has historically operated independently from the sustainability movement. Local economic development
agencies' main concern has been to increase economic growth. There has
been a recent shift in policy and practice for some agencies to broaden their
economic development goals to include equity and environmental considerations. One area of local economic development practice that satisfies the
tenets of sustainability is the support for construction and demolition
(C&D) debris recycling. C&D debris makes up almost half of the landfill-
destined waste stream. For cities and counties that have large redevelopment projects generating significant volumes of C&D debris or those that
have to meet recycling goals, recycling C&D debris is a "low-hanging fruit"
solution. Using data from a national survey of local economic development
agencies, this chapter explores the ways in which local economic development agencies have specifically supported the C&D debris recycling indus-

Global Sustainability Initiatives: New Models and New Approaches
pp. 193–210

try. This chapter has 3 objectives. First, the chapter offers the role and merits of C&D recycling as a sustainable industry. Second, it presents local economic development perceptions and the specific activities in which the agencies have participated to support the industry. Finally, it concludes with a brief discussion on the global opportunities of C&D recycling.

As local economic development agencies seek out new avenues to increase their communities' competitiveness, they are turning to new development models and industries—including those that support sustainability. Traditionally, local economic development agencies have been interested in increasing economic activity at almost any cost. Recently, however, local economic development agencies are showing an interest in alternative development schemes. One of these is recycling-based economic development.

For local economic development agencies, recycling-based development serves two purposes. First, it allows local economic development agencies to meet their traditional goals of wealth and job creation. Second, the ancillary benefits of recycling-based development address the sustainable local economic development goals of environmental responsibility and social equity. This chapter investigates how local economic development agencies support one sector of recycling-based economic development, construction and demolition (C&D) recycling, first, to satisfy their traditional goal of increased economic activity, and second, to take advantage of the broader social and environmental impacts. In addition to presenting the various activities used to support C&D recycling, this chapter reviews how local economic development agency attitudes and knowledge of the industry may influence this support.

Interest in recycling-based development stems from the industrial ecology model in which waste is a valuable commodity in the free market. In this model, industries use waste as inputs for production rather than virgin materials. Firms that primarily utilize raw materials deemed as "waste" or "debris" are classified as waste-based or recycling-based businesses. These businesses are gaining more attention in the local economic development field as research and publications reveal the extent to which the industry contributes to local economies. For example, a 2001 National Recycling Coalition study estimated the recycling and remanufacturing industries represented over 56,000 establishments, employed over 1 million people, and generated over $236 million in annual revenue (Beck, 2001). These industries also support above average wages for their workforce. Since the 2001 study was published, the recycling industry economy has grown and likely increased its economic impact.

The simple collection and sorting of recyclable materials scratches only the surface of the economic development potential of this industry. Economic impacts increase fourfold with the (re-)manufacture of the recovered materials (Beck, 2001; California Integrated Waste Management Board, 2004; Waste to Work Partnership, 2002). The manufacturing processes not only add value to the recovered materials (e.g., salvaged lumber into furniture), but also provide higher wage jobs and greater capital investment for facilities and equipment. Nationally, indirect impacts from the recycling and remanufacturing industries include approximately 1.4 million jobs and $173 billion in revenue (Beck, 2001). Ancillary benefits of recycling-based industries include: reducing the need for additional landfill or incinerator capacity, lower emissions from those facilities, reduced groundwater pollution from landfill leachate, and reduced need for virgin materials (Kane, 2004; Leigh & Realff, 2003). Recycled products, when manufactured domestically, have the ability to compete with imports as raw material extraction, and transportation costs and tariffs can be avoided. Furthermore, Ackerman and Mirza (2001) suggest that communities with significant amounts of waste material and availability of low-wage labor can use recycling-based development as a comparative advantage.

Still, the recycling industry has long battled the perception that it is primarily an environmental activity. Unfortunately, many local economic developers' prevailing attitude is one that perceives recycling as an environmental cause, "service," or the "right thing to do" (e.g., Kelley, 2006; Norton, 2006). Ewadinger and Mouw (2005) offer, "in an ideal world, we would measure a recycling company's success based on its positive environmental impact. In a market-based economy, however, success is measured by a company's ability to start-up, grow, and remain financially solvent" (p. 27). Without witnessing a strong preexisting market to absorb and process the salvaged goods, local economic development agencies may be hesitant to invest their energies in or target recycling as an industry.

The attitudes toward recycling-based development and knowledge of the industry and related conditions may have an impact on local economic development agency support for the recycling industry. Limited knowledge about an industry translates into misunderstanding and oversight of the potential economic benefit to the community.

A caveat for recycling-based development that must be mentioned is the concern over environmental justice with the location of recycling facilities (Ackerman & Mirza, 2001; Bowen & Wells, 2002; Hattam, 2003; Pellow, 2002). If not properly located, collection, recycling, and processing facilities may bring unwanted noise, dust, and traffic into an area. Local economic development agencies must therefore be aware that despite good intentions, the environmental justice issue is a constant concern and must be addressed in policy and program implementation.

A number of local economic development agencies do target the recycling industry to help their communities become more competitive. These agencies use their economic development arsenal (discussed later) to reduce the barriers faced by the recycling industry. For instance, economic development incentives would help to overcome the gap mentioned by Ackerman and Mirza (2001) between strict economic success/failure models and the more robust measure of environmental responsibility or social equity. Specific economic development tools vary by agency based on the conditions faced in each agency's region. Though these tools are hallmarks of traditional local economic development strategies, they are adapted to fit the needs of the recycling industry.

CONSTRUCTION AND DEMOLITION RECYCLING

Stimulating additional local economic development agency interest in the potential economic benefit of recycling is an understanding that the recycling industry is comprised of much more than aluminum cans, plastic bottles, and newspaper. In cities such as Baltimore, Atlanta, Detroit, Philadelphia, Flint, Albany, and New York, large redevelopment projects designed to rid urban blight involve the demolition of thousands of buildings ("County to Seek Flint Demolitions," 2001; Liquori, 2004; Pagano & Bowman, 2000; Whitman & McCoy, 2000). These buildings generate enormous amounts of demolition debris straining landfill capacity and creating economic leakages. Recycling of construction and demolition debris poses an attractive economic development opportunity.

In addition to private redevelopment efforts, local economic development agencies participate in large-scale, publicly initiated redevelopment projects. Local governments earmark tens of millions of dollars to demolish thousands of these buildings (e.g., Baltimore 5000 Project, Genesee County Land Bank Demolition Program, and the Philadelphia Neighborhood Transformation Initiative). These funds send the demolition debris,[1] classified as waste material, to landfills. While removal of these structures allows for much-needed new investment in decaying urban cores, communities must construct new facilities when landfill space is near capacity. Funding these new facilities drains financial resources; developing these landfills may constitute underutilization of land resources; and locating proper hazardous waste disposal sites can be costly. Recycling this material can support revenue generation within the community as well as provide cost savings for local governments.

For communities engaged in redevelopment projects, C&D recycling can address equity, environmental, and traditional local economic development issues. C&D recycling programs often employ at-risk or hard-to-employ persons, providing them with skills training and apprenticeships (Yost, 1999). Many C&D recycling programs were formed to address workforce development in disadvantaged communities (see Leigh & Patterson, 2004: Hartford Stowe Village, Washington, D.C. Ivy City/Trinidad Project, and The ReUse People). As discussed earlier, C&D recycling reduces landfill-related environmental problems and the need for virgin resources. As part of the recycling-based industry, C&D recycling jobs have higher wages than landfill-related jobs and average manufacturing job wages (Beck, 2001).

In total, C&D debris makes up 45% of landfill destined waste per year. Within the waste stream, demolition waste accounts for 48%, renovations 44%, and new construction 8% (U.S. Environmental Protection Agency, 1998). C&D recycling takes materials that would be otherwise destined for the landfill and creates new products through salvage and reuse, remanufacture, or reconstitution of the original materials. The most regularly recycled materials are wood, brick, asphalt, concrete, and gypsum. Additional items salvaged can be resold at a discount or as high-end materials (Leigh & Patterson, 2004).

The national recycling rate of C&D debris a decade ago was estimated between 20 and 30% (U.S. Environmental Protection Agency, 1998). In certain projects, C&D recycling has accelerated since then, as green building projects have demonstrated higher potential recycling rates, upwards from 70% (Freymann & Tessicini, 2003; Ludwig, 2003; Triangle J Council of Governments, 1995; U.S. Environmental Protection Agency, 2000). While many C&D materials are suitable for recycling, the C&D recycling industry faces many challenges in industry development and maturation. Among these challenges are: subsidies for virgin materials, low landfill tipping fees, apathy toward waste generation, labor intensive processes, weak or non-existent markets, and barriers to entry for recycling businesses all stymie the growth of the industry at large (California Integrated Waste Management Board, 2004; Discovery Economic Consulting, 2001; National Association of Home Builders Research Center, 2001).

While some of these barriers extend beyond the scope of what many local economic development agencies can influence, the identification of these barriers offers local economic development agencies and other government agencies specific policy and market intervention opportunities to alleviate the problems that hinder C&D recycling. For example, one of the market deterrents for C&D recycling is the increased labor-intensive process per ton of material for recycling versus disposal. Increased labor costs can drive up recovery costs. The National Association of Demolition Contractors estimates that the recovery rate for concrete, the largest component for demolition sites, is 75 to 85% for private demolition projects, while only 20 to 30% of debris is recycled for public projects. NADC suggests that the reason for lower recovery rates is higher average wage rates required at public sector projects (Fox, Zachary, & Swarbrick, 1998). Public sector projects require contractors on federal projects to pay prevailing wages (Leigh & Patterson, 2004). While the initial cost of the recovery may have increased, larger economic development goals of job creation and workforce training are satisfied.

Local economic development agencies often use incentives to entice business development. If addressed to the C&D recycling sector, these incentives can offset the undervaluation of salvaged materials, the underpricing of transporting and land-filling these goods, the underpricing of natural resources and energy used to extract and process virgin materials, and the cost of labor in salvaging material (Discovery Economic Consulting, n.d.). Many of the incentive policies address land developers and businesses directly (e.g., demolition permit fees, landfill taxes, recycling, or diversion rebates). While these are effective means of transforming the market, the demand for goods through the development of the C&D recycling industry is also important. For example, demolition permit fees and environmental fees discourage land-filling of C&D debris, but they do not directly support the industry development side.

TRADITIONAL LOCAL ECONOMIC DEVELOPMENT ACTIVITIES

Historically, local economic development practice has operated independently, and with little acknowledgement of the concept of sustainability. Whereas sustainability implies the balance between economic vitality, environmental responsibility, and social equity, the majority of local economic development activity concentrates on one aspect—economic vitality through wealth creation (Wolman & Spitzley, 1996). This wealth creation is usually accomplished using traditional activities, such as the attraction of new businesses or the retention and expansion of existing businesses, financial assistance, market development, and infrastructure investment. While these traditional activities can be used to fulfill sustainable local economic development goals, the primary focus on wealth creation without consideration of the environmental and equity impacts often leads to growth that dismisses social and environmental impacts.

There are some local economic development activities emerging in practice that reflect sustainable local economic development goals. These activities include building regional collaboration, workforce training, targeting of green/environmentally responsible industry, and environmental management. Though sustainability has found its way into local government, business, and planning discourse, the mainstreaming of sustainable local economic development has yet to happen. As sustainability expands and begins to impact the way in which local economic development agencies perceive quality of life and competitiveness, the agencies will seek activities that allow them to simultaneously satisfy their traditional goals of wealth-creation while adding environmental and social benefits.

RESULTS

There is evidence that support for sustainability-compatible activities, such as C&D recycling, is finding its way into local economic development agencies to help achieve their goals of economic competitiveness. This section discusses the results from a national survey of local economic development agencies on how their particular agency has supported or is supporting C&D recycling as an economic development tool.

Data Collection

To determine local economic development agency level of support for C&D recycling, a national survey was conducted of U.S. local economic development agencies with populations of 100,000 or more ($n = 663$). The usable survey total was 207 responses or 31.2%. These response rates are consistent with other surveys of economic development agencies (e.g. International City/County Management Association, 2004; Levy, 1993; Reese, 2006). The responding agencies represent 39 out of 49[2] surveyed states, cities, and counties of varying population sizes with a majority of respondents representing cities and counties with populations between 100,000 and 200,000. The mean population was 326,647, with populations ranging from 100,224 to over 9 million persons.

The survey results were supplemented by secondary data. These data were collected from government documents, the U.S. Census of Population (U.S. Census Bureau, 2002b), the U.S. Economic Census (U.S. Census Bureau, 2002a), County Business Patterns (U.S. Census Bureau, 2004), local economic development agency organizational materials, official reports, pamphlets, and Web sites.

Attitudes and Knowledge About Recycling

Agencies' attitudes, awareness, and knowledge about the recycling industry and its characteristics in each jurisdiction suggest that attitudes toward recycling as a contributor to local economic development are changing. Not surprisingly, as recycling has traditionally been associated with the environmental movement, a strong majority of local economic development agencies perceive recycling as an environmental activity (75.5% of respondents agreed or strongly agreed with this statement). However, approximately two thirds of respondents agreed that recycling should be treated as a potentially valuable economic activity. Yet, almost 28% were ambivalent about the potential value of recycling.

Agencies also expressed their opinions on whether C&D recycling as an industry can improve economic conditions and whether C&D recycling is considered to be a valuable industry for their economic development program. While a slight majority of the respondents thought C&D recycling could improve the economic conditions of the community, there was more ambivalence about the C&D recycling industry as a valuable strategy for *their* economic development program. This suggests that although the agencies may consider C&D recycling to be beneficial, they are less certain that their own communities would benefit from targeting this strategy. This hesitancy may stem from understanding current conditions of the recycling industry and of the potential for recycling activity. These conditions include but are not limited to: state recycling goals; state level programs and incentives for the recycling industry; landfill capacity and tipping fees; and the availability of redevelopment projects to supply construction & demolition debris.

State Level Recycling Goals

Only seven states did not have state-level recycling goals: Alaska, Arizona, Kansas, Oklahoma, Utah, Wisconsin, and Wyoming. Most states do not have mandatory goals or penalties. Instead, recycling goals are optional. The range of recycling goals varies from 25 to 70%. The mean recycling rate goal was 37.85% (American Forest and Paper Association, 2008). Of the 207 responding agencies, 85 (41.2%) were located in states with recycling goals of 50% or more.

These recycling goals of 50% or more could be difficult to achieve. For example, the California Integrated Waste Management Act (AB 939) required that California counties and cities meet the state goal of 50% waste reduction by the year 2000. Recycling municipal solid waste only impacted recycling goals by 25%. To make up the difference, the local governments needed larger volume recyclables. In some cases, construction and demolition debris recycling was used as a valuable strategy to reach that goal.

The link between the recycling goals and the relevance of C&D recycling for the community's local economic development is still not well established. When the respondents were asked whether the local governments they serve have to meet state requirements or local recycling goals, over 50% were uncertain. Almost 38% of respondents stated their local governments did have to meet recycling goals while only 18% were certain their local government did not have to meet the goals. Of those agencies that knew their local government had to meet recycling goals, only 23% agreed that C&D recycling was a valuable strategy. This suggests a missed opportunity for regulation to stimulate local economic development. The requirements for recycling could be harnessed in the community to serve as a local business stimulant providing raw materials, business activity, and job creation while simultaneously serving an environmental purpose.

State Level Programs and Incentives

The respondents were also asked about their knowledge of state economic development programs and state incentives to support the recycling industry. Thirty-five percent answered positively that their state had economic development programs to support the recycling industry. When asked whether there were state incentives, only 29% answered affirmatively. While there may be more programs than incentives to support the recycling industry, the number of uncertain responses was high. The data suggest there is a lack of knowledge for state-level recycling support which could then be transferred to the local level as a form of support for the industry.

Landfill Capacity and Tipping Fees

Theoretically, tipping fees or the fees levied on landfill-destined waste should serve as a market mechanism to encourage recycling, and thus the local recycling industry. When the fee is higher, the waste becomes more valuable and alternatives to simple land-filling would be pursued. Higher fees would then be an incentive for C&D recycling activity. The tipping fees range from $18.30 per ton to $60.52 per ton, and the median tipping fee was $31.17 per ton. In some jurisdictions tipping fees were well over $100 per ton. In reality, however, the median tipping fee per ton was actually lower for the states in which the agencies supported C&D recycling ($29.59).

Landfill Characteristics

Another issue for agencies to consider is the cost and availability of land-filling construction and demolition debris. Overall, there was little concern and much uncertainly over landfill capacity status. Thirty-five percent of respondents were uncertain of the status of their landfills, and 43% did not think landfill capacity was a problem. A number of respondents indicated that waste is currently shipped outside their jurisdictions. This waste, along with its recyclable components, represents an economic leakage. Perhaps because this industry is not well-developed or the benefits of it are not well-recognized, this leakage does not constitute a concern for local economic development agencies.

Another mode of supporting the local market for C&D recycling is the banning of C&D debris from regular landfills. A majority of respondents (60%) were uncertain whether any materials were banned, while 38% knew some materials were banned, but not what type of materials. Only two respondents indicate C&D debris was directed to special landfills or other disposal facilities.

Secondary data indicate that Massachusetts recently passed a ban on construction and demolition waste and Florida requires that C&D waste be recycled. Mostly, however, C&D debris is sent to separate landfills where it may receive further processing. The limited knowledge of the respondents signifies that knowledge of banned materials does not play an active role in influencing agency support for C&D recycling activities.

Redevelopment Projects

As stated previously, large redevelopment projects generate significant quantities of C&D debris, thereby taxing local landfill capacity. This debris can supply recovered materials for the C&D recycling industry. Forty-two percent of respondents stated there were redevelopment projects in their jurisdiction that required demolition of existing buildings. Sixty-five percent of those respondents that had redevelopment projects in their jurisdictions were involved in the project. This high level of involvement in redevelopment projects suggests there are opportunities for the local economic development agencies to support the C&D recycling industry in conjunction with these projects through policy and program requirements to connect the C&D recycling industry directly with these projects. For example, the agency could require C&D recycling in lieu of demolition and land-filling of the C&D debris. They could also network the C&D firms with the architects and redevelopment contractors. Yet only 19% of those agencies with large-scale redevelopment projects felt C&D recycling would be a valuable strategy or supported C&D recycling in any manner.

Twenty-six percent of respondents were uncertain if there were redevelopment projects in their jurisdiction. This uncertainty suggests a number of local economic development agencies lack knowledge about the physical redevelopment activities in their jurisdictions. The limited knowledge can adversely affect the ability of agencies to introduce and support C&D recycling.

Activities to Support C&D Recycling

In addition to attitudes and knowledge affecting support for C&D recycling, the actual activities conducted by agencies in support of the industry is revealing as to how these agencies actually implement support for the industry. The number of agencies who actually supported recycling is fewer than those who viewed it as a valuable activity. Fifty-three percent of respondents acknowledged that their agency had supported development of the recycling industry. Almost 30% admitted they had not supported the recycling industry and 16% were uncertain. The range of actual recycling industry support activities was broad. A number of the activities related to traditional business assistance, such as recruitment and expansion of firms and financial assistance. By using traditional tools, the agencies exhibited their ability to adapt to support these industries. The local economic development agencies also used tools associated with sustainable local economic development. Education, job retention, and strategic partnerships are examples.

Survey results identified the types of activities that local development agencies undertake to support C&D recycling. These results were then categorized based upon the activities typically associated with the traditional and sustainable local economic development approaches to illustrate how local economic development agencies are actively supporting this industry. Data on the agencies' attitudes toward recycling as an economic development tool were also collected to gauge the level of interest and resultant impact on the agencies' support for C&D recycling.

Four types of traditional tools were used to support C&D recycling (Table 10.1): (1) recruitment of businesses, (2) site or location assistance, (3) marketing, and (4) financial assistance. All of these are commonly used by most local economic development organizations. Recruitment of, and location assistance for, C&D recycling firms suggest local government interest in this industry and the desire to help reduce the difficulties these firms encounter in the market. When local economic development agencies recruit a particular sector or firm, they often pair this recruitment with incentives and other assistance measures. These measures, such as marketing and financing, are intended to level the playing field and create opportunities for the industry in the local and regional market.

Marketing is an opportunity to strengthen existing industry linkages and to increase market share. By promoting the services of an existing

Table 10.1.   Activities Used to Support the Recycling Industry

Local Economic Activities		Percent of Supporting Agency Open-Ended Responses
Traditional activities	• Financial assistance	16.5
	• Locational analysis and assistance	9.2
	• Recruitment	7.3
	• Setup or expansion of firms	7.3
	• Marketing	2.6
	• Small business development	1.8
	• Infrastructure analysis	1
Sustainable activities	• Grants to support research	3.6
	• Educational programs	2.6
	• Strategic partnerships	1.8
	• Incubator space or other facility provision	1.8
	• Job retention assistance	1
	• Venture capital	1
	• Dedicated recycling industry staff members	14.7
	• City or county run recycling programs and/or requirements	11.0
	• In house procurement policies	5.5
	• Brownfield projects	3.6
	• Supported business that use recycled waste	3.6
	• Waste to energy or cogeneration plants	2.6
	• Targeted industry strategy focused on recycling	2.6
	• Enterprise zone for companies who use recycled-content materials	1.8
	• Required recycling in demolition projects	1.8
	• Support companies that build green affordable housing	1

firm, the local economic development agency can help to avoid economic leakages and also increase local sales and tax revenues—thus satisfying the revenue generation goals of most local economic development agencies. Marketing can also encourage agglomeration economies and thereby strengthen market differentiation.

Financial assistance is another widely utilized traditional tool. Two of the fundamental problems facing the recycling industry are latent subsidies for virgin materials and the small business failure rate. Recycling is inefficient because of the subsidies placed on virgin materials. Although local economic development agencies may not directly contribute to those particular subsidies, they can help to level the playing field by providing financial assistance to recycling-based businesses, such as C&D recycling. Recycling businesses are also mainly characterized by small firms that require large amounts of fixed capital. Machinery for sorting and processing the materials can cost hundreds of thousands of dollars. Financial assistance in the form of revolving loan funds, grants, and low interest loans can alleviate some of the initial start up costs.

These tools, associated with the traditional local economic development approach, are broad enough to fit the needs of many industries, including the C&D recycling industry. Jepson and Haines (2003) claim that some tools, such as marketing to attract investment and financial incentives (e.g., industrial revenue bonds and industrial development bonds), subsidize expansions that are not consistent with the sustainable development approach. But if these tools were used to support an arguably sustainable industry, such as C&D recycling, there is no indication based on this research that they could not be considered compatible.

Traditional tools are not the only ones used to support C&D recycling. Tools associated with sustainable local economic development approaches were also recorded. These tools ranged from moderately common activities to innovative activities that were specifically tailored to C&D recycling. The activities included encouraging and supporting brownfield redevelopment, creating builders' guides for C&D recycling, and requiring C&D recycling. Workforce training is a supply-side mechanism used and is consistent with the equity component of the sustainable development model. By incorporating workforce training through C&D recycling, local economic development activities exhibit flexibility in using a popular activity to serve this particular industry.

Brownfield redevelopment projects are models for sustainable local economic development because they reclaim land for reuse and thereby limit sprawl. Often, demolition must occur on brownfields to make way for new construction. On these sites, the U.S. Environmental Protection Agency strongly encourages C&D recycling (U.S. Environmental Protection Agency, 2006). Likewise, the green building movement has consistently encouraged brownfield redevelopment (U.S. Green Building Council, 2006). A major component of the green building guidelines is waste minimization. C&D recycling is recognized as an integral component of waste minimization and resource conservation. C&D recycling in brownfields address the barriers for the industry by increasing activity in the sector and developing markets for the products.

Local economic development agencies also specifically created some new tools to address the needs of the C&D recycling industry. These tools were often formed in partnership with other agencies to directly address the barriers the industry faces. Builders' guides, for example, were offered through the planning and development offices and also made available through the economic development offices to interested developers and relocating industries. These guides, along with other promotional campaigns, help with public and industry education and training.

Similarly, local ordinances that require C&D recycling were also joint efforts as they are ultimately approved through the local governing body. These activities were intended to rectify the barriers of unsupportive local ordinances and absence of local mandates.

Such tools represent a shift in the way local economic development agencies perceive and act on their goals. The partnerships between departments show recognition of the need to integrate activities. Instead of focusing on the firm (to expand it) or jobs (to increase them in raw numbers) or wealth (to increase in absolute terms), these agencies have taken a broader view on how to improve quality of life through environmental and social change. These types of activities require an entirely new mindset and scope of activities. Some of these agencies were housed in planning; some had an emphasis on sustainable industries.

Only 8% of the respondents had staff members dedicated to supporting the recycling industry. Of those agencies, the number of staffers dedicated to recycling-based development ranged from 0.25 full time equivalents to 5 employees, with a mode of 1. A few agencies indicated partnerships with government agencies and in those agencies there were dedicated staff members. Another agency indicated that all staff would handle presented recycling industry opportunities.

Local economic development agencies are using their existing tools and creating new ones to support C&D recycling. Though the support for C&D recycling is somewhat limited, survey results manifest an increasing interest in sustainability, recycling-based development, and the willingness to be flexible for what opportunities arise.

CONCLUSION

C&D recycling represents a sustainable local economic development option for communities seeking to increase their economic competitiveness by taking advantage of local resources. It creates economic activity through collection, sorting, processing, remanufacturing, and sales. It improves social equity by providing jobs and training for low-skilled or hard-to-employ workers and can also provide training in the construction trades. It reduces environmental impact through diversion of materials from landfills back into the market and reduces the need for virgin material extraction.

Though this industry is not widespread, there is evidence that local economic development agencies are willing to support businesses in this field. Agencies use their traditional tools of business attraction and retention, site or location assistance, financial assistance, and marketing to help C&D businesses. They also employ more progressive tools such as workforce development, interagency collaboration, brownfield redevelopment, and outreach.

Though the existing support for C&D recycling is limited, the general attitudes toward C&D recycling are positive. To increase the C&D recycling industry presence and local economic development support for it will require addressing a number of attitudinal and knowledge obstacles. First, as mentioned above, general attitudes toward recycling-based development are favorable; however, these attitudes don't always translate into action. Increasing awareness of the economic, social, and environmental benefits of the C&D recycling industry may assist in improving perceptions of the industry. This may be accomplished through agency education, networking with other agencies, and the dissemination of best practice models.

Second, once the benefits of the industry are better understood, the barriers to entry for new C&D related businesses, and the overall institutional barriers, can be addressed by the local economic development agency. Uncertainty plagued the survey responses in terms of what conditions impacted the recycling industry. Addressing this uncertainty will help agencies focus their tools on improving supply and demand networks, ensuring adequate infrastructure, assisting in marketing of goods and services, and offering workforce training. To ease this transition for traditional agencies, these activities are all compatible with the conventional activities undertaken by local economic development agencies.

Once the industry and its barriers are understood, the agencies can make connections between various development activities and their ability to support and be supported by C&D recycling. For example, the large-scale redevelopment projects offer valuable materials for the C&D recycling industry—and the C&D recycling industry offer valuable savings and potential job opportunities for the redevelopment projects. Connecting these various programs help to reduce economic leakage and in turn support local economic development competitiveness.

While this study examined C&D recycling in the United States, there are opportunities around the world for similar activity. In rapidly growing regions, development and construction pressures generate copious amounts of C&D debris. Sometimes this debris is absorbed into the informal market, but most often it is sent to landfills. When the debris does not enter the secondary market, national and local governments have to contend with disposing of this waste and losing the potential economic, social, and environmental benefit of recycling the material.

Europe has perhaps the most developed recycling programs, but the best C&D recycling practices are limited to a few countries: Denmark, Germany, and the Netherlands (Leigh & Patterson, 2006). In these countries, much of the support for C&D recycling has come from national governments that set waste reduction levels and thus create a market for C&D recycling. Unfortunately, not much is known about the role local economic development agencies play in supporting the industry at the local level—whether or not they help to address market and institutional barriers. The lessons learned from this U.S.-based study will hopefully serve as a baseline for other local development efforts that include C&D recycling. Those lessons being that attitude, knowledge, and tools are all essential elements for supporting this sustainable local economic development activity.

NOTE

1. Debris from these projects includes materials such as wood, brick, tile, concrete, asphalt, gypsum, steel, other metals, glass, plastics, windows, doors, plumbing and electrical fixtures, vegetation, and soils.
2. No cities or counties in Wyoming met the population criterion; therefore no agencies in Wyoming were contacted to participate in the study.

REFERENCES

Ackerman, F., & Mirza, S. (2001). Waste in the inner city: Asset or assault? *Local Environment, 6*(2), 113-120.

American Forest and Paper Association. (2008). State recycling goals and mandates. Retrieved June 12, 2008, from http://www.afandpa.org/Content/NavigationMenu/Environment_and_Recycling/Recycling/State_Recycling_Goals/State_Recycling_Goals.htm

Beck, R. W. (2001). *U.S. recycling economic information study.* Washington DC: National Recycling Coalition.

Bowen, W. M., & Wells, M. V. (2002). The politics and reality of environmental justice: A history and considerations for public administrators and policy makers. *Public Administration Review, 62*(6), 688-698.

California Integrated Waste Management Board. (2004). Possible barriers to C&D reuse and recycling in California. Retrieved June 12, 2008, from http://www.ciwmb.ca.gov/condemo/Survey/RRSurveyCats.htm

County to seek Flint demolitions. (2001, October 17). *The Flint Journal,* pp. A-4.

Discovery Economic Consulting. (2001). *Using tax shifting and tax incentives to promote the deconstruction/renovation industry.* Retrieved June 12, 2008, from http://www.dec.bc.ca/resources/tax_shifting_incentives.pdf

Ewadinger, M., & Mouw, S. (2005). What's good for the planet is good for the environment. *Business, 27*(3), 27-29.

Fox, J., Zachary, J., & Swarbrick, K. (1998). *Constraints and opportunities: Expanding recovery in the demolition industry.* Santa Barbara, CA: Community Environmental Council.

Freymann, V., & Tessicini, J. (2003, November). *Planning for construction waste reduction*. Paper presented at the U.S. Green Building Council International Conference and Exposition, Pittsburgh, PA, U.S. Green Building Council.

Hattam, J. (2003). Eco-equality. *Sierra, 88*(2), 51-52.

International City/County Management Association. (2004). *Economic development survey*. Retrieved June 12, 2008, from www.icma.org

Jepson, E. J., & Haines, A. L. (2003). Under sustainability. *Economic Development Journal, 2*(3), 45-53.

Kane, A. (2004, Summer). Reclaimed opportunities: Planning for recycling-based economic development. *News & Views* [Economic Development Division of the American Planning Association], 8-14.

Kelley, R. (2006, August). Trash to treasure: Recycling as a moneymaker, panelist at National Association of Development Organization's annual training meeting.

Leigh, N. G., & Patterson, L. M. (2004). *Construction and demolition recycling for environmental protection and economic development*. Retrieved June 12, 2008, from http://cepm.louisville.edu/Pubs_WPapers/practiceguides/PG7.pdf

Leigh, N. G., & Realff, M. J. (2003). A framework for geographically sensitive and efficient recycling networks. *Journal of Environmental Planning and Management, 46*(2), 147-165.

Levy, J. M. (1993). What local economic developers actually do: Location quotients versus press releases. *Journal of the American Planning Association, 56*(2), 153-160.

Liquori, D. (2004, November 26). Venerable hotel becomes symbol of decay in Albany. *New York Times*, p. B5.

Ludwig, A. (2003, November). *Achieving 50% and 75% waste diversion—There is more than one way to divert! U.S.* Paper presented at the Green Building Council International Conference and Exposition, Pittsburgh, PA.

National Association of Home Builders Research Center. (2001). *Report on the feasibility of deconstruction: an investigation of deconstruction activity in four cities*. Washington, DC: U.S. Department of Housing and Urban Development Office of Policy Development and Research.

Norton, M. (2006, August). *Trash to treasure: Recycling as a moneymaker.* Panelist at National Association of Development Organization's annual training meeting.

Pagano, M. A., & Bowman, A. O. M. (2000). *Vacant land in cities: An urban resource*. Washington, DC: The Brookings Institution.

Pellow, D. N. (2002). *Garbage wars: The struggle for environmental justice in Chicago*. Cambridge, MA: MIT Press.

Reese, L. A. (2006). The planning-policy connection in U.S. and Canadian economic development. *Environment and Planning C, 24*(4), 553-573.

Triangle J Council of Governments. (1995). *WasteSpec: Case studies*. Retrieved June 12, 2008, from ftp://ftp.tjcog.org/pub/tjcog/regplan/solidwst/wastspeccs.pdf

U.S. Census Bureau. (2002a). *Economic census*. Retrieved June 12, 2008, from http://www.census.gov/econ/census02/

U.S. Census Bureau. (2002b). *U.S. census of population*. Retrieved June 12, 2008, from http://www.census.gov/main/www/cen2000.html

U.S. Census Bureau. (2004). *County business patterns.* Retrieved June 12, 2008, from http://www.census.gov/epcd/cbp/view/cbpview.html

U.S. Green Building Council. (2006). *Leadership in energy and environmental design.* Retrieved June 12, 2008, from http://www.usgbc.org

U.S. Environmental Protection Agency. (1998). *Characterization of building-related construction and demolition debris in the United States.* Washington, DC: U.S. Environmental Protection Agency Solid Waste and Emergency Response, Franklin Associates.

U.S. Environmental Protection Agency. (2000). *Building savings strategies for waste reduction of construction and demolition debris from buildings (EPA530-F-00-001F).* Retrieved June 12, 2008, from http://www.ilsr.org/recycling/buildingdebris.pdf.

U.S. Environmental Protection Agency. (2006). *Construction & demolition debris recycling—An integral part of Brownfield cleanup and redevelopment. Online presentation.* Retrieved June 12, 2008, from http://www.epa.gov/reg5rcra/wptdiv/solidwaste/debris/brownfields/c_and_dd_reuse_and_recycling_in_brownfields_redevelopment.pdf.

Waste to Work Partnership. (2002). *Making waste work: Creating new jobs in the Pacific Northwest using waste materials.* Portland, OR: Center for Watershed and Community Health.

Whitman, D., & McCoy, F. (2000, February 21). Raising hopes by razing highrises. *U.S. News & World Report,* p. 28.

Wolman, H., & Spitzley, D. (1996). The politics of local economic development. *Economic Development Quarterly, 10*(2), 115-150.

Yost, P. (1999). Construction and demolition waste: Innovative assessment and management. In C. J. Kibert (Ed.), *Reshaping the built environment: Ecology, ethics, and economics* (pp. 176-194). Washington, DC: Island Press.

CHAPTER 11

WRESTLING WITH THE HARD REALITIES

Unintended Consequences and Disappointing Outcomes in a U.K. Water Project

Sam Wong

This chapter introduces and challenges the notion of "sustainable technology" and issues around it, such as governance and institutional constraints. It raises questions about who controls technology and how technological interventions intertwine power inequalities. Drawing on the United Kingdom's first-ever combined rainwater and greywater systems in northwest England, it politicizes the idea of sustainable innovations by examining the distribution of costs and benefits among the elderly council house tenants as the end users. Using a "subjectivity-institutions-structure" framework, the chapter shows that the success of building "pro-poor" sustainable water technologies depends on how people are motivated in trying new devices and how they are involved in choosing the *right* kinds of innovations. It calls for building pro-poor sustainable technological interventions in general and illustrates the value of basing such interventions on an understanding of people's subjectivities, institutional arrangements, and the structural con-

Global Sustainability Initiatives: New Models and New Approaches
pp. 211–231
Copyright © 2008 by Information Age Publishing
All rights of reproduction in any form reserved.

straints surrounding poor people. It argues that using frameworks like the subjectivity-institutions-structure one can help in setting reasonable targets about sustainable development without compromising livelihoods and well-being.

INTRODUCTION

The notion of sustainable development has brought a new perspective to the role of technology in achieving poverty alleviation, improving well-being, and altering people's proenvironmental behaviors. Before the 1970s, technological interventions were largely characterized as top-down, expert-led, large-scale, and one size fits all. Since the 1990s, the idea of "appropriate use of technology" has gradually entered mainstream thinking in the development discourse (World Bank, 2000). Projects promoting sustainable innovations, both in the developed and the developing countries, have tended to be context-specific and sensitive to local needs. Indigenous knowledge has been celebrated (Chambers, Pacey, & Thrupp, 1989). Capacity building is considered crucial to the continuity of technological improvements. The impact and change brought by technological interventions should be gradual and incremental in order to allow local people to make appropriate adaptations, and the process of achieving technological transformation should be bottom-up and participatory in nature in order to create a sense of ownership (Uphoff & Wijayaratna, 2000). These principles for developing successful introductions of new technologies have emerged to address limitations of past endeavours (European Commission, 2005; World Bank, 2008).

There is ample evidence to show the positive impact of this approach on the ground. For example, using case studies in Jordon, Faruqui and Al-Jayyousi (2002) show that the effectiveness of using greywater to irrigate farmlands lies in site-specific factors, such as topography and availability of greywater. Postel, Gonzales, and Keller (2001) report that the use of small-scale drip irrigation, rather than building big dams and large-scale irrigation pipeline systems, reduced poverty for water users in some poor rural communities in sub-Saharan Africa because the drip technology was both affordable and flexible for poor farmers and smallholders.

However, following basic principles for introducing technologies that are developed to contribute to building locally and globally sustainable communities, what might be called "sustainability technologies" or "sustainable technologies," does not always guarantee success. Doing so can fail to protect the environment on the one hand and risk undermining the livelihoods of poor people on the other. For instance, Wong (2007) notes that, although community-based solar home systems may offer an alternative to grid-based electrification to rural populations, his case studies in Bangladesh show that solar home systems can widen poverty gaps between the poor and the less-poor within communities when the latter have stable jobs to pay for energy while the former have not.

The current discourse of sustainable technology may, as critics argue, place too much stress on personal commitment, epitomizing the agenda of neoliberalism—in which governments off-load their responsibilities to private and nongovernmental actors (Feenberg, 1999). As a consequence, the concept can become dangerously overindividualized and overromanticized, as it embodies the assumption that the benefits of technological innovations will be shared equally by all. In reality, however, certain people face more struggles in their everyday lives and have much less power than others in influencing the outcomes of technological developments. This critique is well summarized by Maniates (2002) in highlighting the limitations of any focus on individual citizens: "when responsibility for environmental problems is individualized, there is little room to ponder institutions, the nature and exercise of political power, or ways of collectively changing the distribution of power and influence in society" (p. 45). This argument resonates with the literature of environmental justice, highlighting the uneven distribution of environmental costs and benefits within communities along lines of class, gender, race, ethnicity, religion, and other aspects of socioeconomic status (Schlosberg, 2004). Drawing on their research in developing countries, Cornwall and Gaventa stress that a disproportionately heavy burden can be placed on poor and marginalized individuals (2001, p. 32). Informed by a gender perspective, Jackson (2005) warns that the advocacy of sustainable technology encourages more labor- and time-intensive lifestyles. These lifestyle changes, wittingly and unwittingly, exert additional burdens on women in particular.

Another criticism suggests that the practice of participatory governance, characterized as a great level of civic engagement, deliberative and open discussion, and a high degree of transparency and accountability, may not necessarily challenge social and environmental inequalities (Cleaver & Franks, 2005) since it plays down the "highly differentiated experiences of citizen duties and agency" (Bullard & Johnson, 2000, p. 385). Sharp (2006) argues that the problems of the notion of sustainable innovations lie in the fact that the concept is not politicized enough, so that questions, as to who makes the decision around the choice of innovations, who controls the technology, and how competing interests and priorities are resolved are inadequately interrogated. In her words, using sustainable innovations to alter people's proenvironmental actions remains top-down in nature: experts first define what sustainable behavior is and then identify ways to encourage it in the populace.

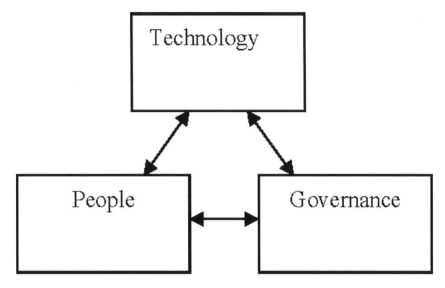

Source: Inspired by Murphy (2006).

Figure 11.1.   Joseph Murphy's "people-technology-governance" nexus.

Joseph Murphy offers a more specific and theoretical challenge to sustainable technology. Coining the term "governing technology for sustainability" (2006), he proposes a "people-technology-governance" nexus in conceptualizing the complex relationships between humanity, technology, and nature.

Murphy suggests that technology can be seen as a means to achieve sustainability, but the process of selecting technology is not apolitical. He challenges technological determinism, and argues that manageability of technology cannot be divorced from social forces and cultural contexts. It, therefore, needs to take people and governance into account. The component of people implies the multiple identities of people and the complexity of their various motivations for adopting sustainable innovations. He criticizes the rational choice model for oversimplifying human actions. He suggests that most of our decisions are not made consciously, and we tend to follow routines, habits, and social conventions in our everyday lives. He defines governance as the relationships between the state and people. The shifting emphasis from government to governance not only marks the changing role of the state, but also the roles of the market, NGOs, and community. While the state is now generally expected to create an enabling environment for the public-private partnership, communities are encouraged to participate more actively in the decision-making process. The institutional arrangements shape, and are shaped by, how people and technology interact.

Building on these criticisms, this chapter proposes a "subjectivity-institution-structure" framework which offers a contextual approach to sustainable technology. This framework places emphasis on the dynamics and complexity of the interplay between subjectivity, institutions, and structure. *Subjectivity* is about how people perceive the functions and meaning of sustainable innovations. It enables us to investigate what values, assumptions, and motives people hold about technology and sustainability. *Institutions* are social norms and rules embedded in our everyday practices. Norms and moral principles, such as the right way to do things, can be as powerful as financial and regulatory incentives in shaping people's choices in sustainable innovations. *Structures* provide the historical and sociocultural contexts that enable and constrain technological improvement. This framework, aims to be "pro-poor" since it examines what impacts the advocacy of sustainable technology have on the livelihoods of the poor. It's pro-poor nature arises from two emphases. First, the emphasis on structure explicitly examines who gains and who loses through specific interactions. Second, when the research concerns the lives of poorer people, the emphasis on individuals' subjectivities, means that their subjectivities are explicitly taken into account. This framework also highlights the unintended consequences that may arise in the process of promoting sustainable innovations.

This chapter draws on a case study involved with sustainable water innovations in elderly people's homes in the northwest of England. A combined greywater and rainwater system and a collective rain-harvesting system were implemented for 34 single tenants who lived in their own flats and bungalows. They were characterized as old (generally above 60 years of age) and poor (most of them relied on state benefits). These new systems were anticipated to both improve the environment (by using less water) and to improve the tenants' livelihoods (by reducing their water bills). As the analysis below shows, as the application of the new technology did not proceed completely as expected, the tenants' lack of involvement in the design or management of the innovations became an issue.

This chapter seeks to demonstrate how the application of a subjectivity-institution-structure sustainable technology framework provides a strong and nuanced analysis of this case, demonstrating its potential to provide insights in relation to other areas of environmental innovation and governance. In particular, the paper attempts to achieve three things. First, that the success of sustainable technology hinges on people's perceptions about the changing environments surrounding them over time and how they feel about making changes. The complexity of subjectivity is demonstated by exploring the meanings and practices of hygiene in the use of greywater and rainwater. Second, that sustainable technology is institutionally embedded, mediated by the "right way of doing things." This institutional embedding is illustrated by showing how tenants' green behaviors are shaped by norms of social respect and a strong desire for community harmony in the process of participation. Third, that it is important to stress that people are the end users of the technologies and that their sense of ownership of the technology is an important factor in its possible contribution to their lives. Keeping the selection process transparent, exchanging information openly, and promoting active participation at every stage can foster a stronger sense of ownership and minimise the negative feelings when problems arise.

Following this introduction, the paper elaborates the subjectivity-institution-structure framework and provides details of the case study. The sustainable technology is then interrogated through the subjectivity-institution-structure framework. Finally, the paper concludes by proposing how the subjectivity-institution-structure model offers a framework for better interventions in promoting sustainable innovations.

SUBJECTIVITY-INSTITUTION-STRUCTURE FRAMEWORK

The goal of the subjectivity-institution-structure framework is to support analysis and to guide practice. The contextual approach of the framework provides ways for thinking about sustainable innovations which are intended to overcome some of the criticisms cited above, and hopefully are successful in doing so,

The paper draws on Carolyne Ellis and Michael Flaherty's subjectivity theory (1992), Mary Douglas's institutional thinking (1987), and Derek Layder's conceptualization of social structures (1994) to build this framework. The framework places emphasis on the dynamics and complexity of interplay between individuals' subjectivities, institutions, and societal structures. The concept of subjectivities is crucial to our understanding of the human-nature relationships. Ellis and Flaherty define subjectivity as "emotions, meanings, situations, experience, motivations, perceptions, hopes and fears" (1992, p. 1). The recognition of the multiplicity of subjectivities, they argue, is necessary for the exploration of the "interconnections among emotional, cognitive and physical experiences" (p. 4). Their theory acknowledges the (partial) capability of human beings in negotiating meanings, interpreting their roles, and improvising on resources in order to deal with unexpected events in the flux of their everyday lives. To avoid romanticizing human agency, Ellis and Flaherty stress the need to contextualize subjectivity in social contexts and circumstances. They underline the significance of incorporating subjective experiences into the analysis of institutions, and highlight the analysis of the structural forces that shape emotional experiences across time and space. And, as Sofoulis (2005) suggests, the dual nature of subjectivity—transformative and reactionary—offers opportunities as well as obstacles in promoting sustainable technology.

Douglas's theory of institutional thinking explores the relationships between individual minds and social institutions. Defining institutions as rules, norms, and conventions, she challenges the rational choice models by explaining how our everyday practice, experiences and modes of social relations are connected to institutional aspects, such as values, routines and habits. She argues that it is not institutions in themselves that act, but the people who make them up. Although it is people who take actions, institutions take over the thinking process for us all. In her own words, "social institutions encode information. They are credited with making routine decisions, solving routine problems, and doing a lot of regular thinking on behalf of individuals" (1987, p. 47). She views subjectivity and structure as being linked through institutions and expressed in social practice.

Shove (2003) applies a similar concept of institutions and studies how social norms and technology coshape each other. She argues that domestic water consumption and the choice of domestic appliances are related to the level of comfort, cleanliness, and convenience that are socially-expected. She suggests that specific practices, such as showering, are reflections of wider social conventions, such as keeping clean. Similar to Douglas, she takes a less functional and less conscious approach to institutions, stressing that we follow our habits and routines to carry out daily tasks without our conscious scrutiny. It is thus critical to study "how new practices become normal" (Shove, 2003), and how routines and social values reproduce everyday practices and societal structures

Layder (1994) defines structure as "structured patterning of social relationships and reproduced practices over time and space … and the power relations that underpin them" (p. 140). Structures show hierarchies of social control, such as class, gender, and ethnicity, that affect the distribution of resources and power between individuals. Structures provide the historical and sociocultural contexts that both enable individuals to take actions and constrain them in doing so. According to Layder, structures are linked to subjectivity and institutions because "the subjective realm of social action is both formed and constrained by the reproduced practices which constitute the institutional domain of modernity" (p. 216).

This subjectivity-institution-structure framework can be useful in exploring the intertwined relationships between individuals, society, technology, and the environment in part because it problematicizes the notion of technology and opens up the implicit assumptions underlying the choice and application of specific technologies. In contextualizing the process of social and ecological connectedness of individuals, it also helps put power in the center of the sustainable technology debate. Since it politicizes technology by highlighting the uneven distribution of costs, benefits, and risks among stakeholders, it unravels the power dynamics, such as who makes what decisions on which technology.

CASE STUDY: SUSTAINABLE WATER INNOVATION PROJECT IN NW ENGLAND

An environmental demonstration project located in the northwest of England was started in 1998 and completed in 2002. The environmental improvements were part of the regeneration of 34 properties. Some of these tenants stay in a residential care center while others in individual bungalows. The majority of the tenants were old and poor. Seventy percent of them are over 60 and rely on housing benefits.

This demonstration project was recommended to us as a possible case study for this paper by a former master's student who worked in an organization that played an active role in the project. In addition to its accessibility, other factors contributed to the attractiveness of the project as a case study: It contained multiple sustainable innovations; won numerous community regeneration awards, and seemed to have had few problems. Finally, most stakeholders were willing to work with us.

Our research objectives were to explore how plans for the implementation of these sustainable water devices were initiated and developed and to identify and examine the factors that enabled and hindered the implementation of the technologies. In the research, 10 stakeholders were interviewed, including the developer, architect, surveyor, plumbing service providers, residential manager, carer, and tenants. Secondary data, such as the Scheme Design Report and meeting minutes, were also drawn on to enrich our understanding.

The principle of sustainability was not embedded into the project at the earliest stage of planning. However, when the developers realized that they needed extra funding to implement the project, they quickly reviewed all of the design process and put sustainable features into the wording of the documents so they could apply for a European redevelopment grant. In their application, they stressed the need to conserve water and energy. They also explicitly stated that this objective could be achieved by using technologies to change people's behavior.

The project started off with one main design group, including architects, developers, and engineers, but the large number of participants made the work unmanageable. The group was then divided into small design teams, specializing on specific issues, such as water, energy, and construction materials. As was true of the initial main design group, these design teams were composed of experts only.

The design teams looked at the technologies available in the United Kingdom and elsewhere in Europe. They discussed what maintenance backup would be required and what practical issues might arise for the tenants. They finally chose a bundle of sustainable technologies, ranging from photovoltaics and solar water heating to waste recycling and composting. In the realm of sustainable water innovations, the project included what the developers' claim is the first U.K. implementation of a combined greywater and rainwater system as well as a communal rainwater collective system.

The decision-making process for choosing these innovations was very complex. It was affected by three main factors: site assessment, technical feasibility, and socioeconomic factors. Site location and characteristics both facilitated and constrained the implementation of these sustainable features. Bungalows with photovoltaic panels, for instance, were built facing south in order to maximize sunlight. The criterion concerning technical feasibility and readiness ruled out the use of wind turbines in generating electricity because the small-scale wind-turbine technologies were not ready at that time. Social acceptance and perception of risk affected how far new technologies could be tested on the ground.

Sustainable Water Innovations

This chapter focuses on only the water innovations of the project. The combined water systems were implemented in the first phase of the project (1998-2000). The flushing of toilets was designed to draw initially on recycled greywater collected from baths and showers, with rainwater backup when the greywater was depleted. The rainwater harvesting system collected rainwater from roof areas for external taps and toilet flushing. It was also connected with the tenants' washing machines. While all 34 properties had access to the rainwater harvesting system, logistical constraints meant that only 12 were fitted with the combined water system. Owing to the technical problems, the combined greywater and rainwater systems were scrapped in the second phase (2000-2002). Instead, a communal rainwater supply system was set up which served 22 properties. Rainwater was collected mainly for the purpose of gardening.

In interviews, various stakeholders gave the strong impression that residents had been actively involved with the Project. The developers claimed that: "I wouldn't have done it without the residents' involvement at all" (interview, 09/01/06, transcript, p. 25). Tenants were invited to go for a trip to the Centre for Alternative Technology in Wales and attended the training programs. These activities were intended to educate tenants and enable them to have a better understanding of the technologies.

However, other interviews and the available documentation show that tenants' participation was partial, selective, and instrumental. The tenants were not involved in the process of choosing sustainable technologies because they were generally perceived as not technically competent to do so. In interviews, the developers stated explicitly: "that was a basically a technical process and there was not that much point in involving them" (interview, 04/08/05, transcript, p. 21). The chairman of the community center, rather than one or more tenants, represented the tenants at the monthly team meetings.

One example of the problems the tenants experienced with the sustainable technologies occurred with the flushing of toilets. To make the sustainable water innovations attractive, the developer persuaded the tenants of the benefits of the system through arguing that it would save them money. However, the combined greywater and rainwater system was found faulty shortly after implementation in 1998. The combined system was designed to collect greywater from baths, showers, and washing basins, with the toilet-flushing system drawing initially on recycled greywater, backed up by rainwater, when the greywater was depleted. Because each property in the project was occupied by only a single elderly tenant, it turned out that the greywater generated from their baths and washing was often sufficient to meet their daily toilet flushing needs. As a result, the system rarely called for rainwater back up. Because the rainwater system was designed to shut down automatically if rainwater was not called for within 28 days, the backup system would shut down automatically and there would be no reserve water to flush toilets when the need arose. This lack of backup water supply became a serious problem when tenants had a party or their family stayed for the weekend. In addressing the problems, the affected tenants were instructed to turn the taps on or to take longer showers in order to create sufficient greywater to allow toilets to be flushed.

Such inconveniences and the resulting grievances brought about an "antitechnology feeling" among the affected residents. They felt like guinea pigs subject to an experiment with the new water equipment. In interviews, the professional stakeholders accused the tenants of being technologically ignorant. A surveyor put it: "we had a tenants' meeting and the end-users' understanding of it [the combined water system] is absolutely terrible" (interview, 13/10/05, transcript, p. 21). Facing strong resistance, the developers decided to scrap the system and put all toilets back on mains water. However, the 12 affected tenants were not informed about this decision.

The following analysis applies the subjectivity-institution-structure framework to three aspects of sustainable water innovations. First, it considers differing ideas between experts and tenants about the cleanliness of rainwater and greywater. Second, it considers the role of institutions in choosing the "right" kinds of sustainable innovations. And, third, it considers perspectives on appropriate participation in the decision process.

COMPLEXITY OF SUBJECTIVITIES

One of the lessons that can be drawn from this case study is the intricate relationships between the application of technology and the characteristics of the user groups. Although the poor, and sometimes the elderly, are often stereotyped as marginalized social groups who generally lack a sense of agency and aspiration to make environmental changes, this case study showed a different picture. Developers and other professional stakeholders did not initially consider the poor and elderly tenants to be obstacles to sustainable development. They believed that the success of sustainable water management did not hinge on particular social groups, but depended on whether the technologies were implemented in a user-friendly and less-intrusive way, and on choosing a technology that minimized the behavioral change required of end-users (interview with developer, 09/01/06, transcript, p. 15).

To encourage tenants to welcome the new water system, the developers highlighted the potential of the innovations in cutting tenants' water bills. This strategy of promoting sustainable technology by providing financial benefits showed a resonance with the arguments by Barnett, Doherty, Carr, Johnstone, and Rootes (2006) that people from marginalized groups are often "mobilized by practical consideration and financial benefits," and that they will understand and recognise environment good if policies and technologies are "made cheap and easy for members of disadvantaged groups" (p. 26).

The task of shifting patterns of citizenship toward eco-friendly norms, however, was far more complex than simply offering financial rewards and penalties. It related to the broader social and economic practices that were connected to sustainability. In this case study, tenants made a strong link between their understanding and use of water and the meaning and practice of "hygiene." Their perceptions about water hygiene mediated what kind of water could and could not be shared. These perceptions should have shaped how sustainable water innovations were designed and implemented. For instance, tenants had a strong feeling that greywater is "personal waste" which should not be shared with their neighbors. Therefore, the combined greywater and rainwater systems should, arguably, be designed to be individualized and self-contained. Rainwater, in contrast, came from the sky and was clean enough to be collectively used, therefore the rainwater harvesting system could be run in a collective way. This observation resonates with ideas by Medd and Shove (2006). They suggest that investigating water consumption should not simply measure how much water each household uses, but should situate water users within a wider set of domestic practices and daily routines.

The case also demonstrates a clear contrast between different groups' subjective ideas about the nature of "clean" water. From the developers' perspective, water provided from rain and from other people's treated greywater was technically clean, and perfectly suitable for use in clothes washing. The use of such water would not only reduce pressure on local water services, but it would also reduce the tenants' water bills. For the tenants, however, such water was a cause of suspicion. They thought rainwater was not clean enough to wash clothes and that would also leave a bad smell in their clothes. For example, a tenant argued that:

> He [the technician] had attached my washing machine to the rainwater. They shouldn't have done, it was against the law. And I washed my clothes for six months in dirty water. It wasn't purified. (Interview with tenant, p. 5)

In a similar vein, using other people's greywater was regarded as dirty. Finally, water was a relatively small part of the tenants' household budgets but a very important part of their daily lives. Compared with energy and heating expenditures, savings on water costs were a lower priority but inconveniences might be regular events.

MULTIPLE IDENTITIES AND ENVIRONMENTAL PERCEPTIONS

In highlighting the innovations' potential to cut water bills and in offering financial incentives, the developers reinforced the tenants' role as consumers and underpinned the rational choice assumption that people's behavior in water consumption is primarily or exclusively a response to water price levels. The decision-making process of the technology users, however, is complex and is shaped by a wider range of socioeconomic-cultural factors. Apart from being citizens and consumers, the elderly tenants in the case study were also grandparents, neighbors, friends, and community members.

For example, their identity as grandparents suggested that allowing grandchildren to play with water was consistent with their desire to be "good" grandparents, but doing so might be in conflict with being a "good" environmental citizen. On one reported occasion, some tenants hosted Christmas parties for their families and friends. The breakdown of the combined greywater and rainwater system during that time meant that there was no water to flush toilets. This did not just cause embarrassment, but made them feel bad about not being a good host. In addressing the problems, the engineers told them to turn the taps on or to take longer showers in order to create greywater.

> Tenant: When I said I'd no water and I'd ring and he'd say, "Well, just let your, your erm, shower run." I said, "Well, what's that got to do with anything?" "Let it run down," he said. I said, "Well, how long will it take to let your water run down?" So, therefore, I wasn't going to save a penny, was I? (Interview, 16/12/05, transcript, p. 21).

The tenants found the engineer's proposed suggestion ridiculous because greywater, from their perspective, was generated from purposeful actions, such as washing hands, and should not be created in order to make up for the system's inadequacies.

The case study also suggests how behavior and attitude changes are highly related to people's subjectivity. Subjectivity is about people's perceptions about their surroundings, the ascribed meanings toward their environments, and their feelings about the actions they can take. From this perspective, how people perceive the change of the environment around them, over time and place, plays a crucial role in ecological citizenship. In explaining the limited success of the sustainable water innovation project, an engineer blamed a popular perception held among the elderly tenants that the environment had improved through the decades, rather than deteriorated. He suggested that:

> They come from a different age. I mean, I can remember when [an anonymous city] was black; every building in [an anonymous city] was black, and these people are older than me! They've lived right through it when they had smog.... So, they're not really worried about the environment: they'd done their bit, they've lived through all the worse part of it, so, to them, this is a lot cleaner than what it used to be. (Interview, 09/01/06, transcript, pp. 30-31)

Since the perceived and visual improvement of the city and the surrounding buildings were in contrast to the claims about deteriorating environmental situations, asking tenants to save water and to help the environment did not make sense to their living experience.

In a nutshell, this example suggests limits on how powerful environmental awareness might be in influencing people's action. For example,

Drevensek's (2005) claim that "it is only when people (namely, citizens or the lay audience) know what is going on in the environment at the local, regional, national or even global level that they can play an active, responsible role in shaping policy making in line with their own wishes and needs" (p. 227), may suggest that awareness is the one key factor in mobilizing action. While demonstrating that people's understanding about their surroundings is an important factor in influencing their decisions and actions, this case did not provide evidence that helping citizens to grasp a deeper understanding of their environment, as the project sought to do, will necessarily lead to desirable environmental outcomes, as Drevensek seems to suggest.

INSTITUTIONAL THINKING

A key step in promoting sustainable technology involves helping individuals to get access to information, so that they can make purposeful decisions about their actions (Barnett et al., 2006). The idea that an environmentally concerned citizen needs to be an "informed" citizen is evidenced in this case study. Tenants had a 1-day visit to the Centre for Alternative Technology in Wales. The purpose of the trip, according to the architect, was to educate the tenants about sustainable development and to enhance their acceptance of alternative water devices. Despite good intentions, the assumption that more education and better knowledge about sustainable technology leads to more environmentally responsible behavior is problematic since it fails to consider adequately the role of institutions in shaping sustainable innovations. The following discussion argues that sustainable innovation is institutionally embedded. Institutions, defined as social values and cultural norms, both enable and hinder our ability to make informed decisions when it comes to engaging in "green" behavior.

The Right Way of Doing Things

Institutions are a set of social practices embedded and reproduced in our daily habits and routines. The power of institutions, in Douglas' words, is that they "think on our behalf" (1987). This insight does not mean that human beings are "cultural dopes" who do not reflect on their actions, but that we often leave "common sense" and social conventions to make decisions for us without our close scrutiny. In the project, water system designers attempted to reduce potable water consumption by connecting the rainwater supply with tenants' washing machines. However, the tenants were very angry about this arrangement. They thought rain-water was not clean enough to wash clothes and that it would also leave a bad smell in their clothes. Facing such strong resistance, the engineers were forced to reconnect their washing machines with the main supply. This example demonstrates that our preferences are historically and culturally shaped. Unsustainable practices, such as using highly treated potable water to wash clothes, have become "the right way to do things" and thus become normalized and embedded in our daily practice and thinking. As the case demonstrates, providing us with more green information or offering us wider choices of sustainable technologies may not be sufficient to disrupt the embedded nature of our ungreen habits.

The current literature on sustainable technology also recommends active involvement of members of the public in the decision-making process that affects their lives. This recommendation assumes that collective action fosters a sense of empowerment, and participation ensures legitimacy and sustainability. Despite good intentions, people exercising their rights to participate do not exist in a vacuum: their involvement is embedded in social relations. It is the very minutiae of social life and relationships, as Cleaver (2004) argues, that shape the forms citizenship can take (p. 272). For example, the elderly tenants in our case study were very content to ask their chairperson to represent them in the steering committee of the project. Although ordinary tenants were allowed to attend the committee, they did not see it as appropriate since their action might risk disrupting the collective harmony of the community. The norm of social respect and the desire to be accepted, therefore, constrained them from getting more involved in the decision-making process.

The faith in participatory governance also needs caution. Many studies show that citizens should have a say in the decision making and their active participation will generate more collective action. However, a preference for formalized participation brings with it the danger of disregarding other channels and mechanisms through which poor or marginalized people can make their influence felt. Most tenants in the case study were not included in the "formal" decision-making settings, but this fact does not mean that they were totally excluded from the process. In interviews, a tenant suggested that their opinions were often passed to the management through the manager and carers. These informal channels appeared to offer safe and efficient routes for them to get heard, with respect to the ways they experienced the new water systems. Furthermore, maintaining good personal relationships with the managers and carers allowed them to seek immediate help more effectively. For instance, when the combined greywater and rainwater system did not work, the tenants were formally instructed to report the problems directly to the company by phone. Owing to the location of the company and complicated personnel arrangements, technicians did not make their visit within a week. To avoid nuisance and delay, tenants rang the carer to seek help. Since the carer had received basic training in plumbing, he could visit the tenants and try to sort out their problems within hours.

These "informal" arrangements may provide poor people a feasible alternative to formal participation, which may demand more time than they have to spare, or, as in this example, risks challenging existing and effective social relations. However, they discriminate against people who do not have dense social networks. They also risk reinforcing social inequalities. For instance, some tenants felt that they needed to maintain good relationships with the carer, otherwise they could not get the immediate assistance when they needed it. Such feelings give the carer a great deal of influence in the establishment.

STRUCTURES: CONSTRAINTS AND ENVIRONMENTAL INJUSTICE

In discussing sustainable consumption, Seyfang (2005) warns that individuals are not necessarily able to act on their ecological preferences to influence the market owing to a diversity of obstacles, such as affordability, availability, and convenience of sustainable products (p. 296). The idea of constraints is also relevant to the discourse of sustainable technology. As discussed in the previous sections, the participation of the elderly tenants was constrained by normative values, such as the norm of conflict avoidance. Their discontinuous attendance at group meetings (due to poor health), low level of self-esteem (resulting from their poor educational background), a general deficit in human capital, and a lack of the "right" kind of language also hindered them from articulating their needs in formalized public fora. Most had a poor educational background and lacked the self-esteem and familiarity with "business" language to represent themselves confidently in a committee meeting.

> Tenant: They really treated you as though, you know, "She's a pensioner. She's, well, they're stupid." But ... pensioners have got common-sense if they haven't got ... I don't profess, you know, to have any brains, because I didn't, I didn't get my 11+ [selection exam at the end of primary school]. I had brothers and sisters who did and went to high school/grammar school and what have you. I didn't!" (Interview, 16/12/05, transcript, p. 31).

All of these factors reinforced the idea that the elderly tenants were "technically incompetent," providing the professional stakeholders with legitimate reasons to exclude them from involvement in the design committee's choice of alternative technologies.

This critique leads to Dobson's thesis about asymmetrical environmental responsibilities (2003). He challenges the assumption that the dialogic relations between stakeholders are necessarily fair and that environmental responsibilities should be shared equally by all. He urges a close examination of the distribution of costs and benefits among different groups in citizenship since some people, in reality, have much less power than the others. Therefore, they should not accept the same level of duties in achieving sustainable development. The poor and elderly tenants in the case study consumed very little potable water in their everyday lives. Given their low potable water use, their savings from the greywater system would be minimal in comparison to the potential savings of people of other ages and other social groups, we need to ask if it is morally right to ask them to play guinea pig to test the innovations. Is it environmentally just to ask them to take more responsibilities when they have already encountered numerous resource and institutional constraints on their lives and when they are so unlikely to benefit from what is learned from their experiences?

CONCLUSIONS AND POLICY IMPLICATIONS

Reducing unsustainable practices by introducing sustainable technology has good intentions. However, this case has identified some conceptual problems that warn us to avoid advancing an ideal, but ultimately unachievable, notion of sustainable innovation, based on an inadequate understanding of subjectivity, group participation, and governance. This chapter has demonstrated the usefulness of the subjectivity-institution-structure framework in reconceptualizing the meaning of sustainable technology. The sustainable water innovation project in northwest England illustrates the notion that sustainable innovation cannot be properly understood by focusing exclusively on the technology, but must be analyzed against the background of broader psychological, institutional, and societal dynamics.

This chapter has three themes. The first theme is the intricate relationships that exist between technologies and their users and the importance of attending to those relationships when policymaking. The willingness of the developers to try new water devices on poor and socially marginalized people helps to challenge the stereotype that these social groups are useless when it comes to understanding adoption of and adaptation to technology. The experiences in this case study show that class, income, and age are not necessarily correlated with the acceptance of new technologies and illustrates some of the reasons why such a correlation might not exist.

Before new sustainability-related devices are installed, it is crucial to consider seriously the potential users' characteristics, social background, and cultural practice. These factors play a crucial role in affecting how well the systems work for the people involved. In the case study, the engineers imported the German hybrid water systems, but they did not pay adequate attention to the family size and characteristics of the tenants. For instance, the social housing was occupied with single elderly tenants. The greywater generated from their baths and washing was often sufficient to meet their sanitary needs. However, the system design was such that if backup rainwater was not called for within 28 days, the rainwater system would shut down automatically. As a result, this caused nuisance to the tenants because there was no water to flush toilets if they had increased demand, for example when visitors called. This problem worsened the relationship between tenants and the workers who did the repairs and undermined the tenants' trust about the sustainable technology.

The second theme relates to the dangers of focusing on any single source of human motivation when attempting to move toward a more sustainable world and to the dangers of providing misleading information about possible benefits. In "selling" the water system to the tenants, the developers assumed that the desire to save money would be the dominant factor in the tenants' response to the system. They used water-bill reduction as a way to encourage the tenants to try new technologies. Using financial incentives to promote participation, however, was not necessarily an effective strategy because other factors were also important, the financial impact was small, and the likelihood of a backlash was large. The financial incentive built up high expectations, and when the users did not receive any financial benefits, the disappointments contributed to their grievances and made them feel like guinea pigs for the new water experiments. Furthermore, developers and equipment suppliers admitted in the interviews that small-scale rainwater and drainage systems have no great cost advantage because annual savings are out-weighed by the high initial capital and maintenance costs. Therefore, caution should be exercised about focusing on only a single factor in designing for implementation of sustainable technologies, and whatever is promised as a benefit should definitely be deliverable. In this instance, the extent of money saving by sustainable water interventions, especially at a small scale, should not have been exaggerated.

The third theme relates to the involvement of the users of sustainable technologies. In this case study, the users were not involved in the process of choosing the technologies. This exclusion stemmed from the professional stakeholders' perceptions that the users were not technically competent in understanding the merits and demerits of each device. Because of their poor social background, they were considered as short-termist who cared only about financial benefits rather than about environmental benefits. The users were also perceived as having strong antitechnology feelings. Telling too much to the users about the risks of the sustainable devices was considered as an obstacle to technological advancement. In addition to increasing the dangers that poor choices would be made by the experts acting in their self-imposed isolation, the downside of not allowing the users to choose the water technologies was that they did not feel a sense of ownership and control. The interviews for this study revealed that the elderly tenants were not as technically ignorant as the professional stakeholders expected. They showed a basic understanding about greywater recycling and the problems of the hybrid water systems. When they learned that the developers wanted to scrap the hybrid systems and put them back on the mains, they were very angry because they were not even informed about the decision.

To conclude, this chapter has shown that the success of building pro-poor sustainable water technologies depends on how people are motivated in trying new devices and how they are involved in choosing the right kinds of innovations. One of the implicit assumptions underlying the subjectivity-institution-structure framework is that poor people bear disproportionately high costs in fulfilling their commitments to the environment and face more constraints in exercising their rights to a clean environment and in participation in decisions about how that environment will be achieved. Building pro-poor sustainable technological interventions is of great importance. By understanding poorer peoples' subjectivities and the institutional arrangements and structural constraints surrounding them, this framework can be helpful in setting reasonable targets for their involvement in sustainable development initiatives and avoid further victimizing them or compromising their livelihoods and well-being.

REFERENCES

Barnett, J., Doherty, B. B., K., Carr, A., Johnstone, G., & Rootes, C. (2006). *Environmental citizenship: Literature review*. Bristol, United Kingdom: Environment Agency.

Bullard, R., & Johnson, G. (2000). Environmental justice: Grassroots activism and its impact on public policy decision making. *Journal of Social Issues, 56*(3), 555-578.

Chambers, R., Pacey, A., & Thrupp, L. (1989). *Farmer first: Farmer innovation and agricultural research*. London: Intermediate Technology Publications.

Cleaver, F. (2004). The social embeddedness of agency and decision-making. In S. Hickey & G. Mohan (Eds.), *Participation: From tyranny to transformation? Explor-*

ing new approaches to participation in development (pp. 271-277). London: Zed Books.

Cleaver, F., & Franks, T. (2005). *Water governance and poverty: What works for the poor?* Bradford, United Kingdom: Bradford Centre for International Development.

Cornwall, A., & Gaventa, J. (2001, February). Bridging the gap: citizenship, participation and accountability. *PLA Notes, 40*, 32-35.

Dobson, A. (2003). *Citizenship and the environment*. Oxford, England: Oxford University Press.

Douglas, M. (1987). *How institutions think*. London: Routledge.

Drevensek, M. (2005). Negotiation as the driving force of environmental citizenship. *Environmental Politics, 14*(2), 226-238.

Ellis, C., & Flaherty, M. (Eds.). (1992). An agenda for the interpretation of lived experience. In *Investigating subjectivity: Research on lived experience*. London: SAGE.

European Commission. (2005). *Doing more with less: Green paper on energy efficiency*. Brussels, Belgium: Commission of the European Communities.

Faruqui, N., & Al-Jayyousi, O. (2002). Greywater re-use in urban agriculture for poverty alleviation—A case study in Jordan. *Water International, 27*(3), 387-394.

Feenberg, A. (1999). *Questioning technology*. Oxon, England: Routledge.

Jackson, T. (2005). *Motivating sustainable behaviour: A review of evidence on consumer behaviour and behavioural change*. London: Sustainable Development Research Network.

Layder, D. (1994). *Understanding social theory*. London: SAGE.

Maniates, M. (2002). In search of consumptive resistance: The voluntary simplicity movement. In T. Princen, M. Maniates, & K. Conca (Eds.), *Confronting consumption* (pp. 199-236). Cambridge, MA: MIT Press.

Medd, W., & Shove, E. (2006, April). *Traces of water workshop paper 5: Imagining the future*. Paper presented at the Traces of Water Workshop, UK Water Industry Research, London. Retrieved July 17, 2008, from http://www.lec.lancs.ac.uk/cswm/download/TWW5_Report.pdf

Murphy, J. (Ed.). (2006). Governing technology for sustainability. In *Governing technology for sustainability* (pp. 203-220). London: Earthscan.

Postel, S., Gonzales, F., & Keller, J. (2001). Drip irrigation for small farmers—A new initiative to alleviate hunger and poverty. *Water International, 26*(1), 1-13.

Schlosberg, D. (2004). Reconceiving environmental justice: Global movements and political theories. *Environmental Politics, 13*(3), 517-540.

Seyfang, G. (2005). Shopping for sustainability: Can sustainable consumption promote ecological citizenship? *Environmental politics, 14*(2), 290-306.

Sharp, L. (2006). Water demand management in England and Wales: Constructions of the domestic water user. *Journal of Environmental and Planning Management, 49*(6), 869-889.

Shove, E. (2003). Converging conventions of comfort, cleanliness and convenience. *Journal of Consumer Policy, 26*(4), 395-418.

Sofoulis, Z. (2005). Big water, everyday water: A sociotechnical perspective. *Journal of Media and Cultural Studies, 19*(4), 445-463.

Uphoff, N., & Wijayaratna, C. M. (2000). Demonstrated benefits from social capital: The productivity of farmer organizations in Gal Oya, Sri Lanka. *World Development, 28*(11), 1875-1890.

Wong, S. (2007, August). Making sustainable technology work with the poor. Paper presented at British Council, Dhaka.

World Bank. (2000). *World development report 2000/2001: Attacking poverty*. New York: Oxford University Press.

World Bank. (2008). *World development report 2008: Agriculture for development*. New York: Oxford University Press.

ABOUT THE AUTHORS

Ann Armstrong has been a lecturer at the Rotman School of Management for the past 8 years. She is the director of the social enterprise initiative there. In that role, she is responsible for increasing the school's involvement in the nonprofit/social enterprise sectors. Ann designed a course titled, Entrepreneurship with a Social Mission, which debuted in fall 2006 and has been teaching a course on nonprofit consulting for some years. She also teaches in the governance essentials program of the Institute of Corporate Directors as well as in the MBiotech program. Ann is working on an Social Sciences and Humanities Research Council-supported research project that looks at the social economy of Ontario and is also "Canadianizing" a management text. She received her PhD from the University of Toronto.

Paul Barnes is a deputy director and research leader (risk and crisis management) of the Information Security Institute and senior lecturer within the School of Management at the Queensland University of Technology, Brisbane, Australia. His teaching and research interests cover resilience in critical infrastructure systems, sociotechnical threats, and the application of business continuity management across institutions. He serves on the editorial board of the *International Journal of Business Continuity & Risk Management*. He has undergraduate qualifications in environmental science and a PhD in risk and organizational analysis from Griffith University, Brisbane, Australia. He has completed projects across the public and private sectors including the Asia-Pacific Economic Cooperation economies on trade security, threat assessment, and counter-terrorism capacity building needs. In addition to coordinating funded research in continuity planning and aviation security, he is a cochief investigator in an Australian research Council Linkage grant examining the airport metropolis and its interfaces. He has worked in the public sector in public safety and emergency response planning, corporate risk management, and national security policy development.

Pierre Bertrand was the general manager and treasurer of Evergreen. He joined Evergreen in 2007 bringing a strong interest in the nonprofit sector and 20 years of experience in the financing and consulting sectors. Pierre leads Evergreen's planning, finance, risk management, human resources, information technology, and facilities management functions. He provided financial, risk management and legal leadership for the Brick Works. Prior to Evergreen, Pierre held a variety of positions to the senior management level with Export Development Canada and the Business Development Bank of Canada. Pierre has also worked in strategic planning, federal provincial consulting and a variety of management consulting services to high-growth and nonprofit organizations through Ernst & Young and his own consulting firm. Pierre holds an LLB and MBA from the University of Ottawa and has been involved in a variety of volunteer activities most recently joining the Governance Committee of the Sherbourne Health Centre.

Geoff Cape is a founder of Evergreen and has acted as the executive director since its inception in 1990. He was also inducted as a senior fellow by the Ashoka Foundation for his innovative approach to social entrepreneurship. In 1999, Geoff was selected as one of Canada's Top 40 Under 40 by the Caldwell Partners and the *Globe and Mail Report on Business Magazine*. He was honored with the governor genera's "Golden Jubilee Medal" in recognition of significant contributions to Canadian society. In 2007, he received the inaugural Schwab Canadian Social Entrepreneur of the Year award. Geoff is an author and public speaker on urban planning and innovation in the nonprofit sector. Geoff has a masters of management from McGill University, and has a bachelor of arts from Queen's University.

Michael B. Charles has a PhD from the University of Queensland and is a senior lecturer with the Graduate College of Management, Faculty of Business and Law at Southern Cross University, Tweed Heads, Australia. He is currently a cochief investigator on a large Australian Research Council Linkage grant examining the airport metropolis and its interfaces. In addition, he is coleading the development of a rail corridor sustainability planning system as part of his applied research work with Australia's Cooperative Research Centre for Rail Innovation. His current research interests include transport and energy policy, public values in infrastructure, public management, and risk and crisis management.

Matthew J. Drake is an assistant professor of supply chain management in the A.J. Palumbo School of Business Administration and John F. Donahue Graduate School of Business at Duquesne University. He received his PhD in industrial and systems engineering from Georgia Tech in 2006 with a concentration in economic decision analysis. His major research interests include the economic analysis of collaborative supply chain performance and the development of ethical supply chain policies and practices. He is a core instructor in Duquesne University's Sustainable MBA program. His recent research has been honored with best paper awards by the Production and Operations Management Society and the Northeast Decision Sciences Institute.

Mark E. Ferguson is an associate professor of operations management in the College of Management at Georgia Tech. His research interests involve many areas of supply chain management including supply chain design for sustainable operations, contracts that improve overall supply chain efficiency, pricing and revenue management, and the management of perishable products. He is the coordinator for the focused research area on dynamic pricing and revenue management. Two of his papers have won best paper awards from the Production and Operations Management Society and several of his research projects have been funded by the National Science Foundation. Prior to joining Georgia Tech, he had 5 years of experience as a manufacturing engineer and inventory manager with IBM.

Laura Fitzpatrick received both her PhD and MA in economics with a specialization in development from the University of Notre Dame. Currently an associate professor of economics at Rockhurst University, she focuses both teaching and research in the global arena with the development of courses and programs in economics, culture and politics of the developing world, political economy, global economic issues, and global studies. Particular areas of research interest include food security and its sustainability, and the impact of theoretical determinism on the achievement or lack of achievement of success in reaching development goals.

Jenni Goricanec is in the final stages of submitting her dissertation for her PhD at The Royal Melbourne Institute of Technology, Australia. She is currently a researcher in the School of Engineering at the University of Melbourne introducing a transdisciplinary subject—in both content and pedagogy—into a multidisciplinary program. She also cofacilitates "integrative conversations" with second year masters' students at *oases* Graduate School, where as an academic board member she has been active in establishing accreditation and seeking funding through grant application and establishing partnerships with businesses. Her consulting practice The Wicked Innovation Practice uses the ideas of wicked problem solving, action research, sociotechnical systems and actor-network theory to innovate. Her previous work includes establishment of a new cross-university academic program—the master of sustainable practice, program leadership, as well as teaching into this program and cross-organizational change to improve product development in a national organization and solution outcomes in an international organization that was traditionally product focused.

Roger Hadgraft is a civil engineer with more than 15 years involvement in engineering education research. He has published many papers on engineering education, with a particular focus on problem/project-based learning and the use of technology to support learning in this way. He was instrumental in introducing a project-based curriculum into civil engineering at Monash University, commencing in 1998. From 2002-06, his work at The Royal Melbourne Institute of Technology was in curriculum renewal to embed graduate capabilities, specifically through a stream of project-based courses/subjects in civil, chemical and environmental engineering. He has consulted on problem-based learning to many universities, nationally and internationally. Roger has been a member of the Australasian Association for Engineering Education Executive since 2001 and is its 2008 president. In February 2007, Roger was appointed at the University of Melbourne as director of the engineering learning unit to assist in the introduction of the new Melbourne model in engineering, to support new project-based learning courses and new learning spaces and to improve teaching quality across the Melbourne School of Engineering. He has been involved in issues of sustainability for the last 5 years, introducing new undergraduate subjects and a master's program based on adult learning principles.

Seana Irvine has been Evergreen's program director since joining the Evergreen team in 1997. She is currently helping to develop the Evergreen Brick Works project, particularly focusing on developing the on-site programming. She is the author and editor of numerous publications focusing on environmental and urban health. She serves on the board of several nonprofit organizations including The Stop Community Food Centre and the Ontario Smart Growth Network. Seana has worked in the public sector for the Toronto and Region Conservation Authority and National Capitol Commission and as a consultant specializing in environmental communications and public consultation. Seana has a masters of environmental studies from York University and an honors bachelor of environmental studies from Trent University.

Tim Keane received his PhD in public policy from Saint Louis University, and his MBA from the University of Richmond. He is currently the director of the Emerson Center for Business Ethics and an assistant professor of management at Saint Louis University. Dr. Keane's experience includes 20 years with a Fortune 100 consumer packaged goods company. He left the company in 1999 to launch a software venture that developed advanced mobile computing solutions for customers such as Frito-Lay. After selling the company in 2003, Dr. Keane entered academe. He was selected as a Kauffman Scholar, and began exploring social entrepreneurship as an area of research to leverage his background and education. In 2007, he was a delegate to the Skoll Forum at Oxford University. In his role with the Emerson Center, Dr. Keane researches causal factors related to ethics issues across various sectors.

Mari Kondo earned her MBA from Stanford Graduate School of Business and PhD from Kyoto University, Center of Southeast Asian Studies, studying about the management in the Philippines. She is an associate professor at Ritsumeikan Asia Pacific University in Japan. Prior to that she was an associate professor at the Asian Institute of Management in the Philippines. In Japan, she teaches corporate social responsibility and business ethics, human resource development in Asia Pacific (undergraduate); strategic management, international business management, and international political economy (graduate school). She has been conducting an annual corporate social responsibility and development seminar for Japanese executives since 1998, and is considered as a pioneer in Japan on this topic.

Lynn M. Patterson earned her PhD from the Georgia Institute of Technology in city and regional planning. She is an assistant professor of geography at Kennesaw State University where she teaches courses in economic, cultural, and world geography. Her primary research interest is in sustainable local economic development. Her most recent work linked sustainable business practices with sustainable entrepreneurship in Argentina. She also continues her research on construction and demolition recycling as an opportunity for economic development. Prior to entering academia, Lynn worked in local economic development in both the private and public sectors.

Dawna L. Rhoades is a professor of management in the College of Business at Embry-Riddle Aeronautical University in Daytona Beach, Florida where she teaches international business, strategic management, and international aviation management. Her research interests include airline strategy, intermodal transportation, and sustainable transportation. Her work has appeared in such journals as the *Journal of Air Transport Management, Journal of Air Transport World Wide, Journal of Transportation Management, Journal of Managerial Issues, Managing Service Quality, World Review of Science, Technology, and Sustainable Development,* and the *Handbook of Airline Strategy.* She is the author of a recently published book titled *Evolution of International Aviation: Phoenix Rising* and the editor of the *World Review of Intermodal Transportation Research.*

Bonnie A. Richley is completing her PhD in organizational behavior at Case Western Reserve University where she also earned her MSc in organizational development and analysis. Her work involves positive change with expertise in appreciative inquiry; the significance of values for individuals and organizations; the role of innovation in creating business/ social models; executive coaching as a trainer and master coach; and adult learning theories and competency development. She was a visiting professor at Escuela Superior de Administración y Dirección de Empresas Business School in Spain for 2 years and is currently teaching action learning at Case Western Reserve University where she is also a master executive coach. She has 15 years experience working in various international venues.

Ushnish Sengupta is an MBA graduate of the Rotman School of Management, University of Toronto. He received his undergraduate degree in industrial engineering from the University of Toronto, and started his career as a human factors engineer. Ushnish is cofounder of Net Impact Rotman, an organization whose goals include applying MBA skills to social issues. He is also cofounder and research director at Rotman Nexus, an organization that provides business consulting services to nonprofit organizations and social enterprises. Ushnish's research interests include social enterprise and social return on investment, and he has presented case studies at a number of international conferences, including Business As An Agent of World Benefit in 2006, and the Social Enterprise Alliance gathering in 2007. Ushnish's current focus includes healthcare, information technology, and environmental policy.

Martin Stack received his PhD from the University of Notre Dame. He is currently an associate professor of management at Rockhurst University where he teaches courses in international business, international management, and corporate strategy. He has published in a number of journals including *Business History Review, Business Horizons, Journal of Economic Issues,* and *SAM Advanced Management Journal.* In addition to his interest in sustainability, he is working on a book on the internationalization of healthcare.

James A. F. Stoner is professor of management systems and Chairholder of the James A. F. Stoner Chair in Global Sustainability at Fordham University's Graduate School of Business. He earned his BS in engineering science at Antioch College in Yellow Springs, Ohio, and his MS and PhD in industrial management at MIT, in Cambridge, MA. He has published articles in such journals and periodicals as: *Academy of Management Review, Harvard Business Review, Journal of Development Studies, Personnel Psychology,* and has authored and coauthored a number of books (approximately 20) including *Management* (first-sixth editions, 1978-1995); *Fundamentals of Financial Managing* (2002, 2006) and *Modern Financial Managing: Continuity and Change* (1995, 2001, 2006). In 1992, Fordham University established the James A. F. Stoner Chair in Global Quality Leadership, with the initial funding provided by a gift of more than $1 million from one of Jim's students (Brent Martini) and his father (Bob Martini) in acknowledgment of Jim's teaching, research, and contribution to their and their company's work in identifying and adopting world class management approaches. In 2005, the name of the chair was changed to the James A. F. Stoner Chair in Global Sustainability to reflect the evolution of Jim's teaching and research. Jim's current projects and interests include inquiring into new ways to bring about organizational and societal change and transformation in a sustainable world. In mid-2003, he started exploring the role of spirituality in individual and organizational excellence and transformation and in achieving a global business, social, and political environment that is sustainable and just. He has recently been teaching management and organizational transformation to petroleum company managers in Siberia and to MBA students and senior managers in Japan. He has consulted with a broad range of companies, including Bell Labs, Richardson-Merrill, Bergen Brunswick, Arthur D. Little, Inc. Email: stoner@fordham.edu

Charles Wankel is associate professor of management at St. John's University, New York. He received his doctorate from New York University. Dr. Wankel has authored and edited many books including the best-selling *Management* (3rd ed., Prentice-Hall, 1986), *Rethinking Management Education for the 21st Century* (IAP, 2002), *Educating Managers with Tomorrow's Technologies* (IAP, 2003), *The Cutting-Edge of International Management Education* (IAP, 2004), *Educating Managers Through Real World Projects* (IAP,

2005), *New Visions of Graduate Management Education* (IAP, 2006), *Innovative Approaches to Reducing Global Poverty* (IAP, 2007), the *Handbook of 21st Century Management* (SAGE, 2008), *Being and Becoming a Management Education Scholar* (IAP, 2008) *University and Corporate Innovations in Lifelong Learning* (IAP, 2008), and *Alleviating Poverty through Business Strategy* (Palgrave, 2008). He is the leading founder and director of scholarly virtual communities for management professors, currently directing eight with thousands of participants in more than 70 nations. He has taught in Lithuania at the Kaunas University of Technology (Fulbright Fellowship) and the University of Vilnius (United Nations Development Program and Soros Foundation funding). Invited lectures include 2005 distinguished speaker at the E-ducation without Border Conference, Abu Dhabi and 2004 keynote speaker at the Nippon Academy of Management, Tokyo. Corporate management development program development clients include McDonald's Corporation's Hamburger University and IBM Learning Services. Pro bono consulting assignments include reengineering and total quality management programs for the Lithuanian National Postal Service. Email: wankelc@stjohns.edu

Sam Wong (s.wong@leeds.ac.uk) is a lecturer in the School of Earth and Environment at the University of Leeds, United Kingdom. His research interests lie in sustainable technology, water governance, natural resource management. and institutional arrangements. He has published a book on social capital and community participation (Amsterdam University Press, 2007). His most significant peer-reviewed papers are published in *Environmental Politics*, *Urban Studies*, and *Progress in Development Studies*. He has obtained research grants from the Engineering & Physical Sciences Research Council, the British Council, and the British Academy, totalling £144K. He is currently researching interboundary water governance in Ghana, Burkina Faso, and China, and sustainable technological interventions in India, Bangladesh, and England. He is a grant reviewer for the Natural Environmental Research Council and a contributing editor for the *Journal of Technology*. Having previously worked as a full-time journalist in Hong Kong for *five* years, he enjoys public engagement and interdisciplinary research collaboration.